Confirmation

Engaging Lutheran Foundations and Practices

Confirmation

Engaging Lutheran Foundations and Practices

Foreword by Margaret A. Krych

Fortress Press   Minneapolis

CONFIRMATION
Engaging Lutheran Foundations and Practices

Scripture quotations from New Revised Standard Version Bible, copyright © 1989 Division of Christian Education of the National Council of Churches. Used by permission.

Cover design: David Meyer
Cover photo: Chip Porter/TSI
Text design: Cathy Spengler Design

Library of Congress Cataloging-in-Publication Data

Confirmation : engaging Lutheran foundations and practices /
    contributors, Robert L. Conrad . . . [et al.].
        p.   cm.
    Includes bibliographical references.
    ISBN 0-8006-3157-9 (alk. paper)
    1. Confirmation—Lutheran Church. 2. Lutheran Church—Doctrines.
I. Conrad, Robert L., 1931-
BX8074.C7C66   1999
264'.041082—dc21   99-19139
                                                                CIP

The paper used in this publication meets the minimum requirements of American National Standard for Information Sciences—Permanence of Paper for Printed Library Materials, ANSI Z329.48-1984.

Manufactured in the U.S.A.   AF 1-3157

03   02   01   00   99   1   2   3   4   5   6   7   8   9   10

CONTENTS

FOREWORD

This book is alive—alive with a vibrancy of excitement about ministry with youth and, above all, confirmation ministry. The authors are all professors of Christian education in Lutheran seminaries, and the book reflects their deep personal commitment to the role of confirmation ministry in the church. This is a book that is theoretical and practical, paying attention to the variety of contemporary practices in congregations and yet holding a solid continuity with the past heritage of the church. It answers questions such as, What's happening in congregational confirmation ministry today? Why do we have confirmation? What is it? How might we think about confirmation ministry in our own congregation?

The book calls us to reflect on the joyful but serious words we hear at each baptism we witness:

> Bring them to the services of God's house . . . teach them the Lord's Prayer, the Creed, and the Ten Commandments . . . place in their hands the Holy Scriptures and provide for their instruction in the Christian faith, that, living in the covenant of their Baptism and in communion with the Church, they may lead godly lives until the day of Jesus Christ (*Lutheran Book of Worship*, p. 121).

The pastoral and educational ministry that is confirmation is grounded in the gospel, the good news of God's forgiving love in Jesus Christ communicated through word and sacrament. In baptism, that proclaimed word incorporates the baptized into the Christian community, the assembly of believers gathered around word and sacrament. So baptism is the beginning of God's confirming work through the Holy Spirit. In this understanding that confirmation is a process that begins at baptism, God's own work through the church's pastoral and educational ministry, Lutherans bring their unique understanding of confirmation to the ecumenical discussion. For Lutheran congregations who use it (and most do), a rite of affirmation of baptism is an opportunity to rejoice in confirmation—that is, the rite is an expression of what God has already done and is doing to confirm the faith of the baptized.

But the rite is not, in itself, confirmation. While this book focuses on Lutheran foundations and practices, several of the authors engage in conversation with other Christian traditions, and it is hoped that the book will be a contribution to the ecumenical discussion of confirmation today.

Confirmation is dear to the hearts of the faithful. Personal and congregational memories of confirmation are treasured. "Tell me about your confirmation," I invite my students—and they share accounts filled with anecdotes and treasured memories. Or, I arrive early as a guest preacher, and am shown around the buildings; ". . . and here are the photos of the confirmation classes from way back," says my guide proudly. Not only individuals and congregations, but also the Evangelical Lutheran Church in America as a body considers confirmation to be important ministry. Soon after its beginning through a merger of three Lutheran bodies in 1988, the ELCA called for a task force to reflect on confirmation and bring a report to the 1993 Churchwide Assembly. Some of the authors of this book were members of that task force. By adopting the report of the task force, the assembly affirmed the important role of confirmation in the lives of believers and in congregations. The 1993 *Confirmation Ministry Task Force Report* is included as Appendix A in this book.

This book is deeply indebted to, and in many ways is a reflection on and outgrowth of, the report brought by the task force to the 1993 Churchwide Assembly as well as a previous study authorized by the predecessor bodies of the ELCA that culminated in the 1970 *Report of the Joint Commission on the Theology and Practice of Confirmation* (a report that the 1993 task force appreciated and affirmed). Therefore, it might truly be said that this book reflects wider wisdom than that of its authors. However, it includes much more material than the Reports and is an up-to-date commentary on the theological foundations and practices of confirmation ministry that offers guidance and a shared vision to all who are involved with working with youth in the church.

Congregations and pastors have been waiting for some time for a new Lutheran book on confirmation. Thirty years have passed since the landmark publications of *Confirmation and Education,* edited by W. Kent Gilbert (1969), and *Confirmation and First Communion: A Study Book*, written by Frank Klos (1968). In the meantime, new patterns have emerged in congregational practices, adolescent research has yielded new insights for teachers, several catechetical curricula have been published, and ecumenical conversations have progressed and demand attention. A new generation of teachers and leaders has arisen and is asking for an in-depth look at confirmation today. And here it is.

Part 1 covers contemporary Lutheran practices—the way things are in congregations throughout the United States. Mary Hughes opens by describing models and stories in congregations that emphasize four different ways of helping persons to identify with the Christian community and participate in its mission. She identifies congregations that emphasize experiencing the faith community, living a life of discipleship, knowing and understanding the faith, and personal growth in faith. Hughes stresses the importance of all of these emphases and encourages a balance among them, while recognizing that the balance will differ depending on the circumstances of the congregation. It is clear that confirmation ministry is alive and well, and that congregations have creative approaches in a variety of settings including the traditional school model, congregational cluster programs, retreats and camps, mentor programs, personalized programs, and "longer and later" programs.

Kent Johnson deals with the changing face of confirmation, especially in the last four decades in the ELCA and predecessor bodies. He describes factors that have accelerated the pace of change, including church studies, educational developments, published curricula, and the particularity of local congregational programs. Johnson highlights individualized, longer and later, and relational approaches to confirmation ministry.

Part 2 focuses on Lutheran foundations of confirmation. Luther Lindberg leads us through the history of confirmation from the second-century baptismal practices through the centuries until today. He gives particular emphasis to confirmation in the Lutheran church and the studies conducted by the Lutheran World Federation and by the ELCA (1993) and predecessor bodies (1970). Lindberg goes on to give contemporary perspectives and ecumenical issues.

Chapter 4 focuses on theological foundations, grounding confirmation firmly in justification by grace through faith. God's confirming work, that is, strengthening believers in faith, is the work of the Spirit through the church. God strengthens faith through word and sacrament, bringing daily the forgiveness of sins through Jesus Christ. Drawing on the 1970 and 1993 studies, the chapter works through the meaning of the ELCA definition of confirmation as "a pastoral and educational ministry of the church which helps the baptized through word and sacrament to identify more deeply with the Christian community and participate more fully in its mission." It concludes with a discussion of the affirmation of baptism rite.

Further drawing on the church's 1970 and 1993 reports, chapter 5 deals with the content of confirmation. The teaching of traditional catechetical and biblical content is set in the context of adolescent cognitive development. The author urges teaching of scripture that relates to the lives of youth, and serious instruction in the catechism that emphasizes law and gospel so that the gospel message may be heard by teenagers and truly be a confession of faith. Mission, discipleship, vocation, worship, and human relationships are considered as content.

Part 3 focuses on confirmation ministry as God's work through community. In chapter 6 Norma Cook Everist writes about the congregation as confirming community, as a church in mission—the mission of Christ. The confirming church is a church of the cross, through the work of the Holy Spirit. Everist encourages congregations to rejoice in diversity and in gifts. Whatever the approach to confirmation ministry, Everist emphasizes the importance of the congregation's commitment to its own approach and to carrying out that approach. She highlights the involvement of parents and the value of mentors and other congregational relationships with youth.

Authors of chapters 7 and 8 look at the adolescent in the community of believers. Robert Conrad speaks of living in the Spirit through word and sacrament; the Spirit given in baptism continually confirms the baptized in faith through the means of grace. In the life of faith, Conrad examines the role of worship and prayer, Bible reading, confession and absolution, and the rite of affirmation of baptism. Diane Hymans explores adolescent development and its implications for teaching and working with teenagers in the church. She describes teenagers today and the developmental tasks of adolescence in ways that will help all those who work with youth in congregations.

In chapter 9 Nelson Strobert places confirmation in the broader context of lifelong education and pastoral ministry in the community of faith. He affirms that such lifelong ministry is the responsibility of all baptized members as well as rostered leaders. Strobert understands catechesis as a lifelong pilgrimage, and illustrates with practical illustrations the journey from early childhood, through childhood and adolescence, young adulthood, middle adulthood, and late adulthood.

In the final chapter of the book, Donald Just emphasizes the importance of educational goals and offers a variety of approaches and teaching methods for use in confirmation ministry in the congregation. Included are classroom settings, later and longer programs, individualized programs, home-based approaches, retreat/camp settings, and presentation/discussion.

Throughout the book, there are some major common themes:

- Lutheran theological foundations: God's gracious activity in Christ, justification, baptism, God's work of confirming in faith through word and sacrament, the working of the Holy Spirit through the church in confirmation ministry;

- continuity with the historical heritage of the church;

- the self-identity of the congregation as a confirming community;

- solid content rooted in scripture, creeds, and catechism;

- the roles of pastor and laity together in confirmation ministry;

- the involvement of parents;

- confirmation ministry as part of lifelong education and pastoral ministry;

- a variety of approaches that pay attention to congregational context.

From this brief overview, it is clear that there is a wealth of material of theological and practical value in the following pages. But, perhaps more important, there is a call to congregations and leaders to pay serious attention to confirmation as the church moves on into the twenty-first century. The spirit of lively energy that permeates the chapters will engage readers in reflecting on their own role in confirmation ministry. And if this encourages them to become more deeply involved and reinvigorates them in their teaching and pastoral ministry to youth, if it moves them to prayer and to action and to wonder at the confirming grace of God in the lives of the baptized, then this book will have done its work. May we rejoice in God's confirming work in the lives of all believers—including our own.

Margaret A. Krych

PART I

Lutheran Practices

CHAPTER I

Confirmation Ministry: Models and Stories

Mary E. Hughes

What is the purpose of confirmation? What will confirmation look like in this congregation? The importance of the answers to those two questions cannot be taken lightly. They provide the confirmation ministry model unique to your congregation.

The Purpose of Confirmation

The definition of confirmation in the Evangelical Lutheran Church in America states that confirmation ministry helps the person "to identify more deeply with the Christian community and participate more fully in its mission."[1] At least four different emphases appear to be at work in Lutheran congregations around the United States as they try to live out that goal. They follow:

- emphasis on experiencing the faith community;

- emphasis on living a life of discipleship;
- emphasis on knowing and understanding the faith;
- emphasis on personal growth in faith.

All these emphases are important, desirable, and appropriate. However, no congregation can treat them all as equally important; there is just not enough time or energy to focus on them all.

However, none of these emphases can be ignored. Each one is to be cherished. Every congregation must decide how to balance the four emphases, a balancing act that most often focuses on one yet includes some attention to all the others. A closer look at each emphasis may help clarify its uniqueness.

Emphasis on Experiencing the Faith Community

It is difficult to become, be, and remain Christian alone. Faith demands community. That is, Christians are always creating and participating in groups of faithful Christians. Community nurtures, nourishes, and nudges their faith. It provides the time and place for worshiping God, for serving others, and for growing personally and within relationships. Confirmation becomes a time when emphasis can be placed on identifying with the Christian community: learning what community means and requires, practicing the skills of community building and membership, and experiencing the richness and rewards of a community of faith.

> Everything we do is aimed at developing relationships. To learn grace, we must experience it. And grace happens in community. We study and learn, of course. But we do it in the context of relationship. By confirmation, every student has met 100 adults within our church: committee people, parents, staff, council, volunteers. We've created a place where our youth bring their friends, feel accepted, pray for one another, get to know their own parents, share their faith in public. (Texas pastor)

The power of relationships within one's faith is the driving force behind the emphasis on faith community in confirmation ministry. Relationships are the basic building block in faith community. In fact, some congregations refer to their confirmation ministry as "relational," and design programs that focus on relationship building.

The methodologies selected for confirmation within these congregations fit the purpose of a community emphasis. Small groups may be used to foster relationships for study, reflection, discussion, projects, and fellowship.

> The small groups facilitate learning. We're not trying to cram stuff into a lecture, but in the discussion after a presentation the group itself facilitates the learning of everyone in the group. (Pennsylvania Director of Christian Education)

Mentors may be assigned or selected to connect the confirmand with role models and caring, guiding adults.

> Our 11th grade students choose mentors, often a couple, and meet with them four times during the year to talk about four topics: faith and work or school, faith and family, faith and social life, and faith and church. (Minnesota pastor)

> In the second year of confirmation the youth choose a mentor. It must be an active participant in the congregation, but not a family member. They all come together at a dinner in the fall, then meet once a month through confirmation. We encourage the relationship between the mentor and student to go beyond those monthly meetings to breakfast together, or youth sports activities. (Pennsylvania DCE)

Time taken to acknowledge and develop relationships is as important as time spent in study and other work. Young persons may be assigned projects that bring them together with others within the congregation—committees, council members, younger students in the church, musicians.

> In addition to the adults who are mentors or group guides, we invite congregational members to share their faith, and that is powerful. A 96-year-old woman came in her wheelchair to talk about what Holy Communion means to her. One woman diagnosed with terminal cancer came with her husband and talked about hearing that diagnosis and the place of prayer in their lives. Young parents who just had a child baptized came to talk about why they did that. The students are really listening—you can tell because they ask good questions of these guests.

> Engaging these adolescents with others in the congregation is a natural outgrowth of that church's goal for last year. Congregational goal: to pass on the legacy of the faith through increased connections of the youth to the extended Christian family—the church." (Michigan church member)

Other congregations have created a confirmation ministry that gives special attention to the young person over several years (sometimes called *longer and later*). Especially through the elementary years the child experiences the attention and nurture of the whole community of faith in ways that are intentional, organized, focused, and systematic.

> We start earlier and help parents take ownership for confirmation. Parents are involved in grades 3–6, and, in fact, all the way through to confirmation. We wait longer to confirm because of the increased maturity; 10th graders are more able to wrestle with questions of life today. (North Dakota DCE)

> Our confirmation program extends over nine years. Most children have received instruction and then their first communion sometime between kindergarten and second grade. In third grade, on Investiture Sunday in October, students, parents, and the congregation sign a paper committing us to participate in confirmation over several years. Students are confirmed in the fall of their 11th grade year after a five-week review of the catechism and Bible. We're enthusiastic about confirmation, and young people remain actively involved in the congregation after confirmation. (Minnesota pastor)

Emphasis on Living a Life of Discipleship

> We don't even call it confirmation anymore . . . we call it Christian Discipleship Training. That's what we want for our young people, that they continue to grow as Christian disciples. So we look for every way possible to learn about, hear about, observe, practice, and experience what it means to be a disciple of Jesus. Last year I gave a "final exam" in my class on the Bible. They expected questions about Job and Moses and Paul. Instead, here were my questions:

> * Tell me about your journey in faith since your baptism.
> * What is there about being a disciple that you do well?
> * What about being a disciple do you want to work on?

> I was amazed at the depth of their reflections. They really had something to say. We want them to live lives of discipleship . . . for the rest of their lives. (Michigan, seminary intern)

Being a disciple is a lifestyle, and not one easily learned. It is learned through study and reflection, action and reflection, modeling, mentoring. Some would say, "To be Christian one must live Christian." The discipleship emphasis focuses on what it means to "live Christian."

The Affirmation of Baptism service in *Lutheran Book of Worship* (the service used for the rite of confirmation) provides a summary of what it means to be a disciple. Those being confirmed respond to the following question:

> Do you intend to continue in the covenant God made with you in Holy Baptism: to live among God's faithful people, to hear his Word and share in his supper, to proclaim the good news of God in Christ through word and deed, to serve all people, following the example of our Lord Jesus, and to strive for justice and peace in all the earth? (*LBW*, p. 201)

We use that question to guide our confirmation program. We want these young people to be able to say, "I do, and I ask God to help and guide me" on the day of their confirmation and to know what that means. So, everything we do is aimed at growing into one or more of those promises. (Ohio DCE)

Emphasis on Knowing and Understanding the Faith

Perhaps the most quickly assumed emphasis in confirmation is on understanding one's faith, and it has a long tradition. Lutherans, following the example of the reformers, have always placed an emphasis on the cognitive content of the faith: knowledge of the scriptures; comprehension of major theological concepts such as grace, justification, incarnation, and gospel; ability to think through dilemmas using the resources of the church.

> Knowing what it means to be a Lutheran is especially important in our neighborhood. These teenagers walk out the church doors into a street that has no concept of Lutherans, and they get asked lots of questions. They get challenged because the people around us are church people but from traditions very different from ours. Our big emphasis is on getting the knowledge in this [confirmation] notebook into the heads and mouths of our confirmands. They are learning to think and talk "Lutheran." (Ohio pastor)

Some congregations are alarmed or disappointed to find young people "illiterate in the faith"; that is, with little knowledge of Bible stories, catechism, or church history. Confirmation becomes a time to focus on that information and its significance. These congregations recognize that confirmation may be one of the first times when students can encounter all that content within an organized learning structure.

Such an emphasis on knowing and understanding the faith does not mean that confirmation must be boring, stuffy, or tedious.

> We learned the books of the Bible through "rap." I can sing the entire Small Catechism because our whole congregation learned and performed it as a church musical. (Ohio confirmation student)

> We don't require memory work . . . we don't have to. But through repetition and singing they remember more than we would require. (Texas pastor)

Learning the content of the faith can fill a lifetime. It certainly requires more than one, two, or three years of confirmation. However, careful planning can insure that students acquire a cognitive framework within which to examine and live out scripture, theology, and history. It is possible to read, study, memorize, and pass tests, yet have little comprehension of that knowledge and little idea of how it fits together. The challenge facing confirmation leaders is to select and organize the desired content, then provide learning experiences through which that content can be engaged effectively; a difficult but rewarding task.

Emphasis on Personal Growth in Faith

> I learned to pray in confirmation. I began to read the Bible every day when I was in confirmation. All that stuff had been explained to me when I was younger, but in confirmation it all seemed to make sense for my life. (Tennessee confirmation student)

Confirmation may be a time when the spiritual and faith life of the young person blooms. Throughout our lives we explore and expand our relationship with God that began in Holy Baptism. Of the times especially ripe for growth in faith, this time is described by those who study adolescent development as when conceptualization can move from the concrete toward the abstract, when growth in faith can move from simplistic acceptance of the values and beliefs chosen by family to struggling with the complexities and ambiguities of the life of faith.[2] This growth includes questioning and doubting the things that might have been assumed at a younger age. It includes separating oneself from simply following the footsteps of parents, church leaders, and teachers and trying to make one's own footsteps. It is a move from childhood faith to adolescent faith. The move to mature adult faith will not happen now, but the probing, challenging, searching, passionate faith of adolescence can be called forth and affirmed. Some confirmation programs seek to engage, support, and guide that move toward and in adolescent faith.

Attention to spiritual disciplines such as prayer, meditation, spiritual retreats, artistic expression, journaling, reading, and devotions is often part of this emphasis on the adolescent's growth in faith. Young people may be introduced to the stories of other persons of deep faith—either living or dead—whose spirituality can inspire and guide the young adolescent.

How Confirmation Might Look in This Congregation

It is a question of format: the organization and scheduling of confirmation. The decisions about format and purpose work hand in hand in creating confirmation ministry in a congregation. Many congregations in Lutheran churches in the United States choose one of the following formats or combine two or more. When formats are combined, one is usually primary and others become secondary. In fact, almost any format can be chosen to focus on any of the emphases described previously.

The most frequently used formats are described here: weekly meetings, special events, clustering, personalized, home-based.

Weekly Meetings

The most widely used format for confirmation ministry brings learners and leaders together weekly or on a regular schedule, perhaps every other week.[3]

> Sunday mornings are the best time for us to meet, no other time works as well. We do lots of other things too, but confirmation starts with our weekly classes on Sunday morning. (Florida pastor)

This format may be chosen because of the power of habit and predictability. It also provides continuity that may be lost when the group gathers less frequently. What is done within this weekly meeting will vary depending on the purpose and emphasis of confirmation ministry in a particular congregation. The time may be a class session emphasizing knowledge and comprehension, and the teaching/learning may be quite traditional or highly creative. The time may be extended to include meals, group time, service projects, trips, or drama, most of which require more than the time available on Sunday mornings.

> Confirmation classes meet after church on Sundays, roughly every other week. After church is convenient for parents; some are group guides in confirmation, others go off to lunch or find things to do in town. And parents take turns providing and serving lunch to the confirmands. We're a downtown church and we do everything possible on Sundays because our members live for miles in every direction but gather on Sundays. (South Carolina DCE)

Special Events: Retreats, All-Day Events, Camp

Confirmation in some congregations is experienced primarily in special events that happen less frequently but last longer. Retreats may be the most popular format in this category. Time away from the ordinary—24 to 48 hours away from home, in a setting conducive to the purpose and emphasis of confirmation—can encourage growth, activities, and relationships unlikely to happen in other settings.

> We have two required retreats every year. One is larger—the retreat includes other churches in the metro area. The other is just us. Last year we studied the Nicene Creed. (Florida pastor)

When overnight retreats are not feasible, congregations may choose all-day events to take advantage of the opportunities to eat and play together as well as study and worship. A surprisingly large number of churches make use of confirmation camp—a week-long experience of confirmation, usually taking place in a camp or retreat setting.

> Everybody here likes confirmation camp. We go to a local Mennonite camp but bring the whole program with us. Of course there are presentations and reading. But there are also crafts and meditative things. There's the pool, the paddleboats, basketball and volleyball, the obstacle course, and the campfires. Students begin confirmation with camp in the summer after the sixth grade, then return after the seventh grade. Their third year of camp comes the sum-

mer before confirmation in the fall. That's two years of confirmation but three years of confirmation camp. (Pennsylvania DCE)

Clustering

When I moved to this city I telephoned other pastors to talk about working together in confirmation. I called a dozen people, and now these three congregations are a confirmation team. There's richness in our teamwork. If I moved to another congregation tomorrow, I would look for other churches to be partners in confirmation. And I would do that whether the church was big or small, rural or urban or suburban. (Ohio pastor)

The best thing that's ever happened to confirmation here has been our joint program with another church 10 miles away. We have more and better ideas, we have lots more energy, our youth are getting to know one another, and we have fun. (Virginia pastor)

For the past 18 years we've participated in a camping cluster program. We do our own thing during the year, but every summer this whole group of churches from across the entire state comes together for confirmation camp. In the fall all the pastors meet and select a theme for the following year, then we divide the preparation among our churches. These young people are learning that the church is more than my congregation, and they meet other Christians from other cities and other settings. (Ohio pastor)

These stories illustrate how clustering may help with the limited resources available to some churches, and how its value extends far beyond efficiency.

Personalized Confirmation

Sometimes by choice and sometimes by necessity, confirmation is structured to meet the unique circumstances, needs, or opportunities of each student. *Personalized* may or may not be the same as *individualized*. Having one or two students is an ideal time to modify a previous program and personalize confirmation to best match the students. Personalized confirmation may take place also within larger groups by giving attention to how the various pieces of confirmation ministry fit together for each person. In this case, not everyone will be doing exactly the same thing at the same time, but students will make choices that work best for them.

Personalization can also happen when the existing approach is working for most but not all the students.

> One girl was not coming to Sunday school at all, or to worship. She just was not participating. We worked it out for her to help teach Sunday school instead, and that went well. (Pennsylvania DCE)

Home-Based Confirmation

Is the home the most valuable learning site for the confirmand? Some congregations have found it to be so. Helping parents or other caring adults to provide stimulating learning opportunities within a familial context brings faith and life together on a daily basis.

> We call it a comprehensive family-centered confirmation program. It begins with birth and lasts through adulthood. Now parents are really partners with the pastors, teachers, and church staff to see that this child is nurtured in Christ's faith. (Arizona congregation member)[4]

Confirmation Practices in the ELCA Today

A 1998 survey of 422 ELCA congregational leaders gives a quick glimpse of the current formats used in confirmation in Lutheran churches. The data cannot be generalized to the entire ELCA, but the results give insight to current practices and trends.[5]

- Most churches (65.3 percent) describe their current confirmation practice as "a traditional school model with an instructor working with youth in a classroom setting." About 18 percent describe their practice as "large group presentation followed by small group gatherings."

- Most churches (62.7 percent) have "regularly scheduled weekday sessions." Almost 27 percent have "regularly scheduled Sunday sessions during Sunday school time." Fifteen percent have "regularly scheduled Sunday sessions, but not during Sunday school time." (Participants checked all that applied.)

- Seventeen percent of churches have confirmation "in conjunction with other congregations," while 83 percent offer confirmation only within their own congregation.

- The rite of affirmation of baptism is celebrated in the 8th grade by almost 50 percent of churches, almost 31 percent in the 9th grade.

- Although confirmation instruction is offered from grades 1 through 12, the great majority of churches have confirmation classes between grades 6 and 10: 6th grade = 23.2 percent; 7th grade = 81.7 percent; 8th grade = 39.8 percent; 9th grade = 10.1 percent; 10th grade = 2.2 percent.

- Although various curricular resources are used, 40.5 percent of these churches develop their own curriculum.

Eight components of confirmation were practiced by a large number of congregations:

- community and congregational service projects: 62.1 percent;

- memory work: 53.9 percent;

- sermon and/or worship reports: 53 percent;

- homework: 52.1 percent;

- retreats: 40.3 percent;

- strong expectations for youth and adult commitments: 38.4 percent;

- mentoring: 33.6 percent;

- confirmation camp: 29.8 percent.

What do such statistics suggest? First, even though the vast majority of churches claim a traditional classroom approach, thousands of churches are using alternative, sometimes quite creative, approaches to confirmation. Second, a variety of settings and formats are used by a large percentage of churches: service projects, retreats, and mentoring are found in more than one-third of these ELCA congregations. Perhaps more congregations are being innovative than claim that innovation. Third, developing one's own curriculum for confirmation requires energy, creativity, and time. That 40 percent of congregations may be developing their own curriculum suggests that many people are making huge investments of themselves into creating and implementing confirmation in the churches of the ELCA.

One final statistic deserves mentioning. Of the churches surveyed, 67.4 percent said, "We have not changed our basic approach [to confirmation] over the last several years." This finding offers both good news and bad news. Some congregations do not wish to invest the energy required to review and change. On the other hand, some congregations, perhaps more than suspected, experience satisfaction in their current program and feel little need to change.

Such survey findings can be a useful barometer to current practice. However, while they describe what is happening, they do not suggest what should be happening or what will be happening in the next decade.

Three Confirmation Stories

CALVARY, TEXAS

"Our intent is to make disciples of Jesus Christ who will in turn 'go and make disciples' of Jesus Christ." Calvary Lutheran Church near Fort Worth, Texas, is a congregation of about 750 members. The "make disciples" goal is stated explicitly, but it is accompanied by another goal of "fostering meaningful, mutually beneficial Christian relationships," because God has called us into community. These two goals reflect a dual emphasis on experiencing the faith community and living a life of discipleship.

What does this emphasis look like in practice? Wednesday nights are for youth group meetings. The 90-minute sessions include group bonding experiences, presentations, and discussion. Each month members of different church committees help focus on a particular ministry of the church. Four parents' nights bring together youth and parents around common yet sticky issues. Over the course of two years, students meet more than 100 adults in the congregation.

> These Wednesday evenings reflect the truth of "the medium is the message." We encourage community; we sit in a circle and sing and talk and pray. It's a small group methodology, and that fits what we are trying to accomplish. My favorite time of the week is that 10 minutes of sharing prayer together at the end of Wednesday evenings. I tell students, "This is the most serious thing we do."

Encouraging signs are evident. Wednesday nights find unchurched visitors returning with their friends. The participation rate is high among students who come, not because of requirements, but because of interest and commitment. The energy level among adults and youth is high.

Bible knowledge is the focus of Sunday school in grades 7 and 8. Confirmands serve as acolytes, crucifers, children's church assistants, and plan and lead Lenten services. Service Saturdays take students into nursing homes, mission centers, and other outreach ministries. Participation in synodical youth gatherings bring together youth from a wide variety of contexts and churches. Before the rite of confirmation students write a paper about their faith, and they share it on Witness Sunday, the week before Pentecost. "That's when we know that good things have happened in confirmation; it's amazing to hear their faith statements."

HOPE, MINNESOTA

At Hope Lutheran Church confirmation ministry extends over nine years. A congregation of about 300 members and located near Minneapolis, Minnesota, Hope is enthusiastic about its own adaptation of a longer and later confirmation format. The process of confirmation ministry keeps the students actively involved in the church and most continue that active participation after the rite of confirmation.

On Reformation Sunday last year, nine students were confirmed. Each of them stood at the pulpit and read a statement of faith he or she had written in the weeks before.

> The congregation's response was very positive. People were amazed at the depth of understanding and faith commitment that 11th graders can make. (Pastor)

The pastor likes confirmation at grade 11. "The maturity difference is incredible [from grade 8 or 9]. These are really young adults."

What does confirmation ministry look like at Hope? Sometime between kindergarten and grade two, after consultation between parents and pastor, most children have received instruction and then their first communion. In the years that follow, children and youth participate in Sunday school, vacation Bible school, worship, and all the ministries of the congregation. In addition, confirmation ministry includes the following:

- Grade 3: On Investiture Sunday in October, students, parents, and the congregation sign a paper committing them all to participate in confirmation over several years. That year, two evening sessions on baptism are held, ending with a Service of Remembrance of Baptism.

- Grade 4: The pastor visits in the homes of all fourth graders, talking especially about family devotions.

- Grade 5: A five-week Wednesday afternoon study session focuses on Holy Communion. During this year student involvement in worship leadership begins and will continue through grade 12.

- Grade 6: A five-week Wednesday afternoon study session focuses on prayer.

- Grades 7, 8, 9: A 10-week Wednesday evening study session is held each year, addressing sacraments, Lutheran doctrine, worship, and mission.

- Grade 10: Students meet weekly for special sessions during Sunday school.

- Grade 11: Students are confirmed on Reformation Sunday after a five-week review of the catechism and the Bible. That year confirmands choose mentors for the year with whom they meet four times discussing the topics of faith and work/school, faith and family, faith and social life, and faith and the church.

This pattern of longer and later confirmation has been in place for about eight years and, while modifications are made, the basic format has remained the same: several short series of weekly meetings over a number of years. The emphasis appears primarily one of experiencing the faith community. This combination of emphasis and format works well to help students know themselves to be members of the church and to continue a lifestyle active in the church into early adulthood.

LUTHERIDGE, NORTH CAROLINA

Lutheridge is an ELCA camp and conference center in the mountains of western North Carolina. Over the last 25 years a program of *campfirmation* has evolved, which now brings more than 500 confirmation students from 180 congregations to Lutheridge for a week of study, worship, fellowship, and fun.

Churches are organized into 19 self-selected clusters of 5 to 25 churches (depending on congregation size, pastor, and tradition) from the synods of

ELCA Region 9. The camp provides housing, logistical planning, meals, counselors, and camp activities designed around the study/activity schedule of a cluster program led by the congregational leaders. Pastors and lay catechists plan those study/activity times, sometimes at a planning weekend at the camp during the preceding months.

Campfirmation clusters are found at Lutheridge eight weeks of the summer, in addition to a full schedule of camping and conference activities for all ages. The program has become so popular that campfirmation weeks are now being offered at two sister ELCA camps in North Carolina.

First Lutheran Church in the Piedmont region of North Carolina takes confirmands entering 8th grade to campfirmation each year. They would take more, but space is limited to 80 students for this cluster of 11 churches from North Carolina, South Carolina, and Virginia. Campfirmation is a week of intentional Christian community focusing on the young person's spiritual journey.

> It's an intense week that cannot be duplicated in any other setting or by our church alone. It is a unique opportunity. (Pastor)

There's 30-plus hours in planned learning events and another 60-plus hours of camp activities. Every confirmand spends hours with his or her own church group and leader, hours with a group of students from other churches, hours with a cabin group of 6 to 8 students with a counselor, and hours with the entire group in camp activities. The Gospel of Luke provides the focus for study and worship. "Many students are hesitant at first, but by the end of the week, no one wants to leave."

A Closing Comment

The church does not tell congregations how to implement confirmation ministry. Instead the ELCA has offered a vision and guidelines, setting congregations free to dream and develop a ministry unique to context, demographics, tradition, personnel, and mission, "to identify more deeply with the Christian community and participate more fully in its mission."[6] No one right way will accomplish that purpose. Instead congregations will continue to search for ways to make confirmation ministry come alive in and for the church.

Notes

1. *The Confirmation Ministry Task Force Report,* Evangelical Lutheran Church in America, Division for Congregational Ministries (September 1993), 1.

2. For further discussion of adolescent faith and adolescent development see chapter 8, "Adolescent Development," by Diane Hymans.

3. ELCA Department for Research and Evaluation (April 1998), Confirmation Ministry Questionnaire.

4. "Confirmation Reformation," *Mosaic* (Summer 1998).

5. ELCA Department for Research and Evaluation (April 1998), Confirmation Ministry Questionnaire.

6. *The Confirmation Ministry Task Force Report,* Evangelical Lutheran Church in America, Division for Congregational Ministries, (September 1993), 1.

CHAPTER 2

The Changing Face
of Confirmation

Kent L. Johnson

Not long ago I met with some acquaintances from my college years. We had communicated by phone and letter since those days, but had not seen each other face to face for a long time. Agreeing to meet for lunch, I came to the crowded restaurant not sure I would recognize their faces. It wasn't long before we found each other. One I recognized right away; the other took awhile. Then, as we talked about college days and what we had been doing since, I discovered more and more characteristics in my friends' faces, characteristics that had been altered over the years. By the time our three hours together were over, and the pictures had been taken, I saw in their faces the friends I had known—changed by the time and circumstances of four decades.

"Confirmation! I just don't recognize it any more. What happened to all the memory work and the Bible study that I used to do?" It's an exclamation I have heard more than once from parents and grandparents who have difficulty seeing in present confirmation programs the face of the one they had experienced. Even individuals involved in confirmation ministry year after year have trouble connecting their adolescent experience with programs of today. Those people who have been away from it for some years are surprised by what they see. The surprise is even greater for those who have the impression that confirmation is something that has been, is, and should be unchanging. The reality is that even though certain basic identifiable features of confirmation have remained constant, it is an area of ministry that has undergone subtle but significant changes since the time of the Reformation. Frank Klos's review of the history of confirmation in his study *Confirmation and First Communion* makes clear the importance of these changes. In the last four decades, however, those changes have come much more rapidly as confirmation programs, and the classes that are a part of them, reflect the current theological, sociological, and educational trends of the day. One of the tasks for those responsible for confirmation ministry is to ensure, in the midst of all those changes, that the constant features that give confirmation its identity are present in the approach offered in the congregation. Among those continuing characteristics are a recognition that baptism is the sole rite of initiation into the church, a sacrament that is not augmented by the rite of confirmation/affirmation; and that confirmation is, of its very nature, a course of instruction centered in the catechism and scriptures.

Factors Accelerating the Pace of Change within Confirmation

Age, health, circumstances, genes, and personal health habits are all factors that influence the rate of change in our human faces. As we get older, the pace of change seems to accelerate. At least two things contributed to the rapid acceleration of change in confirmation over the last four decades: the change in the relationship between confirmation and first communion, and the perceived sociological and psychological needs of the learner in the overall confirmation curriculum. A quick review of both provides a framework for understanding why the face of confirmation seems so changed from what it was in the not so distant past.

The Impact of the Study of Confirmation and First Communion

In 1969 and 1970 the Lutheran Church in America and the American Lutheran Church studied the relationship that then existed between confirmation and first communion. As a result of that study, these Lutheran synods, acting in convention, legislatively allowed for the separation of confirmation and first communion. It was a decisive moment in the radical changing of confirmation. Prior to that action, confirmation was generally, if tacitly, acknowledged to have one central purpose: preparing adolescents for their participation in the Sacrament of the Altar. The rite for confirmation in the *Service Book and Hymnal* made clear that before young people confirmed their faith in the context of the rite, they were not quite considered to be full members of the church and therefore not eligible to commune.[1]

Reaching back to discussion of the sacraments and confirmation carried on at the time of the Reformation, theologians throughout the 1960s had placed a growing emphasis upon the insistence that baptism is the sole sacrament of initiation into the Body of Christ. Having made that argument, these church bodies came to an awareness that confirmation as it was then practiced was both a denial of the singular importance of baptism and an unwarranted barrier to participation in the Lord's supper. In a most successful educational effort of the Lutheran churches in the United States, the adherents of baptismal theology were able to persuade their gathered assemblies to allow congregations to separate confirmation and first communion. With this change, the face of confirmation lost one of the most significant characteristics that had identified it for more than 200 years.

Aware of that impending loss, those who developed the study proposed another definition for confirmation. First articulated in 1969 and 1970, it was affirmed by the Evangelical Lutheran Church in America in its churchwide assembly in 1993.

> Confirmation is a pastoral and educational ministry of the church which helps the baptized child through word and sacrament to identify more deeply with the Christian community and participate more fully in its mission.[2]

In one of the first sessions of "Teaching Confirmation Classes," my class at Luther Seminary, I ask participants to write their own definitions of confirmation and then, gathering students into small groups, direct them to write a group statement that represents a consensus of all in the group. These definitions are written out on chart paper and taped up around the room where they can be compared and contrasted with each other. Participants do this work well. They certainly reveal that they have some theoretical foundation for what confirmation is to be about as well as no small amount of experience with the reality of teaching confirmation classes.

Following that discussion, I project the ELCA's definition of confirmation on a screen and ask for their comments, which generally include several predictable responses. First, they note that no mention of God—Father, Son, and Holy Spirit—is made in the definition. They note that the word *faith* is not there. They comment that the definition assumes that all in confirmation classes are already in the church, members of "the baptized," and makes no mention of outreach or preparation for baptism. Finally, one or more makes the comment: "I don't see anything in this definition that distinguishes confirmation from any other educational endeavor in the church." They also wonder about emphasizing a pastoral dimension to all classes in the church, whether the pastor teaches them or not. Further, and especially for the baptized, isn't the purpose of all education in the church to assist persons to identify more fully with the life and mission of the church, no matter how old they are?

Upon being confronted by my students, I must admit that the definition of the church leaves me somewhat at a loss as to how to distinguish confirmation from any other educational program in the church. Indeed, without a tradition of confirmation present in the church, one with which most of us in the church prior to 1970 were familiar, I would be hard pressed on the basis of the definition to offer many arguments for a particular or distinctive educational and pastoral ministry called confirmation. Preserving in some fashion that tradition as it existed prior to 1970 will be important as the church moves further away from that defining moment.

The definition of 1970 allowed for an almost infinite variety of faces for confirmation as pastors and congregations sought to create a ministry appropriate to, and effective in, their own settings. This wide variety is affirmed in the 1993 statement.[3] As congregations exercised that freedom, the face of confirmation became in some places eventually almost unrecognizable to those who had known it in other places and times prior to 1970.

The Impact of Educational Developments

As evidenced in the study document *Confirmation and First Communion*, emerging psychological, developmental, and educational theories were beginning to influence confirmation. Originators of the study gave substantial attention to the works of Erik Erikson, Jean Piaget, and Robert Havighurst in their recommendations as to the time, purpose, and content of confirmation.[4] For example, Piaget had proposed that humans are not generally able to think abstractly before reaching the stage of formal operations—a stage that begins about the age of 12. Logically, therefore, those arguing for a new face for confirmation in 1969 and 1970 commended postponing the study of Lutheran doctrine, generally agreed to have considerable abstract dimensions to it, until students were well into their teen years.

According to the study, grade 10 became the suggested date for the rite of affirmation of baptism, and curriculum writers quickly began to reflect this awareness in their instructions to teachers: "At this age (that of 13 and 14) the young person begins to use abstract reasoning abilities. However, theology is a highly abstract subject." Teachers were encouraged by the editors of the materials they used to adapt their vocabulary and expectations to the level at which their students could understand and appreciate them.[5]

This outward expression of concern for the learner in confirmation represents a considerable shift in confirmation as it appeared in congregations. This shift doesn't mean that learners had not figured into the structure of confirmation previously. However, after 1970 learners came to play an increasingly important role. Erik Erikson, probably the foremost figure in adolescent psychological/developmental theory at the time these foundational changes were occurring in confirmation, postulated that humans move from birth to death through a series of eight stages. At each stage an individual is faced with a crisis. Confirmation as practiced then and now occurred at Erikson's third stage, that of adolescence, when, according to Erikson, humans are dealing with the crisis of identity. Those who successfully negotiate this stage emerge into young adulthood prepared to deal with the next crisis, that of intimacy. Those who do not become diffused in their identity, not sure who they are, and unprepared for the challenge of intimacy that meets them at the next stage of their development. Confirmation in the 1970s sought to teach adolescents the basics of the Christian faith while, at the same time, helping them to address the crisis of identity that they were experiencing. While other names have been added, readers of this book will soon discover that the impact of Piaget and Erikson on confirmation instruction has hardly diminished in the nearly 30 years since *Confirmation and First Communion* was first published.

Changes in Published Curriculum Materials

One of the responsibilities of a denominational publishing agency is to prepare curriculum materials for use in the educational programs of the congregations of the sponsoring denomination. As such, one can expect that these agencies reflect the present values and convictions of those denominations. Augsburg Publishing House of the former American Lutheran Church and Parish Life Press of the former Lutheran Church in America reflect this commitment to congregations in the confirmation materials they published following 1970 even though they developed slightly different faces for confirmation as the years went along.

It's not possible here to discuss all the confirmation materials they have published since 1970, but a selected overview demonstrates that the face of confirmation they presented to their churches did change. In the midst of those changes, however, these materials remained strongly committed to the centrality of the scriptures and the catechism.

The Face of Confirmation Reflected in Published Materials, 1970–1980

Even before the decision to separate confirmation and first communion in 1970, Augsburg's materials were demonstrating, in the Word, Grace, Faith series, that the official stand of the American Lutheran Church on the subject of confirmation was one that joined old and new features written within an educational structure that was hopeful to the extreme.[6] The overall series contained units covering a full range of biblical and catechetical materials. In recognition of confirmation as a ministry of partnership between congregation and family, each session was made up of three parts: one for the Sunday school hour, one for the "extra" confirmation setting during the week, and one for use at home with parents. The unit entitled *I Am and I Listen* most clearly reflects the influence of Erik Erikson. Session 1 covers the following themes: "My birth dossier tells me who I am"; "God tells me in the Bible who I am"; "The catechism tells me who I am"; and "The liturgy tells me who I am."[7]

These materials made much of teacher/learning objectives (TLOs), which further demonstrated that the editors were moving, or had moved, into the world of educational objectives and their importance in planning every formal learning situation. This unit on baptism wedded in a marvelous way the baptismal theology of the church, the historical and present hope that confirmation would be a partnership between home and congregation, the psychological theories of Erik Erikson, and the educational currents of the day. Though still centered on a cognitive approach to confirmation, the needs and life situations of learners were given a more distinguishable role within confirmation. From then on, the ongoing discussion, even debate, became what is, and should be, the emphasis of confirmation—the learner, the content of the catechism and Bible, or some combination of both. Indeed, these writers and editors were not waiting for the church to give permission to develop a somewhat new face for confirmation. They expected the church to endorse the direction they had already taken, and it did.

Editors in Philadelphia, preparing materials for use in the Lutheran Church in America, were not the least bit behind those in Minneapolis in their development of curriculum materials reflecting educational, sociological, theological, and developmental trends of the day. Catechetics for Today, published in 1980, illustrates the way these writers and editors addressed the crisis of identity, partly evidenced in the use of the pronouns "I" and "me" as indicative of a concern for that issue. For example, the unit entitled *God Comes to Me* includes several session titles with one or the other of those pronouns. Other titles that suggest the same theme are *Belonging by Baptism, Why Belong?* and *Does God Really Care?*[8] The same pattern is reflected in another unit entitled *God Is Love*. Concern for the learner was further demonstrated in the development of supplemental materials that could be used for "mainstreaming students with learning problems."[9] Here the editors were responding to the educational practice evolving in the public schools of including students with "learning problems" in the regular classroom.

Certainly in these materials the notion of confirmation as a broadly conceived ministry was getting full attention. The following statement puts a face on confirmation that had been in various stages of development since 1970, one that balances what confirmation might be.

In addition to catechetics [in the LCA approach, confirmation classes were primarily focused on the catechism] the catechumen probably attends Sunday church school where biblical, rather than catechetical, learnings are stressed. The catechumen also worships and, where early Communion has been adopted, receives Holy Communion. The young person also takes part in the work of the congregation as a lector, acolyte, choir member, usher, committee member, or in other ways. Finally, the catechumen probably participates in a congregational youth group. In all of these ways, the catechumen learns the meaning of the Christian faith and the mission of the congregation.

A good confirmation-ministry effort tries to coordinate all of these elements to give the catechumen broad and varied opportunities to grow and develop as a maturing Christian.[10]

Changes in Confirmation Presented by the Publishing Houses Since 1980

A review of curriculum materials published by Parish Life Press and Augsburg Publishing House during the years following Word, Grace, Faith and Catechetics for Today shows that confirmation was becoming more complex as its agenda became increasingly inclusive. Editors in both Philadelphia and Minneapolis were aware of changes in educational approaches in the public schools, and were especially sensitive to both the church's agenda of teaching the catechism and the scriptures, and that of student needs and life situations.

Affirm, published by Augsburg in 1984, was made up of 20 courses. The *Affirm Planning Guide* most adequately describes the face that the writers and editors were giving to confirmation in this series.

The AFFIRM Series is built around questions and answers. This gives students an opportunity to explore their own beliefs and learn what the church teaches.

AFFIRM has 20 courses: ten 8-session core courses explore questions and answers relating to the biblical and doctrinal heritage of the church; ten 4-session electives concentrate on the questions teenagers ask about how their faith relates to daily life.[11]

However inclusive this curriculum was intended to be of both the agenda of learners and their life situations, and the concerns of the church in teaching the basics of the faith, Affirm was definitely turned in the direction of the latter.

Giving New Life, along with all the resources that went with it, was published by Parish Life Press in 1987. It was a massive effort giving to confirmation the richest possible countenance. A publicity pamphlet introducing Giving New Life asked the questions: "Do you need confirmation ministry resources that encourage home support? provide parent education? and stimulate peer group activities?" If the answers are yes, then these curriculum materials are intended to deliver precisely these things. How could one resist? Historically, these materials would move back in the direction of the Reformation ideal that parents would both teach their children and would be enlisted in the lifelong catechumenate. Educationally and developmentally, teachers were given a solid introduction to the current theories in both areas. Editors encouraged them to think more in terms of student learning rather than teaching, and that teaching adolescents meant dealing with abstract concepts in an introductory sort of way. Identity, teachers were reminded, was a key issue that teens were dealing with, and that relationships with their peers was a prime concern.[12] An array of materials was prepared to accomplish the aims of the Giving New Life series, including The Living Catechism, a collection of materials to be used by students and their parents called Growing in God's Grace, and instructional pamphlets designed to assist pastors and other leaders in congregations to get the program on the move. Aware of the technology looming on the horizon for all areas of education, congregational leaders were given help as to how they could incorporate the computer into the confirmation program. Anticipating the "longer and later" approach that will be described later, Giving New Life stretched over more years—at least from grades 5 through 10. Indeed, one would be hard pressed to find anything in previous faces of confirmation, or ones that were yet to come, that did not find expression in the Giving New Life series. Anyone in subsequent years who thought they were inventing something new can be reminded that in 1987, when Giving New Life reached the desks of pastors and other leaders in the church, few aspects had been left unaddressed—not least a careful consideration of the role that relationships play in confirmation ministry. The editors wrote in the *Planning Manual:*

Confirmation has a strong relational focus: relationships of youth to youth, of the pastor to youth, of adults to youth, of youth to adults, and relationships of youth to God.

The purpose and goals of a vital confirmation ministry program are accomplished within community. A Christian community filled with "tender loving care" nurtures faith and encourages spiritual growth. A confirmation ministry program which effectively includes both pastoral and educational qualities is filled with TLC.[13]

Looking at all those materials now, I wonder how they were first received as they were introduced to the congregations of the church. Was it seen as the beautiful and encouraging approach it was meant to be? I'm confident that it must have been—at least in many congregations. On the other hand, could one also wonder whether that face wasn't almost too much, too overpowering, too challenging, too complex to be taken in? Can a face be too much, too lovely? I think that may have been the case for some pastors and other leaders who did not have the benefit of all the educational theory and practical background that the writers and editors had put into it, or the time and energy to organize and implement the richness of the approach. Materials prepared to introduce Giving New Life to the congregations were excellent, and if anything could have done the job, they were it. Still, is it possible to provide the kind of educational background needed to fully appreciate such materials in three or four sessions? Without that background, it's questionable that many could uncover the full beauty and richness in this face for confirmation created by the writers and editors at Parish Life Press. Though it may not have been expressed explicitly, these materials may have sent a warning to publishers and writers of published materials: keep it simple.

With the merger of the Lutheran Church in America and the American Lutheran Church into the Evangelical Lutheran Church in America, Parish Life Press and Augsburg were brought together to form one publishing house for the ELCA. This joining meant that the writers and editors who had created the varying faces to confirmation were no longer working independently. If those different faces were to persist in the newly merged church, then Augsburg Fortress would have to portray them.

The first new face put on confirmation after the merger was named New Journeys in Confirmation published in 1990. Like Affirm, this series took into account both the profiles that had come into confirmation at least since the publication of Word, Grace, Faith. However, the materials clearly made a greater commitment to the agenda of the church in its teaching of the catechism and the scriptures than to the needs and life situations of adolescents. A two-year program, with one year centered in the catechism and the other in the scriptures, dominated the curriculum. These excellent courses for adolescents and adults reflected an obvious appreciation for solid educational theory. They provided a substantive introduction into the Bible and the Small Catechism. In addition, the series offered a wide range of shorter elective courses designed to address the needs of adolescents. For all its excellence, this curriculum did not present a full frontal portrait of confirmation. It was turned toward the content profile that still tended to dominate the church's traditional idea of confirmation.

Whether sparked by a sense of responsibility to present a variety of faces of confirmation to Lutheran congregations, or an awareness that congregations simply wanted different options from which to choose, or both, early in the 1990s Augsburg Fortress began work on two new curricula that would present two other faces of confirmation. One, Creative Confirmation, first appeared in congregations in 1994 and was unlike other curriculum that had preceded it. It turned confirmation from a profile emphasizing content to one that emphasized the development of relationships among students, and between students and leaders.

Even though the Bible and the catechism remained central to the content of the curriculum, the overall structure of the series and the activities in each session were clearly meant to focus on relationships, experienced in brief soundbites that reflected the rapid pace adolescents have become accustomed to in television programming. Fast-paced and interactive, with an accent on relationships, here in Creative Confirmation was the first curriculum that leaped to confirmation as it had been introduced back in the late 1960s and early 1970s with the Word, Grace, Faith series—a leap that emphasized at least an equal, if not greater, priority on the needs and nature of the learner as it had on the agenda of the church that sponsored confirmation ministries. It's no wonder that those of previous generations didn't quite recognize confirmation as it appeared in Creative Confirmation.

With New Journeys in Confirmation and Creative Confirmation providing opposite profiles of confirmation, editors and writers at Augsburg Fortress set out to give confirmation a straight-on look, which they did in the Living in Grace series first published in 1995. Living in Grace consists of 10 basic courses that emphasize the content of the scriptures and the catechism as they relate to the needs and life situations of adolescents. A sample of titles for the courses illustrates the connections that the writers and editors intended to make between these two agendas: *You're Covered*, a course on baptism; *Up Close and Personal,* a course on prayer; and *Totally God,* a course on the Apostles' Creed. Unlike New Journeys in Confirmation and Affirm where the two agendas were addressed rather independently in core and elective materials for each, Living in Grace was a clear effort to integrate them. And unlike Creative Confirmation, which was designed to be carried on in spaces without chairs and desks and with no materials for students other than the Bible and catechism, the "schoolish" look to Living in Grace was seen as comforting to some, and something of "the same old problem" for others.

Confirmation Development within Congregational Settings

The goal of both Augsburg Fortress and Parish Life Press had been to provide their congregations with curriculum materials that put the best face possible on confirmation. However, it was in individual congregations that confirmation programs took on a particularity that distinguished them from others. While these programs tended, and still tend, to emphasize one aspect of confirmation or another, they did provide a new look that captured the attention of many congregations within the Lutheran church. Only a few that gathered considerable attention can be presented here. The people and congregations that developed these programs were exercising the freedom congregations have always had with regard to confirmation ministry—a freedom made more explicit in 1970 and 1993. What they did was to find an approach that worked so well for them, in the context in which they were working, that the approach was offered to others. Accepting the invitation to look at these confirmation programs, pastors and congregations were equally free to "buy into" these new approaches and/or modify them as they saw fit. Further, it must be noted that the following descriptions arise out of workshops I have attended, conversations I have had with those who developed these approaches, and my observation of them as they have been practiced within congregations.

The Individualized Approach to Confirmation

Most formal education settings include an individualized component—a time when students are given the opportunity to learn separately as individuals. Silent reading and writing assignments completed in class are examples of individualized learning activities. It was the intent of Pastor Andrew Jensen and Mary Jensen, serving at Prince of Peace Lutheran Church in Burnsville, Minnesota, to make individualized learning the dominant feature in the confirmation program. Almost a quarter of a century ago they developed an approach to confirmation that became so popular that hundreds of congregations sent pastors and interested parties to attend the workshops in which it was presented. Many of those congregations adopted the Jensens' idea for their own confirmation programs.

This approach was developed, said the Jensens, because of certain social and educational developments of the mid 1970s, especially in suburbia and in large congregations. Socially, an increasing busyness characterized the lives of adolescents and their parents. The former were occupied by jobs, studies, and other school activities, as well as the desire to exercise some freedom over their own lives, as identified in the Search Institute study on early adolescence.[14] Parents, it was noted, often found themselves in the middle of the busyness of their children's lives, not to mention the hectic pace of their own. What was needed, argued the Jensens, was an approach to confirmation that provided a considerable amount of freedom for those involved in it. It just so happened that the educational theory that would allow for that freedom appeared in the public schools about the same time.

Though not new, programmed learning was coming into vogue in the public schools in the early 1970s. Programmed learning centered on information, packaged into a set of directions and materials that allowed individuals to learn "on their own." What the Jensens created was a set of 16 packets covering a wide range of biblical, catechetical, and practical matters related to the life and mission of the church. Learning centers, staffed by parents and other interested adults, were developed in which audio tapes, overheads, and books were gathered and made available to students when they needed them.

Following the directions in the packet, students—working alone or in small groups—made their way through the packets until they had completed the whole set. At the completion of each packet students met with their pastor to discuss, with other students, what they had learned and any questions they had. When the interview was successfully completed, students were free to move on to another packet of their choosing.

The learning center was open for extended periods one or more evenings a week, and occasionally on weekends. Students could come for longer or shorter periods of time, or not come at all in a given week or month, depending on other obligations they might have. They determined how long they were in the program. With effort, it was possible for students to complete the work in less than a year. Others could stay at it for three or more years. However long it took, no "class" celebration of the rite of affirmation of baptism marked the completion of the program. The rite came when students had completed all the packets and presented themselves for the rite—whether alone or with others.

Many features of the program were especially attractive. First, this approach had no classes for anyone to teach, and therefore presented no discipline matters to attend to. It was a front-loaded program in which leaders/teachers prepared the packets and gathered all the materials and then let the students take responsibility for their learning. Second, it allowed pastors/leaders to spend time with students individually or in small groups, both in the discussions that followed the completion of the packets and as teachers moved about the learning center spending time with those gathered there. Contrary to the criticism that pastors and leaders would be absent from these young people, when pastors and leaders were free from their formal teaching responsibilities, they could move around and talk with these young people, enjoying a less structured relationship. And third, students were free to relate to their peers both in working through the packets and in the youth lounge, which was also open at the same times as the learning center. When students wearied of their studies, they were free to move toward another section of the church that featured soft-drink machines, table tennis equipment, and lounge chairs—all supervised by one or more adults.

Finally, and perhaps most significantly, in this whole approach the emphasis was upon gaining a knowledge of the scriptures and the catechism at the same time that it encouraged the development of relationships among peers and between adults and youths. Here was a happy wedding between a rather avant-garde educational approach with the traditional concern of confirmation that adolescents come to learn the fundamentals of the faith.

Given all the preceding qualities, it's not surprising that many were taken by this approach. In a study of "What's Working in Confirmation" conducted in 1991, I found that of the 35 pastors surveyed, four were using this approach. In fact, one said that before he discovered this approach he had just about given up on confirmation. Nevertheless, when I ask my classes at Luther Seminary about their experience with the individualized approach, typically only one or two out of 25 have heard of it. I'm not altogether sure what led to the almost complete disappearance of this program from the confirmation scene, at least in that part of the world in which I live. Perhaps not all those who were first attracted to it saw its many subtle features and concentrated primarily on the freedom it afforded from actually leading classes with sometimes less than enthusiastic adolescents. It offered so much more, but one had to look closely to see its richness. Then, again, the problem may have been the emphasis on the learning of information, and the apparent lack of emphasis on the building of relationships among peers and between students and leaders. Notice here the word *apparent,* because this approach certainly did stress the importance of establishing relationships alongside the learning of the material. But, if only one aspect was seen by those who were implementing it, it is understandable why the approach lost many of its early enthusiasts. An approach needs more than one feature to make it attractive; at the same time, one feature dominating a face can make it less than attractive. Still, 25 years ago it appeared to be an attractive one for confirmation—a program that is now returning again as pastors and leaders take another look at individualized learning, this time through the use of computers, which could go much further than the Jensens' approach. It could free students and their parents from their trip "down to the church for confirmation."

Though an approach to confirmation totally centered in individualized learning may not be so attractive today, I always urge those in my seminary classes to consider at least its limited use. It can be a good alternative to students who find it difficult to participate in a more classroom-like environment. It's my experience that when students are given a choice between learning individually and in a classroom setting, they most often choose the latter—and do so with a greater sense of responsibility than when they saw it as their only alternative. And I think that the individualized approach is a good way to provide variety to confirmation instruction. A unit centered on information is not difficult to identify and develop for use in confirmation. It could be done during Lent, or some other designated period of time when students already come together at the church for reasons other than study. Students would appreciate the break, I think, and so would the pastor and teachers. It's also an approach that could be taken in one or more of the units in the "longer and later" face to confirmation described next.

The Longer and Later Approach to Confirmation

Somewhere in the mid 1980s, Pastor Richard Holloque and the staff at Olivet Lutheran Church in Fargo, North Dakota, put another face on confirmation. They called it the "longer and later approach," which they intended as a response to the changes going on in the culture. Their concerns, however, were somewhat different from those addressed by the Jensens in Burnsville, Minnesota. First, Holloque was taken by Luther's notions about the "lifelong catechumenate," a notion that keeps surfacing in discussions about confirmation, whatever face one puts on it. Luther, of course, argued that no one, no matter what their age, outgrew the need to learn and grow. If the rite of affirmation of baptism is seen as a graduation out of the church's programs for learning, that need is severely stunted. (Not a few see it as a reason for dispensing with the rite and confirmation instruction altogether and view both as a kind of aneurysm in the educational process that somehow bursts after the rite has been celebrated and involvement in the church seems to die with it.)

Second, that diminishing involvement of course leads to the great concern among many adults in the church that youth, once they have "been confirmed," leave off their participation in the life and mission of the church, putting something of a spoke in the very purpose for confirmation as expressed in its definition given in 1970. Holloque and Olivet Lutheran congregation did not want to discontinue either the rite or confirmation programs. They wanted to develop one that would fit the notions of the lifelong catechumenate, and one that would have an impact on keeping young people involved in the life and mission of the church even after the rite.

Third, Holloque was aware of the developmental theories of Jean Piaget. As in the study *Confirmation and First Communion*, this congregation committed itself to a confirmation program that extended the learning opportunities well into the middle teen years, culminating in the rite of affirmation of baptism in the fall of the students' 11th year of school. Fourth, this approach was attentive to the establishment of long-term relationships among students and between adults and students. By stretching the confirmation program over eight years, students and leaders were given the opportunity to form bonds through a series of activities that brought teachers/pastors together with students and their families and by instituting a mentoring program in the last several months of the program. Finally, this approach focused on the ritual in which students and their families were brought into the center of a worship experience. Beginning with investiture and the presentation of Bibles at grade 3, continuing with first communion at grade 5, and concluding with the rite of affirmation of baptism at grade 11, this approach provided several opportunities for students and congregations to be "affirmed" in the faith.

If the face of confirmation presented in the individualized approach created by Mary and Andrew Jensen seemed too one-dimensional, the one developed at Olivet in Fargo seemed complex. It involved not only an eight-year commitment on the part of parents and students involved in the program, beginning with the public distribution of Bibles and an investiture service at grade 3, but also a four-session course in preparation for participation in the Lord's supper at grade 5, and eight-week sessions on various biblical and catechetical subjects spread out over grades 6 through 10.

A commitment on the part of students and parents that those in the program would faithfully participate in Sunday school and worship services, as well as attend scheduled confirmation classes, is also essential. Just as the Jensens were delighted with what they created in the individualized approach and then offered it to the church at large as an approach that would serve others equally well, so those who developed the longer and later approach were convinced that the face they had put on confirmation would be as attractive to others as it was to them. Both were right to some extent. Like the Jensens before them, Pastor Holloque and his associates were available to tell others about this approach, and leaders in the office of education for the American Lutheran Church, such as Ken Pohlman, provided a platform by which the approach could become known throughout the church. Even though many congregations saw the positive features in this approach, and not a few subscribed to it, it did not, in the perception of this writer, gain the large-scale support that the individualized approach did 10 years earlier.

Written all over this approach to confirmation is the word *commitment* for everyone involved in it—pastors, teachers, parents, students. The level of commitment may be one reason why this confirmation program did not become as familiar to the church as the individualized one. And, like the Giving New Life series, it just may be too complex and extended over too long a time. When I present this approach to my seminary classes, only a few are familiar with it, but most students see its merits. Even if they aren't enamored with all of its features, they see many features there that they do appreciate and hope to include in the programs they develop in the congregations they will serve. At least from my perspective, both the longer and later approach and the approach commended in the Giving New Life series published by Parish Life Press found expression through yet another channel, that of Faith Inkubators.

The Relationally Oriented Approach to Confirmation

The newest face for confirmation that has drawn the attention of a considerable number of congregations is known as the Faith Inkubators approach. It first appeared to pastors and others in the church in an article by Pastor Rich Melheim published in *Lutheran Partners*. In that article he announced that "conformation *(sic)* is dead."[15] Here, indeed, was a bold pronouncement that confirmation programs of the past were not only sickly, but were actually looking up from coffins. Because Melheim was not exhaustive in his explanation as to what he meant by "conformation," one is left to assume that it refers to those efforts in confirmation that look a good bit like a school and have the learning of content—in the case of confirmation, the Bible and the Small Catechism—as their main purpose. In his book *Will Our Children Have Faith?* John Westerhoff made a similar claim with respect to the Sunday school. After describing the typical Sunday school class as an ineffective copy of the public school classroom, focused on the learning of information, Westerhoff exclaimed, "All this must go!"[16] Well, if what has preceded is either dead or must go, what is to take its place? Pastor Melheim had an answer, or a solution, to brighten up the dying, or dead, face of confirmation.

Pastor Melheim served on the staff at Trinity Lutheran Church in Stillwater, Minnesota, where he developed his "Inkubator" approach. As he reflected on the needs of adolescents today and how they are or are not bonded to the church, he concluded that the way most congregations went about providing a confirmation ministry was counterproductive to the aim of nurturing young people in the Christian faith. He took the daring step of putting the content of the catechism and scriptures into an equal, or even a subordinate position, to the needs and life situations of adolescents. And, he argued, the basic need that the church could meet for youth today is the building of solid relationships. It wasn't an altogether new idea, obviously, but to put it as the dominant feature of confirmation was going even further than the editors at Augsburg Fortress had done with their Creative Confirmation curriculum.

Borrowing from his background in camping ministry, Melheim developed a program for confirmation that had the following elements, some of which bore a resemblance to previous confirmation approaches. Twice a month students gather for an opening session centered around lively music, skits, prayer, a brief presentation on the theme of the day, and a good deal of audience participation. After 20 to 30 minutes in the gathering activity, the large group is organized into small groups of four to five students with at least one adult leader. In this activity lies the genius of the approach. Students are led through a discussion of the day's theme using a talk sheet that has been prepared for them. Holloque had seen the value of mentors in his approach, but brought them in only at the end of the overall confirmation experience. For Melheim, the mentors are *a* key, if not *the* key, to the whole approach. Mentors are encouraged to work with the assigned topic for the day, but they also urge students to express their feelings and thoughts about how their life is going, and how it had gone, since they last met.

At the conclusion of the small group discussions, the large group assembles again to sing, pray, and to hear any announcements that need to be made. In addition to these two sessions a month, this approach to confirmation is filled out with a monthly social event organized by the small group and its mentor, and a service project to which the group and its mentor are committed.

It's not surprising that students report that they thoroughly enjoy this approach to confirmation. (Interestingly, the Jensens said the same for their approach—that students appreciated it.) Nor is it surprising that some people miss the dominant features of the scriptures and the catechism in this approach, and wonder if it is confirmation at all. One might look and see only a new and unrecognizable face in this approach; however, several features of the old actually find expression here. Those features include the importance of the role of adults and parents in communicating both the gift and knowledge of faith; the place given to the scriptures and the catechism that runs through the twice-monthly sessions; the significance of community as the context for the expression of faith; and the importance of service in the Christian life. If these aspects seem to recede into the background because of the concern for relationships that dominates this approach, its founder would argue that such is appropriate because it reflects the life situations and needs of the learners at that stage of their lives. At the same time, it can be said that this approach is a rather predictable development given the sociological, theological, and educational setting in which it was conceived some three decades ago, and has now come to full term in the present. One can only wonder what new features and changes will come next in the face of that ministry we call confirmation.

A Closing Comment

In the midst of writing this chapter I was invited to participate in a retreat held at a Roman Catholic renewal center. As with most retreats I'm familiar with, we were left with little time to relax, to retreat. However, I did find time to get away briefly to the center's chapel where I encountered a beautiful stained-glass window. Initially, as I looked at it, I saw nothing but pieces of glass formed together into a brilliant kaleidoscope of color. Then, a little at a time, I discovered symbols taking shape out of the window: a chalice, loaves of bread, fish, the hands of God holding the world, an Easter lily, and a magnificent cross that, once I'd seen it, I couldn't take my eyes from it.

My experience with this window was not unlike my meeting with my college friends. The longer I looked at both, the more I saw the familiarity of the persons, the symbols, that I know and have known for much of my life—concealed by age in the case of the one and by the dazzling array of color in the other. Yet, given time, the character of the faces and the symbols was revealed. Those charged with the responsibility for confirmation in the church at large and within particular congregations have at least a dual responsibility. First, whether they are developing their own program or adopting one developed by another, they must ensure that the constant features of confirmation are present—a confidence that baptism is the sacrament of initiation into the church and a course of instruction that centers in the gospel of Jesus Christ as revealed in the scriptures and affirmed in the confessions of the church.

In addition, leaders in confirmation must see it as a ministry to living persons, most often adolescents, who live in a particular place and time. That place and time is not fixed for all across either the country or the globe. Features of time and place change in terms of how persons learn and in the kinds of issues they must deal with in order to live well. Confirmation ministry must accommodate those changes. At the same time, those changes must not be allowed to so dominate this ministry that the enduring purpose of confirmation is obscured or its real intent is masked. To assist the baptized to grow in faith in the Triune God and in their identification with the life and mission of the church is the goal of all formal education in the church. It can be no less the center of confirmation, whatever other features it may have.

Bibliography

Bergstraesser, Elwin et al. *I Am and I Listen.* Word, Grace, Faith. Minneapolis: Augsburg Publishing House, 1971.

Confirmation Ministry Task Force Report. Chicago: Evangelical Lutheran Church in America, Division for Congregational Ministries, 1993.

DuBose, Edwin et al. *Planning Guide.* Creative Confirmation. Minneapolis: Augsburg Fortress, 1994.

God Comes to Me. Catechetics for Today. Philadelphia: Parish Life Press, 1980.

Hansen, Olaf et al. *God's Grace for God's People.* Word, Grace, Faith. Minneapolis: Augsburg Publishing House, 1967.

Johnson, Kent L. "Confirmation Programs in the Congregation: What Works?" *Word and World* (Fall 1991): 387.

Kadel, Thomas, Gary Dreir, and Mary Sue Dehmlow Dreir. "A Companion for Your Way: The Small Catechism." New Journeys in Confirmation. Minneapolis: Augsburg Fortress, 1990.

Klos, Frank W. *Confirmation and First Communion: A Study Book.* Minneapolis: Augsburg Publishing House; Philadelphia: Board of Publication of the Lutheran Church in America; St. Louis: Concordia Publishing House, 1968.

Lewis, Craig et al. *Living the Lord's Prayer.* The Living Catechism. Philadelphia: Parish Life Press, 1987.

Lohre, Mary and Julie Lindesmith, eds. *Up Close and Personal.* Living in Grace. Minneapolis: Augsburg Fortress, 1995.

Melheim, Rich. "Conformation *(Sic)* Is Dead," *Lutheran Partners,* 17ff, May/June 1993.

Olson, Dennis and Frederick Baltz. *Saints and Sojourners: A Bible Survey.* Minneapolis: Augsburg Fortress, 1990.

Planning Manual. Giving New Life. Philadelphia: Parish Life Press, Division for Parish Services, undated.

Roloff, Marvin. *Affirm Planning Guide.* Affirm. Minneapolis: Augsburg Publishing House, 1984.

Service Book and Hymnal. Minneapolis: Augsburg Publishing House, 1958.

Shenkweiler, Carl et al. *God Is Love.* Catechetics for Today. Philadelphia: Parish Life Press, 1980.

Notes

1. *Service Book and Hymnal* (Minneapolis: Augsburg Publishing House, 1958), 246.

2. Frank W. Klos, *Confirmation and First Communion: A Study Book* (Minneapolis: Augsburg Publishing House; Philadelphia: Board of Publication of the Lutheran Church in America; St. Louis: Concordia Publishing House, 1968), 6.

3. *The Confirmation Task Force Report* (Chicago: Evangelical Lutheran Church in America, Division for Congregational Ministries, 1993), 14.

4. Klos, op. cit., 158–174.

5. Carl Shenkweiler, et al., *God Is Love,* Catechetics for Today (Philadelphia: Parish Life Press, 1980) 5.

6. Olaf Hansen et al., *God's Grace for God's People,* Word, Grace, Faith (Minneapolis: Augsburg Publishing House, 1967).

7. Elwin Bergstraesser et al., *I Am and I Listen,* Word, Faith, Grace (Minneapolis: Augsburg Publishing House, 1971), 13.

8. *God Comes to Me,* Catechetics for Today (Philadelphia: Parish Life Press, 1980), 3.

9. Ibid., 4.

10. Shenkweiler, op. cit., 7.

11. Marvin Roloff, *Affirm Planning Guide,* Affirm (Minneapolis: Augsburg Publishing House, 1984), 5.

12. Craig Lewis et al., *Living the Lord's Prayer,* The Living Catechism (Philadelphia: Parish Life Press, 1987), 10–18.

13. *Planning Manual,* Giving New Life (Philadelphia: Division for Parish Services, undated), 2.

14. Peter Benson et al., *The Quicksilver Years* (Cambridge: Harper and Row, 1987), 36.

15. Rich Melheim, "Conformation *(Sic)* Is Dead!" *Lutheran Partners* (May/June 1993): 17–24.

16. John Westerhoff, *Will Our Children Have Faith?* (New York: Seabury Press, 1976), 7.

PART 2

Lutheran Foundations

CHAPTER 3

Lutheran Confirmation Ministry in Historical Perspective

Luther E. Lindberg

Is the church truly in danger of losing its capacity to transmit some of its most sacred traditions—such as confirmation ministry? The church in history has shown an uncommon and even exciting vitality in its implementation of this form of ministry, but how does this past relate to the future?

Historical Perspective

The intent of this chapter is to provide access to some of the primary historical documents of the church related to confirmation ministry (many of which are either out of print or unavailable), to sketch the history of confirmation so that central issues will become evident, to examine prevailing ideas about the historical parentage of confirmation ministry, and to help the reader gain a sense of the urgency that punctuates confirmation study for Lutherans in North America. Confirmation, for Lutherans, is a big issue and an unsettling idea. An Anglican scholar of the nineteenth century calls confirmation "one of the deepest mysteries of the Catholic Faith."[1] What makes it all the more urgent is that confirmation, for many Lutherans, is a taken-for-granted routine. Such routine, especially when it has a checkered history, tends to foster bad theology and bad practice, even ignorance and ill will rather than insight and commitment.[2] Often the church has found itself in trouble with confirmation because it has not thought enough about confirmation's original meaning and intent. To paraphrase Reinhard Hutter, confirmation practices are the other side of confirmation theology.[3]

History is full of instances of leaders and movements taking confirmation and making of it whatever they thought needed to be done in their minds at a certain time in history, trying to enlist the power and tradition of confirmation in their favor. In this way the church has often become like the rabbit nibbling itself lost from the path, following tuft after tuft of juicy grass. Stephen Sykes reminds us that "signs and symbols express and strengthen the reality they signify but the sign can be present without the reality."[4] Does a universal concept of confirmation—a common definition or practice that can serve as a model or point of reference—actually exist? What, if anything, about confirmation ministry is permanent press—meaning it doesn't wash out with time? Could we be so fortunate that confirmation ministry has been a stable element in the history of the church? Can stability be found in history—either in the early church, the Reformation, or at any later time? Should we expect stability? What or who are the parents of Lutheran confirmation ministry?

The study of history should help us move forward in the maze of confirmation without a lot of hemming and hawing. Steering in the right direction in this endeavor could be likened to rowing a boat. The rower faces backwards and keeps eyes focused on landmarks so that the journey forward will be straight and true. Obviously the rower must also constantly look around at immediate waters and at the destination.

Although the tradition known by the name *confirmation* had its roots in the early church, its flowering for Lutherans was a reflection of the Reformation. Confirmation cannot be seen as a cut flower; we cannot just look at the blossom or petals and say, "This is confirmation." A tradition cannot be severed from its stem and roots in history and in other parts of the world. All the histories we have examined in the writing of this chapter begin by saying that confirmation has been a tangled web, a maze of confusion, a complicated and controverted practice since the beginning. Confirmation is still searching for theology and rationale. Even though its practice has been taken seriously—perhaps too seriously—for centuries, its theology and meaning have seldom if ever been clear. Even when significant confirmation studies have taken place they often have not reached out to congregations. This limited dissemination has led to the occasional notion that a congregation or pastor is free to understand and make rules about confirmation practice in any chosen manner without impinging restrictions. Therefore the question remains: is our understanding of confirmation so murky that we can make of it whatever we choose?

To study confirmation history is to study a bubbling pot. The historical study of confirmation shows that while numerous clusters of interpretations of confirmation come and go, strong threads of consistency and continuity have persisted. The concern for confirmation obviously doesn't belong to Lutherans alone; confirmation is a pre-Reformation phenomenon that was picked up by the Reformers because it was a tradition of the church entrenched in the lives of clergy and lay alike. Martin Luther would have opted not to practice a rite of confirmation, but he fought hard to maintain and improve its catechetical nature. It is impossible to restrict a study of confirmation to Lutheran history and practice. *Confirmation* appears to be a kind of code word for Lutherans that carries the weight of dealing with most of what is needed on the human side of the divine-human encounter. To many it has become a sort of summary of right belief, right practice, and right worship. However deeply confirmation touches on each of these notions, anyone does a disservice to confirmation to elevate it above the sacraments.

Confirmation is one of the lightning rods of criticism of the Lutheran church because it is so diverse in its practice and so lacking in consistent definition and theology. The diversity of thought and confusion surrounding confirmation is not new. Historical study makes it immediately evident that confirmation has had attached to it many different and diverse practices and many different theological rationales. Arthur Repp notes that "one cannot speak of a uniform confirmation practice among Lutherans."[5] David R. Holeton believes that confirmation is in a state of pastoral crisis in many church bodies today.[6] Gerard Austin says that from the beginning confirmation was "a practice seeking a theory."[7] No study of this size could possibly present a complete exposition of all the understandings and practices that have been followed since the early church.

Confirmation: The Baby in Solomon's Court

In his 1993 book Paul Turner writes:

> Confirmation deserves our grief. It is like the baby in King Solomon's court. Two women claimed the child. To determine who was its real mother, Solomon ordered the baby cut in two. Then he listened for which woman wailed, and rescued the baby for her.[8]

If confirmation is the baby, who are its parents? Are the parents the same for Lutherans as for Roman Catholics, Orthodox, or others who practice confirmation? A study of history uncovers many who claim to be its parents. Scholars and church leaders have disagreed from early Christian years and have shaped confirmation ministry in their own image. What does history say?

One recent study has reduced the different understandings of confirmation in a way that is comprehensive and helpful to us. Confirmation has been seen in strikingly different and even contradictory ways as:

- The completion of infant baptism. In this view confirmation is seen as a ceremony in which youth make public decisions to embrace the faith into which they have been baptized and "join the church."

- The ratification of a person's baptism. After rigorous instruction and examination the confirmand makes a personal decision to be committed to the church and is admitted in a public rite to the full privileges of membership. The importance of the confirmand's own personal relationship with God is stressed.

- The sealing of the Holy Spirit. Baptism is "sealed" by the laying on of hands and/or anointing with oil, leading to first communion. Historically, confusion has surrounded the issue of how God's gift of the Holy Spirit comes to persons. The New Testament seems to suggest different possibilities.

- The affirmation of the baptismal covenant in adolescence or the renewal of a covenant at any time during life's pilgrimage when an individual comes to new or deepened understanding and/or commitments in faith. This model sees baptism as the central sacrament.[9] It engrafts one into the body of Christ, the ministering community, and incorporates the possibility of repeatable baptismal affirmations. As people move through life, additional educational and liturgical opportunities refocus this original "ordination" for the congregation.

- The blessing following baptism, welcoming the new Christian into full communion in the church and at the Lord's table. Confirmation is the "blessing" that moves us from baptism to communion. The act of blessing gives identity to the person, as with Abram, Sarai, and Paul. We are blessed to be a blessing.

- The separate, one-time sacrament that imparts the Holy Spirit and imprints a uniquely Christian character establishing identity and effective eternal salvation. In the thirteenth century Thomas Aquinas developed a strong theological position that confirmation is a sacrament. The new "vitality" communicated in the sacrament strengthens the disciple to live in fidelity to the gospel. The sacrament of confirmation must be administered by a bishop or a priest specially empowered to seal with the Holy Spirit.

- The repeatable sacrament (like communion), first experienced in a unified initiation through baptism, laying on of hands, and eucharist, for infants or adults. The sacrament may be repeated at any time in life when the faith of the individual is in need of renewal and focus. We make a mistake when we think that maturity in faith comes at roughly the same time in the lives of all persons.

- The rite that symbolizes and celebrates "life in the Spirit," but is not itself a particular giving or receiving of the Holy Spirit. In this model the renewal of baptism (confirmation) is a rite secondary to the experience of receiving into one's heart and soul the presence of God's Spirit. The important thing is life in the Spirit. It is not the individual or the pastor or the congregation that does the confirming; rather God does the confirming through the Holy Spirit. We do not control when our awareness of the gift takes place.[10]

Confirmation Ministry

The term *confirmation ministry*, however, is relatively new to the Lutheran church where the term *confirmation* is quite old. In one sense, perhaps a chapter on the history of confirmation ministry should begin with the time in history when the term *confirmation ministry* came into common usage. That chapter would begin in 1970 when Lutheran bodies in the United States adopted *The Report of the Joint Commission on the Theology and Practice of Confirmation.* One of the significant results of that study and the actions of the Lutheran bodies is the inauguration of the linking of the two terms, *confirmation* and *ministry.* But even confirmation ministry is not a cut flower; it cannot be severed from the history of confirmation. While the two, confirmation and ministry, have without doubt been used together,[11] perhaps casually, for years, the result of the 1970 actions was to link the terms in common Lutheran usage.

Lutheran Confirmation's Baptismal Parentage

The significant Lutheran studies of the history of confirmation are not known for their extensive attention to confirmation in the years of the early church. They often treat New Testament concerns under the category of theology rather than history. Fortunately studies of the shape of confirmation had been done before it became Lutheran.

Origins

In the time of Jesus and the disciples there was no rite of confirmation.[12] However, baptism included the laying on of hands and marked the coming of the Holy Spirit confirming the baptism. This rite took only a few brief seconds of time. Confirmation is not commanded in scripture and is therefore not a sacrament in Lutheran understanding. Luther noted that confirmation is to be avoided because it has no scriptural basis.[13] Perhaps the closest term we can find in the New Testament that refers to what became known as confirmation is the Greek word *bebaios,* which means "to validate something that has already happened."

We do not find any direct reference to confirmation in the Apostolic Fathers. The Christian literature of the first two centuries is not particularly helpful in describing early confirmation or even baptism. Justin Martyr (Apology, about A.D. 150), however, does describe the rite and doctrine of baptism. He mentions that instruction comes prior to baptism. The Didache (about A.D. 150) notes that being accepted into the church presupposed a period of catechetical instruction. In the time of Tertullian, Hippolytus, and

Ambrose there was no rite of confirmation. Confirmation was a part of the rite of baptism. After candidates were baptized they were "confirmed" with chrism, prayers, the sign of the cross, and the laying on of hands. Aidan Kavanagh's *Confirmation: Origins and Reform* is viewed as an authoritative look at the origins of confirmation.[14] Kavanagh suggests that confirmation in the Western church probably originated as a dismissal that concluded the service of baptism.[15] The earliest allusion in church history to this formal dismissal is found in the influential Apostolic Tradition (about A.D. 215–220) of Hippolytus. Kavanagh assembles evidence that the dismissals regularly consisted of prayer and some form of laying on of hands by the senior minister present. Dismissals were used in a variety of circumstances including baptism and the end of catechetical instruction.[16] Although the dismissal was carried out differently in various congregations of the church of the time, its use was frequent and general. Because the bishop was considered the chief catechist, the bishop carried out the dismissal, the *missa (impositio manuum* or *benedictio)*. In the baptismal *missa* may be found the first indications of what led to what we know as confirmation. The purpose of the *missa* was to conclude and formally close a unit of public worship and the end of the instruction of catechumens. The *missa* gradually turned into a separate postbaptismal rite performed by the bishop, as part of the initiation of new Christians. Wirgman summarizes a portion of the Didache: "After consecrating the oils the bishop apparently left the baptistry and returned into the church, leaving the Presbyter and deacons to administer the baptism, and awaiting the subsequent presentation of the newly baptized to him for confirmation."[17]

By the third century Christian initiation appears to have been a single rite having three parts involving water bath, dismissal (chrism), and eucharist. Kavanagh calls this three-stage process the origin of modern confirmation.[18] Beginning in the third century the bishop of Rome insisted that the baptized receive the sign and seal of the Holy Spirit from a bishop; the practice became widespread by the ninth century. Confirmation by a bishop emerged as the unity of Christian initiation dissolved in the West.[19] Dom Gregory Dix reminds us, however, that the only confirmation many western Christians had in the fifth to seventh centuries in Gaul and Spain was chrismation by a presbyter.[20] The adult catechumenate and confirmation were part of the same piece of cloth in the first five centuries of the Christian church. In the early church confirmation, then, was a part of the rite of baptism. After the candidates were baptized at the Easter Vigil their baptism was "confirmed" with verbal assurance, prayers, chrism, the sign of the cross, and the laying on of hands. This formal action was the second of three parts that made up the final stage of entry into the church; the first was the baptism itself and the last was participation in Holy Communion.

In A.D. 416 Pope Innocent I legitimized a separate postbaptismal anointing, giving it a pneumatic interpretation and basing its practice on the laying on of hands seen in Acts 8.[21] The episcopal action did not yet have a name.[22] The action of the bishop commonly included anointing with oil (chrismation), signing of the cross on the forehead (consignation), the laying on of the bishop's hands and the invocation of the Holy Spirit. These actions were all seen as originating in Acts and Hebrews, but became traditions chiefly in the western church.

The term *confirmation* was actually first officially used in France, probably in a Pentecost sermon by Bishop Faustus, at the Council of Riez (A.D. 439) and the Council of Orange (A.D. 441).[23] These councils were local and not churchwide. Both councils used the term to refer to the action that took place soon after water baptism. The councils decided to give local priests permission to anoint the children they had baptized, but also instructed bishops to visit local congregations to confirm local baptisms and to see that local practices were in order. They did this "confirmation" with a laying on of hands. In earlier history bishops were known to announce to the gathered congregation at the Easter Vigil that a group of catechumens had been baptized in the baptistry, a separate building away from the gathered congregation. The bishop was confirming the baptisms for the congregation through the use of the *missa*.

About A.D. 460 Bishop Faustus of Riez stressed the importance of confirmation being done by bishops, claiming that episcopal confirmation made the baptized "more fully Christian." Kavanagh quotes A. Winkler to show how with Faustus comes the idea that confirmation adds something not present in baptism: "In baptism we are born anew for life, after baptism we are confirmed for battle . . . in baptism we are washed, after baptism we are strengthened."[24] This episcopal action added something that wasn't there previously: that Christian life is a battle against evil and that the strength of the Holy Spirit is additional power for the fight. This idea was to have significant impact on the development of confirmation.

The practice of episcopal confirmation spread gradually in the West. By the Middle Ages the gap between birth and baptism had narrowed to a few days while the time between baptism and confirmation was extended to several years.

THE MEDIEVAL CHURCH

Kavanagh uses the phrase *preservation tendency* to describe how liturgical elements are often preserved even when their original meaning is lost under layers of subsequent interpretation.[25] The phrase describes well confirmation in the West in the Middle Ages.

After about A.D. 1000 the rite of confirmation had already achieved an independent status as a one-time sacrament performed by a bishop. The action that became identified with the rite was consignation with chrism. The medieval theology and practice of confirmation followed the thinking of Thomas Aquinas and was canonized at the Council of Florence in A.D. 1439, the century in which Luther was born. Florence formally identified confirmation as one of the seven sacraments.[26] The Council of Trent (A.D. 1545–1563) anathematized anyone who believed that confirmation didn't need to be done by a bishop.[27] Confirmation was now the official action of the church done by bishops, by which Christians grow in grace and are strengthened in faith. However, confirmation was widely neglected; distant parishes in northern Europe rarely received a visit by the bishop. Confirmation even became a somewhat tongue-in-cheek thing during these years because the episcopal action often became perfunctory; bishops often did their confirming while they were on their horses riding past confirmands who were lined up along the edge of the road (an outsider could sneak into the row and be confirmed). The "good" bishop was the bishop who would actually get off his horse and lay both hands on each confirmand.[28] Robert Jenson has often said that confirmation is the result of episcopal arrogance and bad medieval roads. Wirgman tells how, in England, the Synod of Exeter (A.D. 1287) favored the confirmation of infants and permitted people to apply to "any passing bishop" for confirmation.[29]

Lutheran Confirmation's Educational Parentage

"Confirmation was so generally ignored [in Medieval times] that the rite itself came to be included at the beginning of the pontifical as most candidates for ordination had not been confirmed."[30] In the East the unitary understanding of initiation in which baptism, confirmation, and first communion came together, ordinarily in early infancy, predominated. Most followers of the Reformation in its early years wanted little to do with confirmation because it was considered "Romanizing" and "an offense."

The Reformation, however, gave new freedom and permission for the church to interpret and practice confirmation in the light of reformed doctrine. Erasmus succeeded in poking pins in the sides of both Reformation and Roman Catholic confirmationists.[31] Early on individuals such as John Wycliffe (about 1329–1384) and John Hus (about 1369–1415) and groups, including the Bohemian Brethren (fifteenth century), the Waldensians (about 1200), and the Cathari (eleventh and fourteenth centuries) opposed the standard doctrine and practice of confirmation and made suggestions for change, some of them quite radical.[32]

The historical materials agree that a wide variety of views of confirmation were espoused and practiced by the Reformers. At least six identifiable clusters of emphasis emerged with the Reformation. (Repp may go a little far in calling them "types" because none actually ever existed in separate, pure, and easily described form.)[33] Four of these clusters appeared in the sixteenth century, as might be expected, and the last two in the following two centuries. Today vestiges or reflections of each of these six, as well as other not so identifiable forms, may be found in Lutheran congregations in the United States and across the world. We have picked up and amalgamated aspects of several of these interpretations, giving little thought to consistency or theological foundations.

Four historical studies might be called definitive to the history of Lutheran confirmation. They follow:

- Lutheran World Federation, *Confirmation: A Study Document*, 1963.[34]

- Arthur C. Repp, *Confirmation in the Lutheran Church*, 1964.

- Frank W. Klos, *Confirmation and First Communion: A Study Book*, 1968. (This influential volume includes the preliminary proposal to Lutheran bodies in the United States titled "A Report for Study from the Joint Commission on the Theology and Practice of Confirmation." The book was intended by the commission as a study book to help congregations study the meaning and history of confirmation and to develop confirmation in ways consistent to the history and meaning of confirmation.)

- W. Kent Gilbert, *Confirmation and Education*, 1969.[35]

Although the Lutheran church in the United States and its congregations continue to be perplexed about the meaning and practice of confirmation, these four sources constitute an accurate historical review.

The six Reformation interpretations were identified and sketched in the Lutheran World Federation (LWF) report, given formal names by Repp, and accepted in the work of the joint commission.

In general, the Reformers saw Medieval confirmation handed on to them as a gross misunderstanding and misuse of baptism in that it made confirmation into a sacrament. Therefore the Reformers set out to evaluate the early history of baptism theologically and they chose for their point of departure the New Testament. Their studies led them to different understandings, some destructively radical.

Luther himself criticized confirmation seen as a sacrament and as a supplement to baptism that conferred grace and the added gift of the Holy Spirit. Along with Melanchthon and Calvin he flatly rejected it. This rejection is written into the Lutheran confessions. Luther himself actually had little to say about confirmation as a rite but much to say about it as a catechetical or educational process. He is known to have called confirmation a human invention, monkey business, mumbo-jumbo, and fanciful deception.[36] Although he developed other rites (for example, the Deutsche Messe of 1526), he never prepared a rite of confirmation. M. Reu notes that in 1526 Luther saw worship as opportunity for instruction: "What we most need in our German worship is a plain, simple, clear and succinct catechism."[37] Luther, however, gave some support to colleagues who attempted to revamp the rite of confirmation along evangelical lines but gave strong support to catechetical instruction, especially in connection with both sacraments.[38] Luther noted: "I allow that confirmation be administered provided that it is known that God has said nothing about it, and knows nothing of it and what the bishops say about it is false."[39]

Clearly the Reformers did not all think alike about confirmation. In fact, one gets the feeling that many interpreters picked out rather minor aspects of confirmation—ones that seemed to support their particular likes—and wrapped them in the larger cloak of the tradition of confirmation. The six Reformation emphases are described in the following subsections (the 1970 *Report* provides a brief sketch of each):[40]

CATECHETICAL (CATECHUMENAL OR INSTRUCTIONAL) CONFIRMATION, DRIVEN BY CATECHETICAL INSTRUCTION

This type grew out of the need for instruction and preparation of the young for the Lord's supper but was not limited to those preparing for first communion. No rite was necessary but often the occasion of first communion was accompanied by a simple ceremony. This catechetical emphasis was the earliest Lutheran practice, the most common form in the Lutheran church through its first 150 years, particularly among the Scandinavians and orthodox Germans. In analysis we must be cautioned to remember that no assurance of a worthy reception of the Lord's supper stems from an educational process. Luther is remembered for his strong emphasis on instruction and catechism.

HIERARCHICAL (DISCIPLINARY) CONFIRMATION, DRIVEN BY A VOW OF FAITHFULNESS

This type had its origin with Martin Bucer who developed the first evangelical rite of confirmation. He introduced it in the Hessian churches in 1538–1539 through the Ziegenhain Order of Church Discipline. Bucer combined ideas from Erasmus and Luther and has been considered by many to be the father of Lutheran confirmation, at least in its hierarchical interpretation. Here hierarchical implies the power of the parish clergy in a local congregation. Bucer combined catechetical concerns with Erasmus's emphasis on the importance of the decision of the individual at puberty and the pastoral concern of Luther. Bucer introduced the idea of a vow wherein the young person pledges surrender to Christ and submits to the discipline of the church under the local pastor. Confirmation rather than baptism marks the beginning of membership in the church. This type of confirmation is notable in that it introduced the subjective element into the rite. Sadly, in actuality for many young people confirmation marks the end of association with the church rather than a beginning.

SACRAMENTAL CONFIRMATION, DRIVEN BY A RITE

While the first two interpretations were widely practiced, some congregations returned to a stronger emphasis on the rite that included the laying on of hands and a sacramental interpretation. Bucer's rite was not clear as to whether the laying on of hands actually imparts the Holy Spirit. Those who followed this thinking saw the rite as being of equal status with baptism or communion because it completed baptism and was the door to communion. If, as the Reformers insisted, Holy Baptism and Holy Communion are sacraments, surely confirmation must be. These sacramental overtones of the rite still persist. However, it must be remembered that we cannot assume that God reserves the Holy Spirit until the moment of laying on of hands in a rite.

TRADITIONAL (CONVINCING EVIDENCE) CONFIRMATION, DRIVEN BY THE POSTPONEMENT OF FIRST COMMUNION

Phillip Melanchthon and Martin Chemnitz were strong influences in this interpretation. This understanding of "confirmation without the Roman Catholic abuses" saw confirmation as something unrelated to baptism or renewal of vows. The Saxon Church Order of 1580 notes that catechetical instruction is the true Christian confirmation. First communion happened at a later time, anywhere from a few weeks to several months. In the seventeenth and eighteenth centuries when this type of confirmation was in vogue, first communion might be postponed for as long as two years depending on the progress of the young person. The traditional form of the rite emphasized the laying on of hands and the catechetical instruction that preceded it. The Brandenburg Church Order of 1540 (Bugenhagen) is an early example and shows how many of these interpretations were going on alongside each other. The postponement of first communion lasted in many instances into the twentieth century. However, it was also strongly criticized as Roman by Lutherans who resisted any pressures to conform to the Roman Catholic sacramental interpretation of confirmation.[41] Negative reaction to this view was heavy. The Brandenburg Order was used in Sweden during the latter part of the sixteenth century but was reacted to so strongly that the idea of confirmation itself was abolished altogether.[42]

The Lutheran confessions do not require a rite of confirmation as completion of a deficient baptism. These four interpretations, though quite different and even contradictory, all shared at least the following elements: (a) universal rejection of the Medieval doctrine that confirmation supplements baptism; (b) an assumption or emphasis of education and catechetical instruction before the candidate is presented for confirmation or first communion; (c) an association of confirmation with both the sacraments (except within the traditional form); (d) a young age of the catechumen at the time of first communion (rarely higher than 12) when compared with Lutheran confirmation in the United States prior to 1970. In fact, age was not regarded as important because the major criterion was the young person's readiness to receive the Lord's supper.

Two other schools of thought developed later in the seventeenth and eighteenth centuries.

PIETISTIC (CONVERSION) CONFIRMATION, DRIVEN BY INDIVIDUAL STRONGLY FELT RENEWAL

Parish life in Germany declined during the Counter-Reformation and the Thirty Years War (1618–1648). Catechetical instruction deteriorated along with the rest of parish life. The cause of moribund parish life was taken up in a movement toward Pietism led primarily by Philip Spener (1635–1705) who wanted to bring the head into the heart.

Spener found his most helpful model for confirmation practice and rite in Bucer who fostered a conversion theology with a personal decision and commitment to an elect group of the faithful. In the pietistic interpretation the confession of faith located in the rite became subjective in nature. Confirmation is personal conversion. Subjective elements entered into the examination of catechumens, into the individualizing of the confirmation blessing and into preparation for first communion. The catechumen was supposed to "feel" the new life in Christ. This practice had the effect of raising the age of confirmation to a time when the catechumen was more mature. One problem with this interpretation is that commitment to Christ is a daily not a one-time process. J. D. C. Fisher comments that confirmation was never meant to be an act of commitment in scripture or in the age of the Fathers.[43]

RATIONALISTIC (GRADUATION) CONFIRMATION, DRIVEN BY CULTURAL PRESSURES

As could be expected, the subjective approach prompted a strong reaction. Under the influence of Rationalism with its de-emphasis of the sacraments and its stress on understanding over feeling, scripture, and God's actions, confirmation—the process and the rite—became a festive, cultural, even secular landmark that gave Christian identity to the person. Christianity could be summed up as a series of virtues to be followed. In this kind of thinking confirmation was regarded as the event that gave meaning to baptism. Confirmation became the great festival of youth in which the individual made a dramatic decision, marked by a vow elevated to an oath, to become a faithful member of the church. The examination of candidates was stressed because it demonstrated that the catechumen understood the meaning of the oath of faithfulness. In some Scandinavian countries the practice of a secular confirmation developed in which those not wishing to make a religious profession of faith could participate in the rite in a purely secular way while receiving all the material benefits received by their Christian peers.[44]

In this thinking, confirmation became a rite, a dramatic event marked by long and pleading sermons and lectures by pastors. It became a sentimental event, a time for robes, flowers, parties, gifts, and a sense that the individual was no longer under the tutelage of parents or sponsors but was able now to stand alone in matters of faith and daily life. In this cultural understanding, ideas beyond the scope of the church were added; laws were made regarding voting rights, school attendance, union membership, the privilege of marriage in the church and being a sponsor at baptism. This kind of thinking has been a major influence on current "graduation understandings" of confirmation.[45] In brief, confirmation became necessary if people wanted the rights of first-class citizenship. It became part of the social and national fabric in many Lutheran lands. As such it had a powerful influence on society. During the years of the Cold War in Germany the cultural power of confirmation had built up such momentum that it was replaced by the occupying forces with a "secular youth dedication" process and event (Jugendweihe) in which youth had to participate if they ever hoped to attend university, become apprenticed, or hold government-related jobs. Such thinking is countered by our understanding that no rigid demarcation line falls between youth and adulthood. At best it is a drifting line.

One of the greatest contributions of the Reformation to confirmation ministry, following Luther's lead, was the use of catechisms as primary teaching sources. Although catechisms had preceded Luther, he simplified and strengthened both the form and substance of the catechism and made it a tool for use in the home. He took seriously Paul's words to Philemon about "the church in your house." Luther wrote the Small Catechism for use in the home, thus laying responsibility on the home. In reviewing all that happened around confirmation during the Reformation it becomes clear that the idea and use of catechisms, if not Luther's Small Catechism, is a consistent element.

Confirmation enjoyed an exaggerated and even dangerous esteem in Europe, where it was often seen as the most significant rite in the life of the Christian, but it came to North America including elements of each of the six Reformation models. To make things more complicated, by 1910 American Lutherans were splintered into 24 separate bodies. Luther Reed said that in our early years in America "The [Lutheran] church was confused in practice as well as doctrine, and the abnormal came to be thought of as the normal."[46] The confusion may be seen in the wide variety of confirmation practices and was partly due to the immigration from many European lands, each having its own struggles and traditions with defining and practicing confirmation. As Lutherans began to band together even in spite of the peculiarities of their traditions, confirmation became more and more a patchwork of ideas practiced in the old country. No common understanding defined confirmation or why it was a part of church life other than "it's something we have always done" (Kavanagh's "preservation tendency"). Ethnic and geographic differences held great influence in the minds of parents and following generations of children who had participated in the process and in the rite. The practice of confirmation had actually been dropped in a number of Lutheran lands. However, toward the end of the seventeenth century, with the primary pressures of Pietism and Rationalism and for various other reasons, it had been restored.

What were the prevailing patterns, if any, in the way confirmation was treated in the New World? Three elements stand out: education under the pastor was consistently present; reference to baptism was common; and the process and the rite was seen as preparation for first communion. The 1970 *Report* summarizes:

> Great stress was placed on the solemnity of the vows and their life-long effect. The confession of faith was regarded as subjective in nature. It was said that in the rite the catechumen was assuming the promises that his parents or sponsors had made for him in infancy. Confirmation marked the event in which the child [became an "adult member" and] joined the Lutheran church or a local congregation. The examination was intended to give evidence that the catechumen understood the meaning of the solemn moment. The handclasp was interpreted in one of two ways; either it formalized the vow or it transmitted the rights and privileges that were said to come with the rite. One of these privileges was usually assumed to be the right to partake of the Lord's Supper. The laying on of hands gave dignity to the occasion but was not given a sacramental meaning. It symbolized the gift of the Holy Spirit working through the Word and, in the minds of many of the people, through the importance of the rite itself.[47]

Confirmation was commonly linked (Rationalism) with graduation from required schooling at about age 13 or 14 and seen as the end of formal religious education. Palm Sunday was the most common date for the confirmation celebration, a link with first communion coming during Holy Week. In these practices was a lack of concern for how confirmation was interpreted in other congregations. Little extra-congregational talk was dedicated to it and even less study.

The impetus for a new and thorough study of the meaning of confirmation came with the close of World War II when Lutherans from all over the world met to rebuild a church divided and decimated by national alliances, destruction, and death. National divisions were becoming evident and Lutheran confirmation was being challenged by external forces such as the *Jugendweihe* of the communists. Lutherans joined together to study confirmation. The Lutheran World Federation called for a thorough study of confirmation and issued its first report at its 1963 convention noting that "it is the *theology* of Confirmation which actually is the weak point in the Lutheran Church today."[48] The report was titled "Confirmation: A Study Document" and was intended to be taken seriously by Lutheran churches across the world. Lutheran churches in the United States were involved, and it was recognized from the beginning that confirmation does not belong to Lutherans alone but to other Christian bodies; it is an ecumenical matter. This understanding poses the question as to whether any church body in any land can alone address a situation that belongs to other churches as well. The LWF study document was issued with the reminder that its intention was to stimulate discussion in congregations and countries that might lead to a common understanding of what confirmation is. The report was scholarly, thorough, and laid out a myriad of questions to be addressed in ongoing study. So broad was the scope of the study that it seemed almost to imply that whatever church problem you scratch, underneath is something important to confirmation.

The conclusions reached for study by churches and congregations were significant and even radical. They addressed confirmation both as rite and process.

- Confirmation is part of a larger catechumenate of the church and derives its meaning from infant baptism. Confirmation is elementary instruction during the children's catechumenate.

- In any rite of confirmation the importance of baptism must be clearly expressed. A clear understanding and practice of baptism must be achieved with an understanding that Holy Baptism is complete in itself. Baptismal remembrance is important and needed often. Just so the need to daily renounce the powers of evil.

- Instruction in the faith must be reflected in any rite.
- In any rite it must be clear that the confirming (affirming) of faith is something that must take place every day.
- The confirmation rite is complete in itself and does not happen in stages.
- Proclamation of the word is an important part of the rite.
- Examination is an essential part of the rite.
- The confession of faith is a necessary part of the rite.
- Any use of a "vow" should not be interpreted legalistically or employ "conditional additions."
- Intercessory prayer used in the rite should show that strengthening for the future comes from the baptism of the past.[49]

About a decade before the LWF report Lutheran churches in North America held an important intersynodical seminar on confirmation in Racine, Wisconsin. Although the seminar did not end in specific recommendations for church bodies, it did stimulate a series of conferences and workshops across the country between 1957 and 1960, which heightened the sense of the immensity of the problem being faced and allowed U.S. Lutherans to clarify concerns brought to the LWF study that began in 1961. One element that made these discussions take on more significance was the timing; it was the early years of the Lutheran mergers in the United States. The concern was that we could hardly build strong new church bodies if we were not even sure how present bodies define something as important as confirmation.

As a result of the LWF report, major Lutheran church bodies in North America engaged in a common study, interestingly under the impetus of their Boards of Parish Education. One immediate stimulus for the U.S. study in these prosperous, wide open years, was that curriculum materials for congregations had to be produced on a regular basis. Although concern for the confirmation rite was included in the study, the study concentrated on educational concerns.

Confirmation Ministry: Lutheran Definition

It was agreed that one extremely important element in the resolution of such a deep and thorny problem lay in coming to a commonly accepted definition of what confirmation is. But to arrive at a commonly accepted definition is not an easy matter; we often see in confirmation a practice begun for one set of reasons and perpetuated for another set of reasons.[50] In 1960 a survey was made of Lutheran pastors in an attempt to discover just what the concepts and practices of confirmation were. The responses showed that opinions and practices were extremely if not frighteningly broad—diverse enough to indicate the need for a large-scale study in the United States. The Lutheran Church in America, the American Lutheran Church, and The Lutheran Church—Missouri Synod agreed in 1964 to enter into joint study on the theology and practice of confirmation. The three presidents appointed a joint commission, which included theologians, parish pastors, educators, liturgiologists and administrators to study together and make recommendations to the church bodies for uniform practice suitable in North America at the present time. In 1966 the commission undertook a survey, "Current Concepts and Practices of Confirmation in Lutheran Churches," which was sent to congregations. The survey results indicated that the following concepts were held by pastors and lay leaders. Confirmation was seen as

- a renewing of one's baptismal covenant;
- a personal confession of the faith confessed by one's [parents and] sponsors;
- a public affirmation of one's faith;
- the making of a lifelong commitment to Christ;
- a taking on of increased responsibilities as a member of the church;
- a necessary prerequisite for receiving Holy Communion.[51]

This survey showed grade 8.4 to be the average time for the rite and a general feeling that the age should be higher. Pastors and lay leaders felt that the establishment of a uniform practice with regard to the age of confirmation would be good. Most respondents were not in favor of admitting children to communion before the rite. All in all, such a wide divergence between confirmation understandings and practices was displayed in the feedback that the commission decided to enter into a large-scale, Lutheran churchwide study of confirmation in congregations. It looked as though the church had lost sight of its theology in trying to patch up problems in practice.

The churchwide study program took place in 1969 when Frank Klos's *Confirmation and First Communion* was distributed widely to congregations. The book summarized the work of the commission, contained pre- and post-response forms, proposed a definition for confirmation, and invited wide participation. The study opened up confirmation and informed congregations and pastors and led them to openly change many of their ideas about confirmation and discover reasons for questioning their own feelings about confirmation (for example, the idea that a rite of confirmation is necessary). Either the study book proved to be one of the most effective educational ventures the Lutheran church in the United States has ever taken, or congregations had deep and underlying dissatisfactions with what was happening in confirmation ministry. It cannot be overstated that the 1970 actions signaled drastic changes in the Lutheran understanding of confirmation ministry.

Once participants became immersed in the study, for example, they felt that the commission had not gone far enough in its proposed definition of confirmation. That suggested definition in the study book reads:

> Confirmation is a pastoral and educational ministry of the church that is designed to help baptized children identify with the life and mission of the adult Christian community and that is celebrated in a public rite.[52]

After the commission studied the responses of congregations, it drew up a revised definition that came to the church bodies in the early 1970s.[53] The revised definition read:

> Confirmation is a pastoral and educational ministry of the church which helps the baptized child through Word and Sacrament to identify more deeply with the Christian community and participate more fully in its mission.[54]

The differences between the two definitions are significant. Included now is a clear reference to word and sacrament. Gone is mention of a rite; a rite is not deemed to be an essential part of Lutheran confirmation. Gone is the idea that the church is primarily an adult Christian community. Concern for each individual catechumen is identified as important. Life in the Christian community and the full involvement of youth in the mission of the church is a part of the ministry. Strongly present is affirmation of Luther's theme, "I have been baptized."

A digest of the report and its implications was developed by the Lutheran Church in America, and the American Lutheran Church makes much of the pastoral and educational dimensions and of the good news. It lifts up the following important elements:

- For the first time we have a definition of confirmation.

- Confirmation is a process rather than an event; a ministry rather than a rite.

- Confirmation ministry concludes during the latter part of 10th grade and may be celebrated with a public rite.

- Admission to first communion comes during the confirmation process, in the latter part of grade 5.

- Parents or sponsors are given increasing responsibility in the confirmation process.

- Lay involvement in the confirmation process is stressed to a greater degree than ever before.

- Confirmation is no longer a two- or three-year educational program; it is a 16-year pastoral and educational ministry.

- Holy Communion comes not at the conclusion of confirmation, but is a significant event within the years of confirmation ministry.

- Confirmation has to do with the total life of a congregation—the shape of its pastoral and educational ministry for and with children and youth.

- Celebrations are a part of the Christian life. The entire span of confirmation ministry should be marked by occasional, appropriate rites.[55]

Later action of the Evangelical Lutheran Church in America has underscored some of the chief contentions of the 1970 actions:

- Baptism incorporates into the church. In Baptism people become members not only of the Church universal but of a particular congregation. Therefore all baptisms are entered into the permanent records of the congregation and certificates are issued at the time of the administration of the sacrament.[56]

- Baptism is repeatedly affirmed. The public rite for Affirmation of Baptism may be used at many times in the life of a baptized Christian. It is especially appropriate at Confirmation and at times of reception or restoration into membership.[57]

- The age of first communion may vary. Common mission among the congregations of this church depends on mutual respect for varied practice in many areas of church life including the ages of first Communion . . . There is no command from our Lord regarding the age at which people should be baptized or first communed . . . Out of mutual respect among congregations, children who are communing members of a congregation of this church who move to a congregation with a different practice should be received as communing members.[58]

• Preparation for Holy Communion is recommended.[59]

Richard Robert Osmer, writing from a Presbyterian perspective, has taken note of how the 1970 actions have exerted enormous influence on contemporary mainline Lutheranism.[60] However, even though the church had high hopes that the actions would be studied, taken to heart, and understood by congregations, they did not lead to the widespread study anticipated.

Contemporary Perspectives

Generally speaking, Lutheran confirmation ministry today is recalling its baptismal parentage—at least to some degree. Study of the baptismal surroundings of confirmation in the early church is enlivening congregations across the church.

What forces are shaping confirmation ministry for the present and the future? Do these forces go beyond baptism and education? Even though no simple answer to the question is likely to surface, a number of significant things are happening in the church right now that could influence the shape of confirmation ministry.

The 1970 *Report* is a clear demonstration that commonly guided study carried out in congregations can indeed be a positive shaper of confirmation ministry. However, today the press of member mobility, the busy lives of families and young people, the increasing sense by youth of their need to participate in meeting community and social needs, and the diverse and even opposing confirmation ministry practices of congregations and regional/ethnic clusters are becoming evident. With these factors comes a feeling that we ought to be doing more with confirmation ministry than we are already doing.

One of the hopes of this volume is to stimulate and be a resource for further congregational study and discussion of confirmation ministry by supplying basic study materials. The need for more adequate education of seminary students in confirmation history is also apparent. Plenty of evidence reaffirms that changes in something so central and vital to congregations cannot take place only in books, the halls of church headquarters, and assembly decisions; local impetus and ownership in a thoughtful examination of purpose and practices must be present. Thorough and responsible study that includes not only history but also the many other concerns addressed in the chapters of this volume is needed.

In 1986 the Lutheran World Federation published *Confirmation in the Lutheran Churches Today*.[61] The study once again concerned worldwide Lutheran thinking and practice and showed broad differences among Lutherans but identified significant points of agreement.[62]

The 1993 ELCA Study

The latest official ELCA actions regarding confirmation ministry may be found in *The Confirmation Ministry Task Force Report* adopted by the ELCA Churchwide Assembly in 1993. Although the church had taken significant and drastic action regarding confirmation ministry in 1970, the Church Council of the Evangelical Lutheran Church in America felt the need for and approved a new study of confirmation ministry. This new task force drew heavily on the 1970 *Report* of the Joint Commission on the Theology and Practice of Confirmation, which provided the church for the first time with a definition of confirmation ministry. The term *child* found in the 1970 statement was left out in favor of *baptized persons*. In listening to congregations and carrying out research, the task force built on the 1970 definition and identified a focal question for its study: What is the role of the congregation in affirming youth in Christian faithfulness with an emphasis on lifelong learning and discipleship?[63]

Several things are to be noted about this focus. First of all, it addresses the role and place of the congregation while maintaining high concern for youth, for catechumens, for those going through Lutheran catechetical instruction. Secondly, it picks up the use of the term *affirming* from *Lutheran Book of Worship*, published after the 1970 actions of the churches; in *LBW* one does not find a confirmation service but rather Affirmation of Baptism, a rite to be used not only for confirmation but also for reception into membership and restoration to membership. This affirming of baptism is consistent with the emphasis on baptism in the definitive Lutheran studies. Christian faithfulness is highlighted along with lifelong learning and discipleship. The task force articulated also the need to help congregations and pastors develop a "grace-centered" vision for confirmation ministry. The focus on good news and grace was important for the task force because the catechetical part of confirmation programs can tend to become laden with rules and works-righteousness. The task force explained the Lutheran position: Confirmation ministry is an opportunity for congregations to renew the vision of living by grace, grounded in baptism. This vision is especially important for ministry with young Christians, but it also has lifelong implications.[64]

The task force supported strongly the description of confirmation ministry as a pastoral and educational process. In its study it lifted up the following themes as having special importance:

- the centrality of baptism to our faith;
- the separation of first communion from the rite of confirmation;
- the need for a lifelong process of learning [and] greater emphasis on the entire congregation's pastoral care of young people;
- the challenge to provide genuine opportunities for more profound attachment of youth to the Christian community [which is larger than the local congregation];
- the provision for a variety of rites at significant times in life.[65]

The task force also identified a number of changes in congregational perception and practice regarding confirmation ministry, which had emerged since the 1970 actions. Nine of these were identified as being of special importance:

- Responsibility for confirmation ministry is more and more shared by both lay and clergy.
- Catechetical instruction has broadened to include issues of the wider world.
- Instruction in the Bible and the Small Catechism has recently returned to the fore.
- Increased awareness of learning styles and contexts has generated a variety of approaches, strategies, and techniques.
- Increased understanding regarding developmental stages in both faith and cognition affects both what is taught and how it is taught.

- Though a large majority of congregations invite members to take part in communion before they are confirmed, the age for first communion varies.

- Congregations continue to see the confirmation rite as important even though the meaning remains ambiguous.

- The confirmation rite is seen as an affirmation of baptism, not a completion of it or its competitor.

- Catechetical instruction has been a valued opportunity for experimentation.[66]

The task force developed the understanding that confirmation ministry is an opportunity for congregations to renew the vision of living by grace, grounded in baptism. The whole congregation plays a vital role in this ministry. Everything in confirmation ministry flows from baptism. Confirmation ministry takes place in a living community of faith and is the responsibility of the entire congregation, not only the pastor. No congregation or pastor is an island when it comes to confirmation theology and practice. If it is to be effective, confirmation ministry will involve the use of a variety of persons and approaches and diverse learning models.[67]

The task force made four specific recommendations, which were adopted overwhelmingly (95.4 percent) by the assembly:

- That congregational confirmation ministry be gospel-centered, grace-centered both in content and approach. Hearing the gospel as refreshing, affirming, life-giving good news is important for all members of the congregation.

- That such a confirmation ministry be tailor-made with an emphasis on community building and faith to convey the gospel in the congregation's particular context. Congregations must address the needs of their specific young people and communities while being flexible in addressing varied ages, maturity, and skills.

- That congregations create, or designate, a confirmation ministry team to give shape and direction to the planning and coordination of a pastoral and educational confirmation ministry. Recognizing that reforming confirmation ministry is an ongoing task, the task force urged that a specific group/committee or "confirmation team" within the congregation be designated to provide oversight and continuity.

- That synods, the churchwide organization, and seminaries be in partnership with congregations in developing a broad variety of support resources, such as materials, networks, and trained leaders for confirmation ministry. The term *partnership* is to be taken seriously (congregations, indeed, are not islands). Given present funding patterns in the church where more funding is available at the congregational level and less at the synod and churchwide levels, work in the area of confirmation ministry must be more deliberate and intentional in congregations within a sense of partnership.[68] Partnership must be ecumenical in scope.

The 1993 ELCA *Report* attempted to summarize Lutheran thinking in the United States and includes a number of practical suggestions for congregations. If confirmation ministries in local congregations are to experience greater effectiveness, then the impetus will probably come from congregations themselves and not from some other level of the church. Presently synods, seminaries, publishers of the church, and churchwide agencies stand in responding and supporting partnership roles, and congregations have the responsibility to move things along. It is not the congregation or the pastor who confirm; it is God working through the church.

Broader Concerns for Confirmation Ministry

At the same time congregational and educational loci of confirmation ministry are emphasized, we must not fail to see that confirmation ministry is not a thing owned by congregations or church bodies in isolation; confirmation ministry belongs to history, to the Lutheran church across the world and to other church bodies that treasure it dearly as part of their essential character. In the latter days of this century we are even seeing church bodies not previously claiming confirmation as part of their tradition, looking to confirmation as one way to help them face contemporary problems such as the retention of youth members, the instruction of young people beyond the Sunday church school, and the need to affirm more strongly the power and place of baptism in faith.

The ongoing examination of confirmation by the Lutheran World Federation demonstrated that concern for confirmation ministry is still bubbling across the wider church. A 1995 global report titled *Confirmation*

Ministry Study is notable.[69] Here the "new" term *confirmation ministry* is used in LWF reporting for the first time. This articulation was a demonstration that the Lutheran church across the world is becoming comfortable with the new and dynamic understanding that confirmation is indeed a ministry. The 1995 study was unique in that it addressed new ground in four respects:

- Its focus was deliberately placed on the ministry and voices of Latin American, Asian, and African churches. This focus provided quite a shock for Americans and Europeans, accustomed to having studies focused primarily on their situations.

- The research undertaken utilized interviews and meetings rather than written response forms. Written forms reflect Western thinking.

- The research attempted to get at the concerns of the people involved in confirmation ministry in many different contexts.

- The research reflects a changing view of pedagogy in that it sees education as a partnership between educators and theologians. (Pedagogy is no longer seen only as an instrument of theology attempting to transmit eternal truths.)

This 1995 LWF study was generated by concern across the church over the absence of young people from congregational life and the need to go to them directly to address their lack of involvement in the Christian community.[70] While Lutherans from North America were significantly involved in the LWF research, the results may relate more to the other geographical areas mentioned. What Americans learned was that worldwide Lutheran understandings and practices of confirmation go far beyond even the diversities we see in North America. Common concern for confirmation ministry, however, can be found in three factors:

- a yearning for future generations to experience faith;

- a passing on of the faith tradition of the Bible as summarized in the catechism;

- a sense of authorization by the community.[71]

The issues addressed in the third and last LWF study reflect the concerns of both the 1970 and 1993 actions of the church in the United States but are phrased in refreshingly different ways. Nine such issues were evident:

- a renewed relationship between theology and education or pedagogy;

- an emphasis on the ministry of the laity, . . . pastoral formation and the partnership between pastors and lay teachers;[72]

- the congregation as a learning community;

- renewed evangelical conversation;

- the recovery of the catechism as a conversation between life and faith;

- the role of the family in confirmation ministry;

- confirmation ministry as part of a lifelong journey of faith;

- the importance of the context in giving shape to the ministry;

- the relationship between confirmation, baptism and Holy Communion.[73]

All seven geographical regions of the LWF participated in the study: North America, Latin America/Caribbean, Asia, Africa, Northern Europe, Western Europe, and Central/Eastern Europe.[74] Site research was carried out in 22 countries, six area consultations were held, and eight significant national studies were included. Approximately half of the persons involved were female and 60 percent of the sites, consultations, and studies were in Africa, Asia, and Latin America.[75] The study of confirmation ministry was new to most of the national Lutheran churches involved. Each of five regions (Africa, Asia, Central/Eastern, Western and Northern Europe, Latin America and the Caribbean, and North America) reported observations and recommendations, which were referred to the churches in the regions for study and action. The themes developed by the North America region are stated in a way that applies new terminology and insights to issues already addressed. The four themes:

- The role the congregation plays in confirmation ministry is much more significant than most congregations think. We must not forget the role of small groups in the congregation, especially those that nurture and plan confirmation ministry programs.

- Confirmation ministry and youth education are at their best when they are seen as part of a lifelong journey. Youth education thrives when adult education is strong. Confirmation ministry is only one of several affirmations of baptism that occur over the lifetime.

- Contextualized and tailor-made programs developed by congregations rather than lockstep approaches are encouraged. Even the catechism and the best materials and program ideas need to be adapted to the needs of families and young people in the local congregation.

- We must do more to highlight the importance of young people in the life of the congregation. Attention to the development of the Christian identity of the young person and youth ministry were seen as elements central in the confirmation process.[76]

Evidence for broader interest in confirmation ministry is found also in Robert L. Browning and Roy A. Reed's 1995 book *Models of Confirmation and Baptismal Affirmation*. The book is written by professors from Methodist Theological School and examines the understanding and practice of confirmation in seven major denominations (Evangelical Lutheran Church in America, Episcopal, Presbyterian, Roman Catholic, United Church of Christ, United Methodist, and United Church of Canada). The book notes that the affirmation of baptism is a common element running through major current studies and makes a case for confirmation as a repeatable event. Although the church body studies noted conclude that lifelong learning is an essential part of confirmation ministry, few church bodies, Lutherans included, have made a serious effort to describe what this lifelong process might look like. The 1993 action of the ELCA Assembly does begin to sketch out the process as will be seen later.

Two of the assumptions running through the book were first articulated by Max Thurian in his 1957 book *Consecration of the Layman*. Browning and Reed write: "Thurian used scriptural and historical evidence to argue that confirmation is part of baptism and has no meaning apart from the meaning of baptism. He used historical, theological and pastoral data to argue for a new perspective on confirmation as repeatable and consecratory."[77]

Browning and Reed suggest that an increasing convergence of thought about confirmation and Christian initiation across church bodies is occurring, and they make suggestions for building a holistic perspective of what confirmation could be like in both its educational and liturgical dimensions. They contend that how we approach and practice confirmation ministry indeed reflects our practical theology, our understanding of baptism, our sense of community, and our understanding of faith development. As does the 1970 Lutheran report, Browning and Reed's *Models* suggests that the call for congregations to examine confirmation ministry actually comes out of a continuing pastoral concern to teach and inspire commitment.

The authors identify 13 major liturgical and educational trends in attitudes toward and the practice of confirmation ministry. These trends in themselves are reason enough for us to keep our eyes and attention on confirmation as we approach the next century. Here we note only some trends that have special connection with the Lutheran concerns already cited:

- Baptism, not confirmation, lies at the heart of conversion and commitment. Confirmation is part of the baptismal gift. Confirmation must not demean or lessen baptism. A new recognition has risen of the "unified initiation" practice of the early Christian church in which baptism, the *missa,* and eucharist were all part of the same rite. The sacrament of baptism is the rite of complete belonging and full membership in the church.

- The need for liturgies of commitment continues. Such baptismal affirmations (confirmations) must happen often during life. We make a mistake when we focus on a single age or time for such liturgies.

- The eucharist is the climactic moment of Christian initiation, just as the supper was a climactic experience for the disciples of Jesus. A rite of confirmation, however, should not be made a prerequisite for communion.

- Christian initiation is a communal, congregational experience rather than an individual experience. The recipient of the Holy Spirit is never the isolated individual.

- The new understanding is that education in the church is not for assent to right beliefs but for truth that integrates all of life. It is not just for children and youth but for all Christians. A faith development perspective includes persons of all ages in the confirmation process; it does not end with a single rite. Fresh and creative educational experiences that reflect traditional values are necessary if the catechetical side of confirmation ministry is to be effective.

- The current move is to hold catechetical instruction during late adolescence or early adulthood rather than in the early years of youth. The traditional age for confirmation was set by a schooling model of education. Now, the emphasis is on participation within the whole life of the community of faith in its worship and living life each day as disciples.

- Current thinking stresses bringing rite and process together in confirmation. Rather than being either a rite or an educational process, confirmation is seen as an interlinking partnership of the two. Confirmation has more than one parent. Educational and worship experiences can and should take place with parents, sponsors, and the congregation around baptism, confirmation, and communion. Congregational confirmation ministry programs should include a guiding team of lay members, mentors, and the involvement of the whole congregation so that the brunt of the effort does not fall on the shoulders of the pastor or reflect only a regional or local understanding.[78]

The theme that persists throughout the book is that confirmation is a repeatable experience designed to remind believers of the reality and importance of baptism as they face various stages and situations in life such as initiation into the church, adolescents describing and affirming their baptism in terms of vocation, adults struggling to reassess their lives and commitments, and older adults discovering their baptismal covenant to be a blessing. The authors make it clear in the preface: "We shall show why it is theologically, psychologically, and religious educationally sound to see confirmation as part of the unified initiation, but a sacramental celebration that can and should be repeated at different times in life's pilgrimage when persons have new self-understandings and fresh and deeper commitments to the Christian faith and life."[79] The use of the term *sacramental* is not meant to imply that the celebration is a sacrament in Lutheran terms.

The focus articulated by Browning and Reed is on the rite as well as the process of confirmation. Both the rite parentage and the process parentage of confirmation must be seen. The 1970 Lutheran actions were taken primarily at the suggestion of educators, but the introduction of *Lutheran Book of Worship* and wider ecumenical study has placed emphasis equally on confirmation as a rite.

The broad nature of confirmation ministry is clear also in Richard Robert Osmer's 1996 book, *Confirmation: Presbyterian Practices in Ecumenical Perspective*, which, like *Models*, looks at the history of confirmation and its practice in a number of church bodies. (He includes Lutherans, Presbyterians, Anglicans-Episcopalians, and United Methodists in his study.) Osmer notes how, during the past four decades, American Lutheranism has undertaken a serious and comprehensive examination of the theology and practice of confirmation. Osmer suggests that the conclusions of these church body studies were motivated not only by educational but also by theological and liturgical clarity.

From the 1970 study commission report to the present, then, the Lutheran Church has maintained a practice that stands in continuity with the older Reformation paradigm, although altering it in significant ways. Confirmation has been separated from admission to the Lord's supper. Catechetical instruction is one of several objectives viewed as important to the confirmation program as a whole. Broadly speaking, however, the defining focus of confirmation remains *catechetical*: providing nurture and care that allows youth to confess the faith of the church and more fully take up the responsibilities of the Christian life. Although there are both *professional* and *catechumenal* elements in the new understanding of confirmation, both are subordinated to its catechetical purpose. The way the Lutheran Church has integrated all of these elements in its educational, theological, and liturgical work on confirmation over the past three decades represents an important contribution to the continuing ecumenical discussion.[80]

Osmer's conclusions lead us easily to the renewed interest not only in the Roman Catholic Church but Protestant church bodies in the adult catechumenate of the early Christian church; we are returning to our starting point. David R. Holeton points out that "the vast literature of the past decades on Christian initiation has had a profound effect on confirmation."[81] This interest has undoubtedly been spawned partly by the confirmation ministry actions and discussions going on in many church bodies. Vatican II revived interest in the catechumenate through its 1972 actions related to the Rite for Christian Initiation of Adults, which marked a significant shift in the practice of welcoming new adult members in the Catholic community.

Aidan Kavanagh points out that a fundamental concern of the council was to integrate the three sacraments that made up the initiatory process of the early church. Reform was needed because confirmation had come to be celebrated apart from baptism and after the eucharist was being received. Such practice suggested that confirmation has some sort of autonomy that permits it to fill a variety of needs, which may or may not be related fundamentally to confirmation, namely a puberty rite for young adolescents, a maturity rite for older adolescents or youth, a graduation rite from one or another grade in school.[82] He suggests that the initiatory rites to come from Vatican II had to be considerably different and radical. Even though some of the suggestions being made by Lutherans may seem radical, more dramatic changes are taking place in the Roman Catholic Church (for example, the uncomfortableness of the catechumenate as a lay program of pastoral care). The proposed Rite for Christian Initiation of Adults has immediate connections with confirmation ministry for Lutherans; these arouse lingering Lutheran thoughts that confirmation marks the time of "adult" faith.

The 1963 LWF confirmation study document begins its historical section with reference to the importance of the catechumenate for confirmation history: "The medieval *confirmatio* which the Reformers attacked had developed from the orders of Baptism and of the Catechumenate in the Western Church."[83] The catechumenate was a process of discerning, forming and ritualizing adult conversion to Christ.[84] While it is yet to be seen just what influence these studies might have within the Lutheran understanding and practice of confirmation ministry, serious examination of implications is currently going on. A number of current North American Lutheran studies deserve mention; their influence on confirmation ministry can be seen only later. The earliest of these comes from Canadian Lutherans:

- Frederick P. Ludolph. Living Witness: The Adult Catechumenate. *Preparing Adults for Baptism and Ministry in the Church* (Evangelical Lutheran Church in Canada, 1992).

- Gordon W. Lathrop. Living Witness: The Adult Catechumenate. *Congregational Prayers to Accompany the Catechumenal Process* (Evangelical Lutheran Church in Canada, 1992).

- *Welcome to Christ: A Lutheran Introduction to the Catechumenate* (Minneapolis: Augsburg Fortress, 1997).

- *Welcome to Christ: Lutheran Rites for the Catechumenate* (Minneapolis: Augsburg Fortress, 1997).

- *Welcome to Christ: A Lutheran Catechetical Guide* (Minneapolis: Augsburg Fortress, 1997).

The ecumenical dimensions of the renewed concern for the catechumenate are reflected in significant studies carried out by the Episcopal and United Methodist Churches.[85] An important question is raised: is it possible that the study of confirmation ministry can and ought to be done together by Christian churches?

The Shaping Power of Rites and Hymns

A complete English language history of confirmation is not yet in place. Adequate attention has yet to be paid to English language rites and hymns that have shaped popular piety in the United States. Clearly, a major shift in Lutheran understanding of confirmation ministry has to do with a reclarification of the rite as baptismal affirmation. We sense that the ritual and hymnic aspects of confirmation ministry are once again returning to attention alongside the catechetical.

A number of significant contemporary worship books pick up the theme that confirmation is affirmation of baptism. The 1992 hymnal of the United Methodist Church uses the term *reaffirmation of faith* to describe confirmation.[86] The Presbyterian Church, USA, calls it *reaffirmation*,[87] the 1979 *Episcopal Book of Common Prayer* describes confirmation as "reaffirmation of Baptismal vows,"[88] and the *Book of Worship of the United Church of Christ* uses the term *affirmation of baptism* in connection with confirmation and reception of new members.[89]

In our historical study of Lutheran confirmation ministry we find few references to the liturgical elements that shape confirmation ministry in the minds of the people of the church. *LBW* itself provides us with new historical information. Osmer comments that *LBW*:

> is deeply informed by contemporary liturgical developments and scholarship, particularly in the area of the rite of initiation. Although it maintains continuity with the Lutheran tradition, it also reaches behind the Reformation to the patristic period, bringing together elements of initiation that had long been separated in the Western church: renunciation and profession, water-washing, laying on of hands, prayer for the Holy Spirit, consignation, and Eucharist.[90]

The introduction to *Lutheran Book of Worship* makes clear that a consistent rationale for the building of rites and the selection of hymns has been used. *LBW* was developed with certain goals in mind.

> An examination of the contents [of *LBW*] will reveal the several goals toward which the Commission [Inter-Lutheran Commission on Worship] worked in liturgy: to restore to Holy Baptism the liturgical rank and dignity implied by Lutheran theology, and to draw out the baptismal motifs in such acts as the confession of sin and the burial of the dead; to continue to move into the larger ecumenical heritage of liturgy while, at the same time, enhancing Lutheran convictions about the Gospel.[91]

It was suggested by some that any service following traditional forms might actually constitute a second confirmation, the first taking place in baptism. The rite of Holy Baptism in *LBW* has returned to baptism something that historic confirmation had taken away from it: the prayer for the Holy Spirit with the laying on of hands and anointing. Turner points out that in The

Lutheran Church—Missouri Synod *Lutheran Worship* book, confirmation stands as its own ritual.[92] The confirmation prayer asks for "the Holy Spirit" in a way that could imply that the Holy Spirit is seen as coming in confirmation and membership begins with confirmation.[93]

LBW's Affirmation of Baptism clearly reflects the baptismal parentage of confirmation, but it also reflects reliance on the 1970 decisions of the church regarding confirmation ministry and its focus on instruction in the teachings of the Lutheran church and baptism.[94] The Inter-Lutheran Commission on Worship took seriously and debated long on baptism, confirmation, and first communion. Members were at different places as to whether a confirmation rite should be included. The ILCW blended a confirmation rite into a multi-use Affirmation of Baptism, which served to de-emphasize confirmation as a rite and elevate the significance of baptism. Although some have expressed the opinion that the new rite attempts to do too many things, little pressure has been exerted to separate the three uses of the rite. Affirmation of baptism is not just a new name for confirmation. It is a rite that marks moments when the faith given in baptism finds new expression and when spiritual gifts given in baptism are stirred up to meet new challenges. It changes the emphasis from what I do to what God has already done for me. Such baptismal renewal is needed often and by persons of all ages.

Just as the liturgical actions of a church body reflect and even shape its theology, so hymns both reflect and shape doctrine, scriptural understanding, and practice. Martin Luther is remembered for putting his understanding of the faith both in the form of catechism and catechetical hymns; next to theology, music was Luther's most cherished companion. He wrote at least seven catechetical hymns, a few of which are included in *LBW*. In his Table Talk, Luther calls the Ten Commandments the most important of all teachings, the Creed the most important story of stories, the Lord's Prayer the prayer of all prayers, and the sacraments the most important of all ceremonies. He expressed these in song. His hymns as well as others we use around affirmation of baptism are meant to reflect our deep understanding. Luther's hymns include "All praise to you, eternal Lord" (*LBW* 48), "We all believe in one true God" (*LBW* 374, a paraphrase of the Nicene Creed), "O thou, who hast of thy pure grace" (*LBW* 442, Luther's commentary on the Lord's Prayer), and "To Jordan came the Christ, our Lord" (*LBW* 79, written in 1540 to follow a sermon on baptism).[95] Perhaps the next chapter in the history of confirmation ministry should include the English language worship books of the church, their rites and hymns.

Finally, some questions: Is it our hope or task to pass on to the next generation a more settled and comprehensive view of confirmation ministry? Do we have a clearer understanding to forward than the one common at the beginning of the twentieth century? What clues tell us what confirmation ministry will or should look like in the next years?

We can't change history, but we can do a better job of remembering the baptismal and educational parentage of confirmation ministry. While much of this realization must happen in congregations, confirmation ministry belongs to the whole church—Lutheran and other. Our concept of church is broad; congregations cannot act in isolation or in ways that overlook other congregations, history, or the wider church.

The stability longed for has not yet come. Still too many forces—many conflicting with each other—are acting among us. But the focus on baptism and education, the basic fibers of confirmation ministry, must continue.

Perhaps the most we can say is that confirmation ministry is here to stay but is also still "on the way," still in dynamic tension. Our practices change over time but should recognize our heritage. The difficulty of any historical study such as this one is that readers will look at history and see different things in it. The Daniel Yankelovich organization reminds us that the generations see change with different eyes:

> Each generation views change differently. Xers see it as their best bet for some kind of breakthrough in their prospects. It's not an issue for Matures as long as they can protect what they've accumulated. It confounds Boomers, presenting only greater risk. So celebrate change with Xers, focus on continuity and safety with Matures, provide resources and support for Boomers.[96]

Luther was convinced that we are fundamentally anxious souls "in constant search of *securitas*."[97] But he also sensed that the search for fixed order can lead to idolatrous propensities to "close the circle and fix the universe." We must not be too quick at circling the wagons because they are still on the move.

Confirmation ministry is still a bubbling pot. We can celebrate it while still asking questions about it. David Holeton and others think that confirmation will not disappear: "It has a tremendous resilience. Confirmation can be disowned by exegetes, disproved by liturgists, decried by theologians, and denounced by educators, but it continues. This resilience cannot be dismissed totally as misdirected popular piety."[98] We cannot hope to resolve the issues of confirmation ministry without a careful remembering of baptism and education. Confirmation ministry is indeed a big idea. Being "on the way" is not a bad thing even though most of us do not like to deal with things that are unstable and changing; we prefer the stable and permanent. We certainly aren't at that point in the history of confirmation ministry. Douglas John Hall reminds us that when the people of Israel "settled down" in the promised land something happened to them. They became smug, stagnant, self-satisfied, entrenched, and inflexible.[99] Hopefully the shakings of history will leave what is essential (baptism and education) so that all else will be shaken away (Heb. 12:27). And in this window of opportunity, this "being on the move" toward deeper and broader understanding, we need the constant affirmation of God's love seen in Holy Baptism, and we need to keep learning.

Recent Shapers and Reflectors of Confirmation Ministry in the ELCA

Lutheran World Federation. *Confirmation: A Study Document*, 1963.

Repp, Arthur C. *Confirmation in the Lutheran Church*, 1964.

Inter-Lutheran. *The Report of the Joint Commission on the Theology and Practice of Confirmation*, 1970.

Lutheran Book of Worship, 1978.

Lutheran World Federation. *Confirmation in Lutheran Churches Today*, 1986.

ELCA. *The Confirmation Ministry Task Force Report*, 1993.

Lutheran World Federation. *Confirmation Ministry Study*, 1995.

The LWF studies were part of a planned series of three studies and are worldwide in scope. The others are limited to North America.

Notes

1. A. T. Wirgman, *The Doctrine of Confirmation* (London: Longmans, Green and Co. 1897), 1.

2. David R. Holeton, "Confirmation in the 1980s" in Max Thurian, ed., *Ecumenical Perspectives on Baptism, Eucharist and Ministry* (Geneva: World Council of Churches, Faith and Order Paper 116, 1983), 86.

3. Reinhard Hutter, "The Church as Public: Dogma, Practice and the Holy Spirit," *Pro Ecclesia* (Summer 1994): 354.

4. Stephen Sykes quoting George Lindbeck in Ephraim Radner and R.R. Reno, *Inhabiting Unity: Theological Perspectives on the Proposed Lutheran–Episcopal Concordat* (Grand Rapids: Eerdmans, 1997), 22.

5. Arthur C. Repp, *Confirmation in the Lutheran Church* (St. Louis: Concordia Publishing House, 1964), 155.

6. Holeton, "Confirmation in the 1980s," 74.

7. Gerard Austin, *Anointing with the Spirit* (New York: Pueblo, 1985), 23.

8. Paul Turner, *Confirmation: The Baby in Solomon's Court* (New York: Paulist Press, 1993), 120–121.

9. Robert L. Browning and Roy A. Reed, *Models of Confirmation and Baptismal Affirmation* (Birmingham: Religious Education Press, 1995). Note how Browning and Reed have a broader definition of sacrament than Lutherans do. Here see the importance Luther's definition of sacrament in "The Babylonian Captivity of the Church" (*Luther's Works*, 36:93) had in the Reformation dialogue regarding confirmation. Luther wrote: "We seek sacraments that have been divinely instituted and among them we see no reason for numbering confirmation."

10. Ibid., 12–13. Browning and Reed have been able to summarize the many interpretations into these eight images, which are meant to be helpful characterizations and not a complete listing of all the historical interpretations.

11. The first use this writer has been able to find is from Wirgman's 1897 book, which quotes Dr. Vaughn's book *Epistle to the Hebrews* and the phrase "Confirmation is a gift of ministry." Wirgman, *The Doctrine of Confirmation,* 68.

12. Theodore R. Jungkuntz, *Confirmation and the Charismata* (Lanham, MD: University Press of America, 1983), 5, suggests that Jesus repeatedly went through "confirmations" as in the Transfiguration (Matt. 17:1-8, for example).

13. Repp, *Confirmation in the Lutheran Church,* 16.

14. Aidan Kavanagh, *Confirmation: Origins and Reform* (New York: Pueblo Publishing Company, 1988).

15. Ibid., 3.

16. Ibid., 31.

17. Wirgman, *The Doctrine of Confirmation,* 151.

18. Kavanagh, *Confirmation,* 67.

19. Ibid., 68.

20. Dom Gregory Dix, *The Theology of Confirmation in Relation to Baptism* (Plymouth: Dacre Press, Adam and Charles Black, 1946), 14.

21. Repp, *Confirmation in the Lutheran Church,* 13.

22. Browning and Reed, *Models,* 9–10.

23. Wirgman suggests that it was Leo the Great, A.D. 440, who "may be considered as the first Western theologian who applies the verb *confirmare* to the imposition of hands with its accompanying unction." *The Doctrine of Confirmation,* 248.

24. Kavanagh, *Confirmation,* 69.

25. Ibid., 64.

26. Frank W. Klos, *Confirmation and First Communion: A Study Book* (Minneapolis: Augsburg Publishing House; Philadelphia: Board of Publication of the Lutheran Church in America; St. Louis: Concordia Publishing House, 1968), 44.

27. Wirgman, *The Doctrine of Confirmation,* 348.

28. Holeton, "Confirmation in the 1980s," 69.

29. Wirgman, *The Doctrine of Confirmation,* 337.

30. Holeton, "Confirmation in the 1980s," 69.

31. The humanist Erasmus helped to turn over the soil in the field of confirmation. He emphasized the age of puberty and a rite of personal dedication to the vows spoken for us at baptism. He felt that confirmation was actually "God's chosen instrument for the renewal of the church." Jungkuntz, *Confirmation and the Charismata,* 38.

32. The Waldensians criticized not only the Roman Catholic sacramental idea of confirmation but its accompanying lack of catechization. They reintroduced the practice of laying on of hands (which had been displaced by chrismation) as a sign of the end of catechetical instruction. Some say that they are the originators of the catechetical interpretation of confirmation. The Cathari accused the church of making spiritual things into material things. They advocated baptism by the Holy Spirit and the laying on of hands together with rigorous practices of self-deprecation, which they saw as cross-bearing. Wycliffe and Hus were outspoken critics of sacramental confirmation. The Bohemian Brethren rejected the idea of vows and oaths and advocated a strong Christian discipline. They stood for a simple, pure, and unworldly faith. Infant baptism needed some kind of personal yes to be complete, which means instruction and examination before admission to the Lord's table. Jungkuntz, *Confirmation and the Charismata,* 35–37.

33. Repp, *Confirmation in the Lutheran Church,* 21.

34. *Confirmation: A Study Document.* Commission on Education Report, Document No. 16, Fourth Assembly of the Lutheran World Federation. (Geneva: LWF, 1963). This report is the first of three extensive world studies of Lutheran confirmation.

35. W. Kent Gilbert, *Confirmation and Education* (Philadelphia: Fortress Press, 1969). Yearbooks in Christian Education, No. 1. This book was the first in a series written to grapple with major problems in the field of Christian education. It is significant that this first volume dealt with confirmation. The book was developed in the spirit of the request for a thorough study and analysis of the report of the Joint Commission on the Theology and Practice of Confirmation and the LWF study.

36. Repp, *Confirmation in the Lutheran Church,* 15. Hans Kung recognizes and supports Luther's position at this point. He writes, "There is no indication of any independent sacrament of confirmation [instituted by Christ] as can be shown precisely from Acts 8:14ff. and 19:1ff." Hans Kung, *Theology for the Third Millennium.* (New York: Doubleday, 1988), 88. Confirmation is one of those "other sacraments" that can't be traced back to Christ as can baptism, eucharist, and remission of sins.

37. Quoted in M. Reu, *Catechetics* (Chicago: Wartburg Press, 1927), 86.

38. Repp, *Confirmation in the Lutheran Church,* 16.

39. Von ehelichen leben quoted in J. D. C. Fisher, *Christian Initiation: The Reformation Period* (London: SPCK, 1970), 172.

40. *The Report of the Joint Commission on the Theology and Practice of Confirmation* (Minneapolis, Augsburg Publishing House, 1970), 8.

41. Ibid., 8–10.

42. Richard Robert Osmer, *Confirmation: Presbyterian Practices in Ecumenical Perspective* (Louisville: Geneva Press, 1996), 88–89.

43. J. D. C. Fisher, *Confirmation Then and Now* (London: Alcuin Club/SPCK, 1978), 138–139.

44. Holeton, "Confirmation in the 1980s," 77.

45. Repp notes how he has been influenced by the thinking of Martin Doerne (*Neubau der Konfirmation,* Gutersloh: C. Bertelsmann, 1936) in Germany who argued that then-current practices of confirmation too easily made confirmation terminal when Christian education needs to continue throughout life. Baptism assumes not only lifelong learning but lifelong repentance and contrition. Doerne emphasized continuous instruction and proposed a later confirmation (actually age 21). He called the time of study leading up to confirmation a "catechumenate." Doerne also suggested that the assumption we make that all young persons be confirmed at the same age fails to reckon with normal differences in youth. Repp, *Confirmation,* IV.

46. Luther D. Reed, *The Lutheran Liturgy* (Philadelphia: Muhlenberg Press, 1947), 169.

47. 1970 *Report,* 11.

48. LWF 1963, *Confirmation: A Study Document,* 10.

49. Ibid., 74–77.

50. Frank C. Senn, *Christian Liturgy* (Minneapolis: Fortress Press, 1997), 227.

51. 1970 *Report,* 3.

52. Klos, *Confirmation,* 185.

53. 1970 *Report,* 33. The American Lutheran Church and the Lutheran Church in America both adopted the report at their 1970 conventions. The Lutheran Church—Missouri Synod referred it to congregation.

54. 1970 *Report,* 21.

55. *Confirmation in the 70s* (Minneapolis: Augsburg Publishing House, 1971), 26.

56. *The Use of the Means of Grace: A Statement on the Practice of Word and Sacrament* (adopted by the Churchwide Assembly of the Evangelical Lutheran Church in America, August 19, 1997), 33.

57. Ibid., 34.

58. Ibid., 42–43.

59. Ibid., 46–47.

60. Osmer, *Confirmation: Presbyterian Practices in Ecumenical Perspective,* 95.

61. Riitta Virkkunen, *Confirmation in the Lutheran Churches Today* (Geneva: LWF Department of Studies, 1986). This is the second of the set of three studies.

62. Ibid., 29–30.

63. *The Confirmation Ministry Task Force Report,* Evangelical Lutheran Church in America, Division for Congregational Ministries (September 1993), 1.

64. Ibid., 6. Tom Johnson points out that Erasmus's emphasis on puberty as the right age for confirmation has unfortunately done serious damage to the idea of lifelong learning.

65. Ibid., 2.

66. Ibid.

67. Ibid., 10.

68. Ibid., 14.

69. *Confirmation Ministry Study: Global Report.* LWF Document No. 38 (Geneva: LWF, 1995). This report is the third of the three studies carried out by the Lutheran World Federation.

70. The study by Browning and Reed of confirmation in the Roman Catholic Church showed that "by moving confirmation to late adolescence (ages 14–18) many Catholics believe that they are having more success with less attrition of youth involved in the confirmation programs."

71. LWF 1995, *Confirmation Ministry Study: Global Report,* 11.

72. One point of view suggests that confirmation since its beginning has been a kind of ordination of the laity. Dom Gregory Dix, *The Theology of Confirmation in Relation to Baptism,* 15.

73. LWF 1995, *Confirmation Ministry Study: Global Report,* 11–12.

74. For another helpful look at the worldwide history and practice of confirmation, see Fisher, *Confirmation Then and Now.*

75. LWF 1995, *Confirmation Ministry Study: Global Report,* 9.

76. Ibid., 41.

77. Browning and Reed, *Models,* 1.

78. Ibid., 29–50.

79. Ibid., 3.

80. Osmer, *Confirmation,* 98.

81. Holeton, "Confirmation in the 1980s," 68.

82. Kavanagh, *Confirmation,* 89. "The tradition which associates Baptism vaguely with vaccination and confirmation with leaving school has its theological weaknesses, but at least it is generally understood. We shall not easily get any changes in it accepted by the mass of our people in less than one generation's time, at the least." Dom Gregory Dix, *The Theology of Confirmation in Relation to Baptism,* 40.

83. LWF 1963, *Confirmation: A Study Document,* 20.

84. *Occasional Services* utilizes as its very first offering the service of enrollment of candidates, normally adults, for baptism. *Occasional Services: A Companion to Lutheran Book of Worship* (Minneapolis: Augsburg Publishing House, 1982), 13. It is a clear reflection of the catechumenal process.

85. We note here a few that reflect concerns much like those expressed by our own church.

- *The Catechumenal Process: Adult Initiation and Formation for Christian Life and Ministry* (New York: The Church Hymnal Corporation, 1990), a product of the Office of Evangelism Ministries of The Episcopal Church in the USA.

- Daniel T. Benedict, Jr. *Come to the Waters: Baptism and Our Ministry of Welcoming Seekers and Making Disciples* (Nashville: Discipleship Resources, 1996). This resource and the two that follow are products of the United Methodist Church.

- Lester Ruth, *Accompanying the Journey: A Handbook for Sponsors* (Nashville: Discipleship Resources, 1997).

- William P. McDonald, *Gracious Voices: Shouts and Whispers for God Seekers* (Nashville: Discipleship Resources, 1996).

86. *Services of the Baptismal Covenant: Reaffirmation of Faith* (Nashville: United Methodist Publishing House, 1992), 86.

87. *Book of Common Worship* (Louisville: John Knox Press, 1993), 431–488. Six different uses for the rite are cited.

88. *Book of Common Prayer* (New York: The Seabury Press, 1979), 413–419.

89. *Book of Worship: United Church of Christ* (New York: UCC Office for Church Life and Leadership, 1986), 127.

90. Osmer, *Confirmation,* 95.

91. *Lutheran Book of Worship* (Minneapolis: Augsburg Publishing House; Philadelphia: Board of Publication, Lutheran Church in America, 1978), 7–8.

92. Turner, *Confirmation: The Baby in Solomon's Court,* 42.

93. *Lutheran Worship* (St. Louis: Concordia Publishing House, 1982), 206.

94. *Lutheran Book of Worship,* 198.

95. Marilyn Kay Stulken, *Hymnal Companion to the Lutheran Book of Worship* (Philadelphia: Fortress Press, 1981), throughout.

96. J. Walker Smith and Ann Clurman, *Rocking the Ages: The Yankelovich Report on Generational Marketing* (New York: Harper Business, 1997), 198.

97. Larry Rasmussen with Cynthia Moe-Lobeda, "The Reform Dynamic: Addressing New Issues in Uncertain Times" in Karen L. Bloomquist and John R. Stumme, eds., *The Promise of Luther in Ethics* (Minneapolis: Fortress Press, 1998), 145.

98. Holeton, "Confirmation in the 1980s," 83.

99. Douglas John Hall, *Why Christian?* (Minneapolis: Fortress Press, 1998), 130–131.

CHAPTER 4

The Theology of Confirmation

Margaret A. Krych

The early church knew no such thing as confirmation. Confirmation is the stepchild of the original unitive sense of the church's rites of initiation, which included the water bath, reception of the Holy Spirit, laying on of hands, and chrism or anointing. Baptism was preceded by a period of instruction and exorcism and was followed by the reception of the first Holy Communion.[1] The catechumenate in preparation for baptism was of varying lengths, but came to take about three years.[2] In the West, the water bath was associated with the washing away of sin.

The unitive rite broke eventually apart with the local presbyter baptizing and the bishop at a later convenient time laying on the hands and anointing. Confirming or strengthening therefore became the bishop's work. By the eighth or ninth century the long period between baptism (which, after Constantine, had been primarily in childhood) and confirmation was seen as a sort of completion of what was begun in infant baptism. Over time, then, confirmation became viewed sacramentally, a position Aquinas clearly articulated by declaring confirmation a distinct sacrament in its own right, in which the Holy Spirit is given for strength in spiritual combat so that the baptized may arrive "at the perfect age . . . of the spiritual life."[3] The Council of Florence (1439) declared and the Council of Trent (1547) fixed as doctrine that confirmation is a sacrament. As confirmation became understood as a sacrament, catechetical instruction was less emphasized.

The Reformation reclaimed the emphasis on instruction. Luther insisted that confirmation was not a sacrament. He did not restructure confirmation as such; restructuring was not necessary because the bishop's confirming role had no place in Lutheran congregations. Luther did emphasize instruction and preparation for confession that preceded first communion. And Luther left us the treasure of the Small and Large Catechisms. Educational ministry was high on his agenda in order that the baptized might know what God had done for them in Christ and might receive forgiveness of sins by faith in God's promises.

Melanchthon makes clear that confirmation is not necessary for salvation because it does not have the command of God.[4] And, as long as it is not for the purpose of earning grace, we may put confirmation under Augsburg Confession Article XV, Church Usages that "contribute to peace and good order in the church." *The Confirmation Ministry Task Force Report* adopted by the Evangelical Lutheran Church in America in 1993 says, "While it is true that confirmation is a practice not mentioned in Scripture . . . it was created by the church as a valuable tool for growth in faith. Because of its work through the centuries in helping to shape a Christian's faith, confirmation ministry remains important to Lutheran congregations today."[5]

The lack of emphasis on confirmation in early Lutheranism did not mean that the practice went away. *The Report of the Joint Commission on the Theology and Practice of Confirmation,* published in 1970, gives an excellent, though brief, history of confirmation in the Lutheran church[6] (see chapter 3, "Lutheran Confirmation Ministry in Historical Perspective"). It identifies six strands that came to the United States: the catechetical type, which emphasized instruction and preparation for first confession and the Lord's supper (involving no real rite except first communion); the hierarchical type of Bucer, which included a vow of surrender to Christ and the church's discipline; the sacramental type in which people often thought of confirmation as the beginning of membership in the church; the traditional type with instruction and laying on of hands but not associated with first communion; and two strands from after the sixteenth-century period—the pietistic, which emphasized conversion, confession of faith, and renewal of the baptismal covenant; and the rationalistic, which emphasized examination and oath and was closely related to citizenship and social importance. All six strands variously intertwined in congregational practice at the time of the 1964–1970 Joint Commission on the Theology and Practice of Confirmation. And these strands were to come under serious theological scrutiny by the commission.

A radical shift in thinking in 1970 rejected much that was represented in the six previous strands except the catechetical. The shift also differed from the understanding in other Christian communions. That is, the 1970 *Report* rejected any suggestion that confirmation is something the confirmand does. Also rejected was any suggestion that confirmation can be defined as a rite. Of course, in concert with the Reformation, the commission also rejected any suggestion that confirmation is a sacrament or that it completes baptism. What confirmation is was then defined with these four understandings firmly in place. The 1993 task force welcomed and reaffirmed the approach of the 1970 commission, which since has been studied in a number of ecumenical circles and especially in many Lutheran churches in the Lutheran World Federation (LWF). It is interesting that, while the 1961 LWF seminar raised the question of confirmation on an international level and led to the joint commission report of 1970, the 1970 report in turn raised theological questions for all parts of Lutheranism and stimulated the 1979–1986 world study. This study discovered that most of world Lutheranism reflected positions that were rather typical in the United States before the 1970 report.[7] The international evaluation group, however, was clear that "confirmation should be understood in terms of baptism as the only sacramental initiation into the church. Confirmation does not confer a status different from the membership of all the baptized."[8] That the United States studies and viewpoint then influenced many other Lutheran churches to some extent can be seen in the 1995 Lutheran World Federation *Confirmation Ministry Study*.[9]

The Lutheran position adds a unique proposal to the ecumenical scene in the United States. Richard Osmer has done a great service to the ecumenical discussion of confirmation with his book *Confirmation: Presbyterian Practices in Ecumenical Perspective*.[10] He suggests that, in traditions other than Lutheran, confirmation is variously seen as sacramental, professional, reaffirmation of the baptismal covenant, public confession of the faith, personal confirmation of the baptismal covenant, and commissioning.[11] In the last two or three decades in mainline Protestantism, the desire has been not to devalue baptism or to say that it is incomplete. Where the term *confirmation* is used, its primary connotation is that of a rite. Generally, the sense is that confirmation is something that the confirmand does—whether professing the faith or reaffirming the baptismal covenant. (In some cases, such as United Methodist, some emphasis is also on God's confirming work.[12])

Lutheran Foundations

Evangelical Lutheran Church in America (ELCA) Lutherans do not hold that confirmation is something that one does, but rather something that *God* does. It is God's initiative. God is the subject of confirming even as God is the subject of baptism. And what is it that God does? God confirms or strengthens us in faith; that is, God strengthens us in relationship with God's trinitarian self—a relationship based on the forgiveness of sins by God's own gracious activity in Jesus Christ and received through faith. God does this confirming work through his chosen means by which he imparts to us the forgiveness of sins through Christ. These means of grace are the word and the sacraments of baptism and the Lord's supper.[13] They are the ways in which Christ comes to us, gives himself to us, proclaims to us his promises. God does the confirming work through the church, the assembly of believers among whom the gospel is preached in purity and the sacraments administered according to the gospel.[14] From a Lutheran perspective, then, confirmation is grounded in the doctrine by which the church "stands or falls"[15]—justification by grace through faith.

Justification by Grace through Faith

Justification is the central doctrine of the Reformation. The Augsburg Confession, Article IV, says:

> It is also taught among us that we cannot obtain forgiveness of sin and righteousness before God by our own merits, works, or satisfactions, but that we receive forgiveness of sin and become righteous before God by grace, for Christ's sake, through faith, when we believe that Christ suffered for us and that for his sake our sin is forgiven and righteousness and eternal life are given to us. For God will regard and reckon this faith as righteousness, as Paul says in Romans 3:21-26 and 4:5.[16]

Both the 1970 and the 1993 reports root the understanding of confirmation in this gospel message. The 1970 commission begins the "Theological Aspects of Confirmation" with these words: "The central teaching of the Lutheran church states that God accepts sinners by grace alone, for Christ's sake, through faith."[17] The members of the 1989–1993 ELCA task force welcomed and built on the confessionally based theology they found already in the 1970 *Report*.[18] They echo the preceding statement: "The Gospel, which is the power of the triune God for salvation, is the proclamation that God was in Christ, reconciling the world, a reconciliation freely given to us because God is gracious. God's Spirit leads us to trust this good news that God in Christ has established a right relationship with us."[19]

Lutherans understand that all human beings are sinful and therefore in need of forgiveness. In sin humans are self-centered, elevating themselves to the place of God, lacking trust in God. We are estranged from God, from others, and from our very selves.[20] Sin is an inclination and deep corruption of our whole nature, involving cognition, will, emotions, and actions. Even though we can attain a degree of civil righteousness by our own free will, nevertheless we cannot, by our own strength, attain righteousness before God. By God's mercy we remain God's creatures even though sinners, but we humans bear responsibility for sin and deserve God's wrath and punishment. And, because we remain both sinful as well as saved throughout our whole life, therefore we daily need God's merciful forgiveness. Lutherans believe fervently that persons of all ages need to hear the good news that is answer to this sinful state in which we are born.

And that good news is the gospel, the message of God's merciful forgiveness in which, because of God's act in Jesus Christ, we are treated by God as just in spite of our sinfulness. God is the only one who can recreate us, make us whole new persons. God does not overlook sin but accepts us in spite of our guilt and estrangement. This forgiveness is due solely to God's grace. Human beings do not earn or merit God's mercy. But God freely chooses to act graciously towards us, to reconcile us to himself because of God's unmerited love for us. The Old as well as the New Testament witness to God's mercy, and we see God's love most clearly in Jesus Christ and especially in his death on the cross for our forgiveness. This gift of forgiveness is received through faith, which is itself a gift of the Holy Spirit and for which we ourselves can take no credit. Throughout our lives on earth, we remain sinful as well as saved, *simil justus et peccator*, but God's gracious mercy is extended to us continually so that every day we may return to our baptism and receive the benefits of Christ's atonement. In other words, we stand simultaneously under judgment and mercy, law and gospel.

We are forgiven because of God's work in Christ alone and not because of anything that we have done or can do. Christ has already fulfilled the law on our behalf. God's forgiving mercy in Christ then frees us to live for and to love others. In other words, good works that serve the neighbor flow from faith as a consequence of justification.

The Means of Grace

The good news of the gospel of God's forgiveness of sin must always be central to a Lutheran understanding of confirmation. This good news is communicated through God's chosen means, the word and the sacraments.

> These means or channels through which God's grace comes to us include the Word manifested in such activities as preaching and teaching, and the sacraments, Holy Baptism and the Lord's Supper. Through these means of grace, God reveals and declares to men that he is fully reconciled to all the world. Through them God creates, supports, and strengthens a new relationship with people. This relationship is based on the forgiveness secured for men by God's Son, Jesus Christ.[21]

The Word of God

The word of God is God's self-expression, self-revelation—in fact, the impartation of God's very self. The creative and redemptive word of God is a happening word, an event, a deed, an act.[22] Because the primary way God has spoken and told us who God is and what God is like is in Jesus Christ, Jesus Christ is properly called the *Word of God*.[23] The message about the incarnate Word is one of judgment and mercy, of God's condemnation of sin as well as God's merciful compassion for the sinner, of law and gospel. And we refer to this message also as the word of God.

Because the Bible has its center in this message, we also refer to the Bible as the word of God. It is the definitive written witness to God's word in Christ. And of course the Bible has an important role in God's confirming work through the church. The biblical texts drive teenagers to their knees to ask for forgiveness and remind them that they can do nothing of their own to earn God's favor; the texts also proclaim a God who freely promises forgiveness of sins and who accepts teenagers in spite of who they are and what they have done. The scriptures tell of the great saving works of God who does for them what they cannot do for themselves. God's word speaks of God's judgment and promises. It kills and makes alive. Teenagers, as much as any other age level, desperately need this law-gospel hermeneutical key in reading the scriptures. They need to hear the message of justification by grace through faith just as clearly today as in the time of Paul and in the sixteenth century. Through God's word we receive this good news.[24] Through the word we learn that God freely chose to reconcile us to himself because of grace.

Youth also need to hear the word of God as it comes to us today in preaching, teaching, and sacraments. Through the word, God the Holy Spirit applies to teenagers, as to all age levels, the treasure of salvation, creating faith and giving the promise of forgiveness of sin again and again. Through the word, God confirms or strengthens the faith of the believer. So Christian worship will be central to the lives of children and youth as well as adult Christians. Youth receive the word not only spoken in public worship but also as other baptized Christians speak God's word to one another, including those opportunities in Sunday school and catechetical classes. For this reason, congregations who have education programs simultaneously with their one public worship service shortchange the confirmation process. All Christians need both learning and worship.

The Sacraments

Youth also need to receive the word in sacraments that make visible the word of God enacted. The word connected with physical elements—water in baptism and bread and wine in communion—is a powerful communication of Christ himself. And it is the same word coming to the action in two ways: as command and as promise.[25] Both sacraments proclaim God's gracious forgiveness and mercy in Jesus Christ. They are acts of God in which Christ gives himself to us, encounters us, receives us, forgives us, gives us new life, and strengthens us by the Holy Spirit. Like the preached word, sacraments are means by which God confirms (strengthens) the faith of the believer. They "are signs and testimonies of God's will toward us for the purpose of awakening and strengthening our faith. For this reason they require faith, and they are rightly used when they are received in faith and for the purpose of strengthening faith."[26]

God confirms the faith of the believer within the community of God's people. Sacraments are both personal and communal. In baptism, God claims the individual as God's own child, gives salvation, and makes the individual a member of the Christian community, the church. In the Lord's supper, Christ comes with forgiveness to each believer within the community of God's gathered people around the table.

BAPTISM

The 1970 and 1993 *Reports* strongly emphasize the sacrament of baptism because God begins God's strengthening work in the life of the believer in this sacrament. In baptism the individual becomes a child of God and an heir of salvation. In the Small Catechism Luther lists as the benefits of baptism, forgiveness of sins, deliverance from death and the devil, and eternal life for the believer, according to the word and promise of God. Luther emphasizes that the water does not produce these effects but the word of God connected with the water.[27] For Lutherans the promise of salvation is constitutive of baptism: baptism is a proclamation of justification by grace through faith. We participate in the death and resurrection of Christ. We are drowned to sin and rise to new life by the gracious action of God. Baptism is solely God's work, not our own. Its benefits are received through faith; baptism, in turn, awakens and strengthens faith in the believer.

Lutherans say that baptism is the sacrament of prevenient grace, that is, baptism proclaims God's prior act in the death and resurrection of Jesus Christ for our salvation before we ever asked for it and even before we were born. Infant baptism particularly proclaims God's prior grace for helpless sinful children.[28]

Baptism looks forward to the life of the believer in which sin will be drowned daily by repentance and the new person rise daily to new life.[29] "A Christian life is nothing else than a daily Baptism, once begun and ever continued," says Luther.[30] It is the Spirit's sanctifying work. God the Holy Spirit, given in baptism, strengthens faith—that is, confirms us—and calls us daily back to our baptism, back to the word of promise, back to the cross of Christ for the forgiveness of sin. Sanctification is really the continuance of justification. If tempted to doubt God's promise of mercy, Luther taught that we must respond with, "But I am baptized! And if I am baptized, I have the promise that I shall be saved and have eternal life, both in soul and body."[31] Baptism incorporates us in the priesthood of all believers and gives us a vocation: to speak the word to others, and to pray for and serve the needs of the neighbor in all aspects of our life. Baptism calls us to a life of sacrificial service under the cross, ministering to others and serving God wherever we are called to be in the church and in the world. This vocational emphasis was highlighted in 1993:

> As baptized people, we see our daily life as a place to carry out our *vocation*, our calling. All aspects of life, home and school, community and nation, daily work and leisure, citizenship and friendship, belong to God. All are places where God calls us to serve. God's Word and the Church help us to discover ways to carry out our calling. Youth, especially, face far-reaching decisions about education, marriage or singleness, citizenship and occupation . . . Confirmation can help young people determine how they want to live now and in the future.[32]

Baptism incorporates us into the church. We receive the Holy Spirit and are made full members of the church at baptism and assume all the blessings and responsibilities of belonging to the church, although learning about such responsibilities and privileges is of course a gradual process as the child grows. "Baptism . . . gives the sinner a new relationship with the church. It makes him [or her] fully a member of the church (1 Corinthians 12:13). It gives him [or her] the gift of the Holy Spirit (Titus 3:5)."[33]

The danger of several of the views of confirmation prior to 1970 was their inherent devaluation of baptism, a sense that baptism was not "complete" without confirmation. To suggest that baptism needs completion is to imply that God's word of promise was not fully effective or that the benefits of baptism were not fully given in the sacrament. Both the commission and the task force were at pains to stress that this view is not the case. They asserted that confirmation arises from Holy Baptism, but in no way completes or supplements baptism. The baptized receive fully the benefits of baptism—forgiveness of sins, deliverance from death and the devil, and eternal life. Baptism is a proclamation of justification by grace through faith in which the person becomes fully a child of God and an heir of salvation. The baptized are full members of the church. If an affirmation of baptism rite is used, it is an opportunity to affirm baptism and is usually an important milestone in the life of the young believer, but it does not add anything to baptism. Baptism is entirely complete in and of itself. Nothing else is needed to complete God's baptismal work.

Membership in the Christian church is bestowed on an infant or child through Holy Baptism. When the church, in obedience to its Lord, baptizes a child, it makes him [or her] by that very act a member of the church (1 Corinthians 12:13). The membership begun in Baptism is thereupon experienced in the Christian life (worship, teaching, the Lord's Supper, and service). Membership in the church is not conferred by a later experience nor by a special rite, such as confirmation, but in the way commanded by Christ, through Holy Baptism.[34]

Confirmation ministry does not *complete* Baptism, for Baptism is already complete through God's work of joining us to Christ and his body, the Church. In him is salvation. Moreover, confirmation ministry does not *compete* with Baptism, because confirmation ministry does not save anyone.[35]

Confusion sometimes arises from the keeping of "confirmed member rolls," as if baptized members and confirmed members are somehow different categories of membership. Records of confirmed members are better seen as bookkeeping items, helpful in assessing synodical benevolence and perhaps in gauging the potential leadership strength of a congregation. They may even be a reflection of the seriousness with which a congregation pays attention to God's confirming work through the word. But they are not theological statements. "The different designations of membership that an organization may devise for the sake of order and efficiency merely indicate various levels of rights or responsibilities that the members may have accepted within the organization. But the Scriptures do not speak of various kinds of membership. Baptism makes us members of the body of Christ, the only church of which the New Testament speaks."[36] Theologically, a confirmed member is simply a baptized person who is strengthened daily through God's word. Which is precisely what a baptized member is! Confusion might be avoided if we would normally refer simply to baptized members.

Baptism, then, "is the basis for Christian education and nurture, including confirmation ministry. The Church is to help baptized Christians to live out their Baptism, to grow in knowledge, insight, and faithfulness as servants of Christ. Baptized Christians need to be nurtured in lives of faith, hope, and love, grounded in the pattern of death and resurrection."[37]

THE LORD'S SUPPER

The sacrament of the Lord's supper is a further means through which God confirms or strengthens the faith of the baptized. "The holy sacrament was not instituted to make provision for a sacrifice for sin—for the sacrifice has already taken place—but to awaken our faith and comfort our consciences when we perceive that through the sacrament grace and forgiveness of sin are promised us by Christ. Accordingly the sacrament requires faith, and without faith it is vain."[38] Like baptism, the Lord's supper is a proclamation of justification, a return to the word of promise united with the elements of bread and wine. In the Small Catechism (VI), Luther states that the benefit of eating the bread and drinking the wine are the forgiveness of sin, life, and salvation, and that the person receiving the sacrament is worthy and well prepared "who believes these words: 'for you' and 'for the forgiveness of sins.'"[39]

Lutherans believe that the crucified and risen Lord is truly present in the sacrament to do what he has promised: give himself to us in the eating of the bread and drinking of the wine.[40] The sacrament proclaims the past event of the cross for our forgiveness. The risen Christ gives us his body and blood for our salvation.

This sacrament is a communion with God and with the other members of Christ's universal church. The sacrament strengthens both the individual believers and the community of believers in faith and is an anticipation of the final fellowship of Christ and his church.

The 1970 *Report* distinguished between Holy Baptism as an initiating sacrament, which makes the person a child of God, and Holy Communion as a sustaining sacrament, which maintains and strengthens what was given in baptism. But the report hastens to add that the distinction is one of emphasis and "the relationship is not exclusive or supplementary but collateral."[41]

Definition of Confirmation

Having established this evangelical basis for confirmation, the commission offered the following definition:

> Confirmation is a pastoral and educational ministry of the church which helps the baptized child through Word and Sacrament to identify more deeply with the Christian community and participate more fully in its mission.[42]

This definition was barely changed in the 1993 *Report*:

> Confirmation ministry is a pastoral and educational ministry of the church which helps the baptized through Word and Sacrament to identify more deeply with the Christian community and participate more fully in its mission.[43]

In 1993, the word *child* was removed because teenagers today do not think of themselves as children and because many current congregational programs are "longer and later"—often extending to grade 12 or ages 18 or 19. Such persons are well beyond childhood. The definition from 1993 also has the word *ministry* following "confirmation," doubly stressing that confirmation is essentially ministry and not primarily a rite.

What does this distinction say about an end point to the process of confirmation? In 1970, the task force affirmed lifelong learning but said that the process of confirmation *per se* was the beginning part of that lifelong process, from baptism until the "time of fulfillment" in 10th grade.[44] The commission considered the 10th grader "no longer a child" and capable of assuming mature responsibilities in the life and mission of the Christian community. While the baptized continue to receive lifelong pastoral and educational ministry, nevertheless, the commission saw a change in the way in which 10th graders were able to assume responsibility for giving pastoral and educational ministry to others. Therefore, they suggested that the term *confirmation* cease to be used after 10th grade.

The 1993 *Report* also stresses the lifelong reception of pastoral and educational ministry but does not state a particular "end point" or "fulfillment time" for confirmation. The lack of specified fulfillment serves to highlight lifelong learning and also reflects the trend in many parts of the country to longer and later confirmation programs and perhaps the fact that study of Luther's catechism is more cognitively appropriate to the middle and later adolescent years than the earlier ones (see chapter 5, "The Content of Confirmation"). Because the 1993 *Report* particularly emphasizes the adolescent years, by implication rather than explicit statement, it agrees with the 1970 statement: "Confirmation could be described as an initial stage of this strengthening [work of God through God's word], not as a terminal experience but as a stage in a lifelong process of nourishing through the Word."[45] However, just to complicate matters, the 1993 *Report* refers at one point to "confirmation ministry as a lifelong process"[46] while the 1970 *Report* refers to a "lifelong catechumenate"[47] (a term usually used to refer to the period of instruction before baptism of older children, youth, and adults).

Both reports understand baptism as that which leads to lifelong pastoral ministry and learning. Both presuppose that persons reach a time when they not only receive, but also give of this ministry to others; while children are engaged in such ministry, adults have a more responsible and accountable role in it. Both focus on the period from baptism to young adulthood, even though the Spirit's work of strengthening the believer through the church's word and sacrament ministry continues throughout life, constantly drawing the believer more deeply into the church and its mission.

PASTORAL MINISTRY

Confirmation is a pastoral ministry. Pastoral ministry is not limited to the ministry of pastors. The phrase refers to God's work through the whole congregation, speaking God's word to youth, serving the young neighbor's needs, praying for youth, welcoming them in the congregation, supporting them in their faith journey, rejoicing as they share the privileges of belonging to the people of God, helping them from early childhood to assume some of the responsibilities of the people of God that are appropriate to their age level. "The *pastoral* aspect of confirmation ministry is the loving care which the whole Christian community expresses for the well-being of the child."[48]

Youth need to relate to, and receive pastoral ministry from, persons of all ages. In turn, they give pastoral ministry to others in ways appropriate to their level of maturity. In particular, youth need adult role models of both genders from whom they learn adult behaviors, values, and faith. The church provides many opportunities for such relationships. Confirmation ministry is not limited to catechetical classes. From baptism through young adulthood, congregations provide pastoral ministry through persons who serve in cradle roll ministry, Sunday church school, vacation Bible school, church nursery school, day-care and latchkey programs, day schools, children's groups, youth groups, scouts, children's choirs, youth choirs, bands, orchestras, retreats, camps, counseling services, acolyte programs, workshops, intergenerational events such as potlucks and picnics, and so on. All these activities should be seen as opportunities for pastoral ministry to the baptized, and channels through which God does his confirming work within the church, bringing the word and love and care to young believers.

It is important that youth not only hear God's word, but experience it. Congregations must seek by the power of the Spirit to be the body of Christ where the word of forgiveness is spoken and the reality of forgiveness lived. Group relations and acceptance in the church, though fragmented and marred, can nevertheless point beyond themselves to the acceptance we all need in Jesus Christ.

While affirming the role of the whole people of God in pastoral ministry, the pastor has a particular role in giving theological leadership to congregational pastoral ministry, and in relating as pastor to youth and helping them in their faith struggles. The 1993 *Report* also highlights the ministry of parents as models of faithfulness and guides in Christian life and understanding, and of mentors in witnessing to the importance of vocation.[49] It suggests that the congregation's responsibility is best guided by a congregational ministry team.[50]

EDUCATIONAL MINISTRY

Confirmation is educational ministry. Again, it is God's work through the whole congregation, and lifelong learning requires the congregation's serious commitment to teaching and learning in large and small classes and groups as well as in speaking God's word one-on-one to others. Such a learning process helps baptized persons to know and confess the Christian faith as their own as well as to assume increasingly responsible roles in the life and mission of the church.[51] It helps the baptized identify with the Christian community by developing a deeper understanding of the scriptures and the faith of the church. But learning goes beyond cognitive understanding to involve will and emotion and, in fact, the whole person. In educational ministry, the Holy Spirit through God's word calls youth to faith. In educational ministry youth learn what it means to belong to the assembly that gathers around word and sacraments for the forgiveness of sin. They learn what it means to belong to the priesthood we all share and live out in the world daily.

Congregations provide many opportunities for educational ministry to young people. All are channels God uses to confirm: Sunday church school, catechetical classes, camps, conferences, retreats, schools, libraries, family learning, tutoring, choirs, committees, newsletters, computer programs and Web sites—whatever learning opportunities the congregation can devise. Clearly, educational ministry calls for a budget, and for careful teacher selection, training, and support. Members who serve in such settings can rightly consider themselves agents of God's work of confirmation, and they need the support and prayers of the whole congregation for the educational ministry they provide on behalf of the whole community.

Again, while educational ministry is the responsibility of the whole congregation, the 1993 *Report* also emphasizes the particular role of the pastor in giving theological and biblical teaching and in training others for educational roles in the congregation. It asserts that "equally important is the unique role that pastor plays as an adult model of faith and ministry."[52] Seminary education especially fits persons to provide theological and biblical insights, confessional content, and critique of points of view that contradict the gospel.

THROUGH WORD AND SACRAMENT

Through word and sacrament, confirmation ministry is deeply personal. The word comes to youth as personal encounter, judging and forgiving, killing and making alive. God uses the ministry of the church to speak directly to all age levels to bring his promise and mercy and to give new life. Youth need to gather with the whole assembly in worship to hear the word of absolution, the public proclamation of the gospel, and to receive God's merciful forgiveness at the Lord's table.

> From the days of primitive Christianity there has been a close relation between the celebration of the Lord's Supper and the proclamation of the gospel in Christian worship . . . Proclamation of the death of Christ takes place already when the words of institution are spoken at the celebration, but it is never limited to these. Remembering Jesus and his death at celebrations of the Supper demanded an exposition of the saving event that underlies the Supper and also of the Supper itself that rests thereon. At early Christian worship this exposition seems to have been the task of prophets and teachers."[53]

Youth need to see that the gospel proclaimed in the Lord's supper is the same gospel proclaimed in preaching. That is, that the word comes in spoken and in visible, acted forms, but that it is the same gracious word for the forgiveness of sin.

Before the 1964–70 study, the normal pattern in congregations was reception of first communion after the rite of confirmation. The 1970 *Report* recommended the separation of first Holy Communion from the end of the confirmation process and the reception of communion at an earlier age. Holy Communion was now seen as a part of confirmation, a means through which

God strengthens the believer, rather than a privilege to be granted on completion of a course of study. The report suggested that fifth grade might be an appropriate time but allowed congregations to choose the age they deemed suitable. This flexibility was affirmed in 1993. Naturally, the 1970 *Report* has guidance on the education that precedes reception of communion. It sees this preparation as more pastoral than educational ministry—helping the growing members at their appropriate level of development prepare for a meaningful participation in the Lord's supper. "To receive Holy Communion without understanding would be to perform a meaningless act that would contribute nothing to the process of growth." And, "The child must be prepared for participation in the sacrament so that he [she] receives it with benefit. This preparation involves a basic understanding of the gospel and the nature of the sacrament at his [her] level of expression."[54]

As further ecumenical agreements of various kinds are approved or discussed, youth can rejoice that tables, which have been divisive for so long, are now being shared or that sharing is under discussion. They will be well served if the educational ministry helps them appreciate accurately the points of debate. Correct information can enable youth to avoid uninformed prejudice that inhibits understanding. Seeing how far ecumenical discussion has progressed can help temper youth's impatience at the length of road yet to travel.

The Christian Community

Identifying more deeply with the Christian community is rooted in baptism. In that once-and-for-all yet daily proclamation of God's merciful forgiveness of sin lies the identity of God's people. Youth find here the only identity in which they can receive true comfort even at a time in their development when peers, adults, and the world may condemn and when they themselves are perhaps their own greatest critics. They can also be assured of the community of saints that supports them and speaks the word to them.

The church is the assembly of believers in which the gospel is preached in purity and the sacraments administered according to the gospel.[55] In other words, justification is at the heart of ecclesiology. We gather round the means of grace through which the Spirit calls forth justifying faith, and through which the Spirit confirms believers. It is for the word that we come to the assembly. Some youth may be drawn to the assembly by other interests initially—friends, somewhere to meet, activities. But ultimately the gift God gives to youth as to all the baptized is the fellowship in which forgiveness of sins is proclaimed and we are set free. This word binds believers in a fellowship deeper than any other experience of community that youth may have.

The church is one, holy, catholic, and apostolic. Youth can appreciate that now is an exciting time to be part of the body of believers. Ecumenical relations are making more visible the oneness that is already gift of Christ by virtue of our one Lord, one proclamation of Christ, and one water of baptism. Congregations can help youth appreciate the scriptures and creeds that Christians hold in common and distinguish those matters that still divide and call for discussion between denominations. The church is indwelt by the Holy Spirit who daily renews and strengthens the church, and is a source of comfort to youth. In today's society in which we have easy and instant access through technology to all parts of the globe, the catholicity of the church takes on new meaning for youth. They can literally be in touch with Christians the world over and can appreciate global aspects of mission. Catholicity also reaches back through time, through the centuries, connecting us to believers of all eras. And the church is an apostolic community: we have the apostolic task of proclamation, and we have the apostolic message, the gospel. Youth can participate in the one because they personally know the other.

Simil justus et peccator means that the communion of saints is not sinless, but rather it is that community in which the Spirit daily forgives sins, calling, gathering, enlightening, and sanctifying. Grasping this power of the Spirit can help youth deal with the disillusionment of discovering that hypocrisy and other evils lurk within the people of God.

PARTICIPATING IN THE CHURCH'S MISSION

To share in the priesthood is to approach Christ without a human mediator; it is also to carry into Christ's presence those whom we love and serve. As members of the priesthood, "we stand before God, pray for others, intercede with and sacrifice ourselves to God and proclaim the word to one another."[56] Youth participate in the church's mission as they speak the word to others, and as they pray and serve the needs of the neighbor. Wolfhart Pannenberg reminds us that "Luther's concept [of the priesthood] did not involve religious individualism but specifically the reality of the congregation as *communio.*"[57] It is important that adolescents, at a time when they focus so much on themselves, sense this greater community of faith to which they belong and in whose priesthood they share. The understanding of the mission of the church in the 1970 *Report* includes worship, teaching-learning, witness, and service. The pastoral and educational ministry to the baptized is to incorporate them into this broad ministry. The 1993 *Report* focuses particularly on bringing the gospel to all people and on discipleship.[58] Incidentally, the best evangelists to youth are other youth. When educational ministry is carried out well, youth on fire with their new mature grasp of the faith will share it gladly with others.

More Than One Way

Not everyone will be confirmed. Timothy Lull writes, "It is a mistake to try to make confirmation a universal Christian experience, as it makes sense only within one pattern of becoming a Christian."[59] Persons who are not baptized in infancy and who later hear the word and are called to faith in Jesus Christ may be baptized in later years. In today's post-Christendom era, more and more unchurched persons are converted in adulthood, instructed as catechumens, and baptized. Confirmation assumes infant baptism or the baptism of children. The adult catechumenate and baptism are not usually called confirmation even though clearly pastoral and educational ministries are involved.

In the case of youth and adults who request to be baptized, the church accedes to their request when candidates have already been made one with Christ through the power of the gospel. By their faith the candidates for baptism already share in the death and resurrection of their Lord. The subsequent baptism clearly signifies the new relationship that is theirs by faith, confirming their personal share in the redemptive work of Jesus Christ. In such cases a rite of confirmation is not appropriate. Adults who have already been baptized and instructed should be received by profession of faith.[60]

Similarly, adults baptized in another denomination will, after instruction, be received into the ELCA congregation through affirmation of baptism. But they will not be considered confirmands. These different paths mean that "true" Lutherans are not only those who were baptized as infants and confirmed, but also those who have come into the ELCA by other routes! The adult catechumenate followed by baptism has, after all, a 2,000-year history, and it is with joy that many Lutheran congregations are embracing this practice as a regular part of evangelism outreach.

Lifelong Ministry

Nevertheless, every Christian, by whatever route he or she has journeyed, needs lifelong pastoral and educational ministry, including both biblical and theological education. It means recapturing the value of the catechisms as teaching instruments for adults. Often we have failed to use the Small Catechism with adults because of its wide use in the confirmation process. We need to recover the use of the catechisms with adults—not only those adults who are new to the Lutheran tradition, but also those who have been confirmed members for many years. Luther urged the pastors and preachers to take their office seriously and to teach the catechism to the people, especially to the young. Then, having taught the brief catechism, he exhorted them to go on with a "large catechism so that the people may have a rich and fuller understanding."[61] The church needs well-informed laity who reflect deeply on their beliefs, can articulate them to others, and can relate their faith to everyday life as individuals and as members of society. Catechetical instruction of adolescents would be enriched immeasurably if students arrived already thoroughly versed in the catechism by well-taught parents who in turn had carefully passed on to their offspring not only the text but its meaning and how that meaning could be applied in their family and community living day by day![62]

Affirmation of Baptism

The 1970 *Report* raised the issue of whether a rite was necessary or even desirable as a termination point of confirmation. The commission wanted to emphasize that confirmation is a process and not a rite. It made clear that the process does not require a rite. But it did not say that a rite was undesirable—on the contrary, a rite for the fulfillment of the process was recognized as a possible helpful event.[63] By 1993 it was clear that the overwhelming majority of congregations had continued to use a rite, hence the report commends the use of affirmation of baptism as "of great benefit to the congregation."[64] Both reports recommend a variety of rites be used throughout the confirmation process, marking particular points of growth (1970) or life transitions (1993). The 1993 *Report* makes recommendations for such rites of affirmation of baptism, insisting that such rites must never in any way be considered sacraments and that they should recall, reflect, and honor baptism. They should also be evangelical, involve the community and the faith of the whole church, be participated in voluntarily, and be contextual.

The question then is whether an affirmation of baptism designed for repeated use in congregations as well as for restoration of the inactive and reception of persons from other denominations is also the best rite for use with teenagers. Clearly, its value is that it does point back to baptism and avoids the danger of sacramental interpretation. But it may be attempting to do too many things in the one rite. Teenagers may be forgiven if they see little similarity between their situation and that of persons transferring who have already been confirmed in other denominations. They may see even less similarity between their situation and that of restoring inactive members, especially if the latter have received no pastoral and educational ministry for decades and may, sadly, have had no more than a session or two of preparation prior to the service.

Some distinct features characterize the adolescent situation. A good rite of affirmation of baptism for youth would uphold the importance of baptism and celebrate God's confirming work in their lives through word and sacrament in the congregation. Youth with abstract thinking are able to grasp in new ways the message of the scriptures, to "put it all together" and make theological sense of that which has in childhood necessarily been fragmented by concrete thinking. Joy in the gospel and in God's work for them in Jesus Christ is a fine reason to have an affirmation of baptism service with a focus on youth. But any suggestion of rite of passage, of becoming a true member of the church, of "doing it because we always did it," of reward for years of homework, and so on, are theologically questionable and even abhorrent.

Such a rite would seem appropriate only when youth have had sufficient time and exposure to the Bible and the church's teachings to have come to some genuine grasp of the gospel and its implications. In this case, real questions can be raised about the appropriateness of a service at the end of eighth grade (when it may well be premature even though it is often the current practice). Then, ninth grade? Tenth grade? Later still? When each individual is ready? (For the teen so identified with the peer group this readiness could be difficult to determine.) Whatever time is chosen, one would hope that the emphasis in the rite would be celebration of God's gift of baptism, celebration of the pastoral and educational ministry of the church through which

God has confirmed the young people, and thanksgiving to God for the gospel of forgiveness of sin through Jesus Christ. A strong emphasis on vocation, ministry in the world, and the priesthood of all believers would also be appropriate. The rite is not to be used as a "puberty rite" to gain adult standing in the church; far better for this purpose would be markers such as roles or tasks (such as, being an usher; being able to join the senior choir).

Confirmation as Churchly Practice

Confirmation is essentially a churchly ministry. The local congregation is vitally involved. God does the confirming or strengthening through word and sacraments; no prescribed pattern in the New Testament provides the shape of a program through which God will accomplish this purpose within the church. So, it is entirely appropriate that the congregations choose materials, programs, and other ways of dealing with pastoral and educational ministry with confirmands as may be suitable in their particular settings and age levels. Therefore, the 1993 task force left the program/practices to particular congregations to design while giving broad guidelines about ways that have seemed helpful in churches today. But, it continued the strong focus on those aspects that are not optional and are important for all congregations: the centrality of word and sacraments, and the role of Bible, catechism, worship, and pastoral and educational ministry that involve the whole congregation as well as the pastors.

The 1993 *Report* opened the way for local practices, and the task force thought of all such practices as responsible to the norm of the scriptures and the Lutheran confessions. They assumed that such local practices would be rooted in an ecclesiology that takes account of others in the church. What one congregation does will affect another. When we share ideas, we do so as a church, not for gain, but to help one another and above all to help and serve youth. Sharing procedures that have proven helpful will build up the body of Christ and contribute to the church's whole life, provided ideas are also humbly open to the critique of the brothers and sisters in Christ.

As the church, we shall continue in coming years to reflect together on confirmation. But always such reflection will stand firmly on the Reformation foundation of justification by grace through faith. We can thank God who continues to confirm the baptized through word and sacraments, through the pastoral and educational ministry of the church, which communicates the gospel and helps young people identify with the people of God whose mission is to bring the gospel to the world.

Notes

1. On early baptismal traditions, see Thomas M. Finn, *Early Christian Baptism and the Catechumenate: West and East Syria* in *Message of the Fathers of the Church,* vol. 5, (Collegeville, Minn.: The Liturgical Press, 1992), 4–18.

2. On Hippolytus's stages of catechesis, see Leonel L. Mitchell, *Worship: Initiation and the Churches* (Washington, D.C.: Pastoral Press, 1991), 17–21.

3. Thomas Aquinas, *Summa Theologica,* Part III, Question 72, Articles 1 and 5. The version used here is translated by Fathers of the English Dominican Province (London: Burns, Oates, and Washbourne, 1923). For more on the history and development of confirmation as a sacrament, see Richard Robert Osmer, *Confirmation: Presbyterian Practices in Ecumenical Perspective* (Louisville: Geneva Press, 1996), 55–57.

4. "If we define sacraments as 'rites which have the command of God and to which the promise of grace has been added,' we can easily determine which are sacraments in the strict sense . . . Confirmation and extreme unction are rites received from the Fathers which even the church does not require as necessary for salvation since they do not have the command of God." *Apology of the Augsburg Confession,* Article XIII, 3, 6. The translation used throughout is *The Book of Concord,* Theodore G. Tappert, trans. and ed. (Philadelphia: Fortress Press, 1959).

5. *The Confirmation Ministry Task Force Report,* ELCA Division for Congregational Ministries, adopted by the ELCA Assembly (September 1, 1993), 2.

6. *The Report of the Joint Commission on the Theology and Practice of Confirmation* (Minneapolis: Augsburg Publishing House; St. Louis: Concordia Publishing House; Philadelphia: Board of Publication, Lutheran Church in America, March 7, 1970), 8–10. For the background of the commission's report, it is exceedingly helpful to read the two books issued at the time to help in understanding the study of confirmation: *Confirmation and Education,* edited by W. Kent Gilbert (Philadelphia: Fortress Press, 1969), and *Confirmation and First Communion: A Study Book* by Frank W. Klos (Minneapolis: Augsburg Publishing House; Philadelphia: Board of Publication of the Lutheran Church in America; St. Louis: Concordia Publishing House, 1968.)

7. See, for example, Riitta Virkkunnen, *Confirmation in the Lutheran Churches Today* (Geneva: LWF Department of Studies, 1986), 5–6, 8–17, 20–24.

8. Ibid., 29.

9. LWF Document No. 38 (Geneva: Lutheran World Federation, 1995). For example, in the concluding "Global Perspectives and Themes" and "Challenges and Promising

Approaches for Local Congregations and Churches" (43–58), this author sees strong evidence of the U.S. discussion, although clearly many parts of the world still face serious differences.

10. Robert O. Osmer, *Confirmation: Presbyterian Practices in Ecumenical Perspective* (Louisville: Geneva Press, 1996).

11. Ibid., 98–160. Also, for the Roman Catholic position on confirmation as a sacrament, see Catechism of the Catholic Church 1113, 1210, etc. (New York: Doubleday, Image Book, 1995), 315, 341.

12. Ibid., 111.

13. In the Smalcald Articles (VIII, 10), Luther reminds us that "we should and must constantly maintain that God will not deal with us except through his external Word and sacrament."

14. Augsburg Confession (AC), VII.

15. Eric Gritsch and Robert W. Jenson, *Lutheranism: The Theological Movement and Its Confessional Writings* (Philadelphia: Fortress Press, 1976), 36. See Apology IV, 2 which refers to justification as "the main doctrine of Christianity."

16. *The Book of Concord,* Theodore G. Tappert, trans. and ed. (Philadelphia: Fortress Press, 1959), 30.

17. 1970 *Report,* 13.

18. The books related to the 1970 study soon went out of print and the report itself was not easily accessible. With the advent of the Evangelical Lutheran Church in America, a new task force was appointed to tackle the same issues. Building on the theological position of the 1970 statement it ultimately produced a report adopted by the ELCA Churchwide Assembly in 1993.

19. 1993 *Report,* 3.

20. To use the terminology of Paul Tillich, *Systematic Theology,* vol. 2 (Chicago: University of Chicago Press, 1957), 44–59. For fuller reflection, see Margaret Krych, *Teaching the Gospel Today* (Minneapolis: Augsburg Publishing House, 1987), chapter 3.

21. 1970 *Report,* 13.

22. See Gerhard Ebeling, *God and Word,* trans. James W. Leitch (Philadelphia: Fortress, 1967), 40.

23. John 1:1, 14. Also, AC I, III (Latin text).

24. God's word and justification by faith are integrally related. In his Apology of the Augsburg Confession, Melanchthon writes, "One cannot deal with God or grasp him except through the Word. Therefore justification takes place through the Word, as Paul says (Rom. 1:16) . . . " And Luther says in the Large Catechism (38), "In order that this treasure might not be buried but put to use and enjoyed, God has caused the Word to be published and proclaimed, in which he has given the Holy Spirit to offer and apply to us this treasure of salvation."

25. Apology XIII, 3.

26. AC XIII.

27. Small Catechism (SC), IV.

28. The Augsburg Confession, Article IX, states that "Baptism is necessary for salvation, that the grace of God is offered through Baptism, and that children should be baptized, for being offered to God through Baptism they are received into his grace."

29. SC IV.

30. Large Catechism (LC) IV, 65.

31. LC, IV 44.

32. 1993 *Report*, 5.

33. 1970 *Report*, 14.

34. Ibid., 17.

35. 1993 *Report*, 4.

36. 1970 *Report*, 18.

37. 1993 *Report*, 4.

38. AC XXIV:30.

39. SC VI.

40. The Augsburg Confession, Article X, puts it this way: "It is taught among us that the true body and blood of Christ are really present in the Supper of our Lord under the form of bread and wine and are there distributed and received."

41. 1970 *Report*, 14.

42. Ibid., 18.

43. 1993 *Report*, 1.

44. 1970 *Report*, 28–29.

45. Ibid., 14.

46. 1993 *Report*, 13.

47. 1970 *Report*, 20.

48. Ibid., 21. The 1993 *Report*, 12, has practical guidance on involving the whole congregation in the confirmation ministry program.

49. 1993 *Report*, 7.

50. Ibid., 11.

51. 1970 *Report*, 21.

52. Ibid., 7.

53. Wolfhart Pannenberg, *Systematic Theology*, vol. III, trans. Geoffrey W. Bromily (Grand Rapids: William B. Eerdmans, 1998), 332.

54. 1970 *Report*, 16, 25.

55. AC VII.

56. Paul Althaus, *The Theology of Martin Luther* (Philadelphia: Fortress Press, 1966), 314.

57. Pannenberg, *Systematic Theology,* vol. III, 126.

58. *1993 Report,* 4–5.

59. Timothy Lull, "Continuing Confirmation: The Road Forward," *Parish Practice Notebook,* 32 (Winter 1989): 6.

60. 1970 *Report,* 18.

61. Martin Luther, preface to the Small Catechism, 17.

62. See Margaret Krych, "Teaching the Catechisms in Today's Parish" in *Parish Practice Notebook* (Spring 1991): 34.

63. 1970 *Report,* 31. For a fuller discussion of the whole issue than is possible here, see Margaret Krych "Confirmation: Right or Rite?" *The Living Light,* vol. 25, no. 2 (January 1989): 156–162. Also Margaret Krych, "The Adolescent and Confirmation Ministry," *Parish Practice Notebook,* 32 (Winter 1989): 1–6, from which some of the ideas in this section are taken.

64. 1993 *Report,* 9.

CHAPTER 5

The Content
of Confirmation

Margaret A. Krych

The understanding of confirmation held by the Evangelical Lutheran
Church in America includes all pastoral and educational ministry from the
point of baptism. To describe the entire content of all pastoral and educational ministry to the various stages of childhood, youth, and young adulthood would require several volumes. This chapter will mainly focus on the
educational content appropriate to adolescence, that content more traditionally associated with confirmation. For more insight on pastoral content with
adolescents and the content of lifelong learning you are referred to in chapter
7, "Living in the Spirit," and chapter 9, "Lifelong Education and Pastoral
Ministry."

Content Areas

The ELCA's *Report of the Joint Commission on the Theology and Practice of
Confirmation*, published in 1970, lists three objectives with implications for
content.[1] The Christian community is to help the baptized toward knowing

and confessing the Christian faith, living as children and servants of God, and growing in the life of the Christian community and its mission. It therefore recommends regular opportunities for spiritual growth in knowledge, attitude, and response; special attention to Luther's Small Catechism; opportunity for seeing themselves as part of the congregation and being committed to its purposes; exploration of the meaning of a rite if used; and a continuing plan to proceed further in learning in future years.

The Confirmation Ministry Task Force Report adopted by the ELCA in 1993 is even more explicit. It lists eight characteristics of a strong program, six of which involve content areas while two deal with structure and continuance.[2] The content areas include the following:

- a focus on grace, affirmation of baptism, mission, discipleship, and vocation;
- a focus on the Bible and the Small Catechism;
- the use of resources and guidelines provided by the church;
- an emphasis on human relationships within the congregation;
- integration of the program into the worship life of the congregation;
- an understanding of affirmation of baptism as a lifelong process rather than a once-in-a-lifetime event.

Lutherans throughout the world have remarkable agreement on confirmation content. Serious attention is paid to the scriptures and Luther's Small Catechism. The Lutheran World Federation studies of the member churches in 1979–1986 showed that, "In almost all Lutheran churches Luther's Small Catechism is used in one way or another as a basis for confirmation instruction. However, there are some European churches where this is not the case. Luther's Large Catechism is used in very few churches, and then only in Africa, Asia, and Eastern Europe."[3] The report concludes, "The catechetical content, or more precisely Luther's Small Catechism, has maintained its place as the basic substance of confirmation instruction."[4]

The 1995 global report on Lutheran confirmation ministry did not focus on content but nevertheless gives clear indication that, in Africa, Asia, and Latin America, content involves the Bible, the Small Catechism, and sometimes the hymnal, and that in the Nordic countries and Germany it involves the catechism as well as a religious bibliography that covers the symbols and content of the Christian faith.[5]

New Opportunities in Adolescence

Teaching theological and biblical content to youth brings enormous joy. In early adolescence, youth have new ways of thinking that enable them to deal with biblical and theological content they could not comprehend in childhood. They are able to read and appreciate the Bible, and to think through the implications of faith, in new and personal ways. Typically, adolescents experience a deeper personal response to Jesus Christ and a desire to share the gospel. It is a time to help youth read the Bible as God's personal word to them, yet listen seriously to what others have said about it and dig ever more deeply into its meaning. It is a time to use the catechism to summarize the theological experience of youth as well as that of the church through the ages.

Yet, teaching theological and biblical content to youth also brings particular challenges because of the changes that young people experience in adolescence. In particular, taking account of the changes in cognitive development can mean the difference between rote incomprehensible presentation and clear articulation of God's word in ways that make sense to youth. At this point we shall give attention to cognitive content because many teachers encounter difficulty in this area. The key is to recognize as equally important the relating of content to emotional, social, and physical development. Where possible, these aspects will be mentioned. You are urged to read this chapter in conjunction with chapter 8, "Adolescent Development," and to make connections between content and the many aspects of adolescence in that chapter.

The worldwide studies in cognitive development that began with Jean Piaget and have been continued by post-Piagetian research in many countries through several decades have shown that children's thinking is qualitatively (not merely quantitatively) different from that of adults.[6] In fact, children develop cognitively through a series of stages to the point where, at about 11 or 12 years, they are capable of "abstract thinking," that is, the kind of thinking typical of adults. Because the Bible, the creeds, and the Lutheran confessions all presuppose abstract thinking, the cognitive development of the child and adolescent has important implications for how we teach, what we teach, and when we teach it.

Just as the child's body develops slowly to adulthood, so also the brain and nervous system go through a process of maturation. Piaget proposed that intellectual development reflects brain cell development. The series of stages is invariant for all children, although the actual ages at which stages appear may differ from child to child, depending on genetic endowment and environmental factors. However, in most children, the stages do appear rather closely related to age.

Of the six stages of cognitive development, the first three are sometimes grouped together as the sensorimotor stage. They occur in the first two years. In the fourth or preoperational stage, from about age two to seven years, children develop abilities that have to do with representing things: they use words as symbols, remember the past, and make-believe. *Preoperational* refers to the fact that the child is not yet able to use logical operations due to the inability to reverse their thinking (a characteristic necessary to check reasoning). Preoperational thinking is also "centered": children tend to focus on one part of a problem and ignore other parts, thus failing to consider the relation between the parts or between the parts and the whole. Their thought is often distorted because they try to make reality fit their own desires and because they reason from particular to particular rather than from particular to general or vice versa (as adults do). All these characteristics mean that young children reason in a way decidedly different from adults. Children try to make sense of what they are told, which may result in distortions and misapprehensions of theological and biblical ideas. So, in the confirmation process at young ages, Bible passages must be chosen with attention to age-level appropriateness. Teaching the catechism is simply inappropriate in the preoperational stage, although themes, such as God's love for the child, will reflect catechetical theology.

The fifth stage, concrete operations, lasts usually from 7 to approximately 11 or 12 years of age. The children's thinking is no longer centered; they can focus on the interrelation of parts and wholes. They can think about things and the relations among classes of things. And their thinking is reversible; they can check their mental reasoning processes and so are capable of logical reasoning (operations). In this period children develop the ability to conserve quantity and number, and handle concepts of movement, speed, time, and space. They are able to see the point of view of others, and their ability to generalize develops. They can distinguish fact from fantasy. Therefore, much more of the Bible, of history, and of geography, is appropriate for learning. But children in the concrete stage are still limited to thinking about those things that in principle are perceivable through the senses; therefore they give a sensory referent to every concept, including those concepts that do not have sensory referents from an adult point of view. The children can reason about concrete simile, but not about metaphors in which similarity does not refer to sensory characteristics or objects. Many theological concepts will still be only partially understood or, in some cases, not understood at all. Most parables are beyond their grasp. Some theologically important concepts begin to develop during this period and will be refined further in the next stage—for example, forgiveness takes on a new dimension about the age of nine or ten when children begin to take account of intention in judging moral right and wrong; death is not understood until after the age of ten as that which is irrevocable and the cessation of corporeal life (and therefore resurrection has a different connotation for a younger child than for an adolescent).

About the age of 11 or 12 usually (although sometimes earlier or later), children reach the stage of formal operations or logical thought or abstract thinking. As the final stage, abstract thinking is typical of adults the world over in all cultures. Abstract thinking is not limited to that which is perceivable in principle through the senses. It opens up an enormous number of new concepts, including many theological ones (spirit, justification, eternity, and so on). Persons in the abstract thinking stage deal with abstract constructions, use symbols for other symbols, construct ideals and reason about the future, use complex reasoning, apply principles in theory, and consider propositions about situations that are contrary to what they know to be factually true. They are able to introspect, to think about their own thinking, and to envisage how they and their ideas appear to others. They can deal with global generalizations, and grasp metaphor. Most of these aspects of thought are necessary for mature theological reasoning.

Abstract thinking influences the social and emotional understandings of teens as well as opening up new possibilities for cognitive reflection. The new abilities can be simultaneously exciting and bewildering to the young teenager, opening up new worlds but bringing the loss of the old familiar ways of thinking and replacing them with the new and unfamiliar. And most congregations begin intensive study of content about the very time (or soon after) that this change in thinking occurs. Adolescents need the church to support and help them in using their new thinking skills as they reflect in increasingly mature ways on the gospel.

Teaching Content to Adolescents

At the beginning of this new thinking capacity, youth need careful teaching. It usually takes a year or two for adolescents to develop the new thinking skills to capacity and to operate with facility in the new mode of thinking. Catechetical instruction should continue regularly over an extended period to allow for reflection and repetition. An occasional retreat is helpful in developing relationships, but simply will not do as the major means of communicating theological material: retention is low and insufficient time is available to digest ideas slowly and wrestle with them. Probably ideal would be instruction through weekly classes over a span of three years to allow for long-term, thorough digestion of the riches of our biblical and theological heritage.

In the concrete thinking stage, children assign literal and concrete meanings to the theological terms they hear. Teachers therefore must be prepared to spend time in unteaching misconceptions. Otherwise, new teaching will be laid over the old and misconceptions will remain that will cause further misunderstandings and confusion. Of course, teaching carefully the appropriate conceptual material to children in the preoperational and concrete stages will reduce the amount of "unteaching" needed in the teenage years.

Teachers need to use traditional technical language—or theological jargon—sparingly and explain it fully and slowly. They also need to teach the simpler, more concrete concepts first and then gradually introduce those abstract principles that are more complex. Illustrations that use analogy, metaphor, and parable are helpful for young abstract thinkers. Frequent review and repetition are necessary for retention.

In the early adolescent years, students can handle only a certain amount of complexity. They are grasping the Christian faith in a holistic way for the first time. Given conflicting ideas, they will ask, "But which is the right one?" Therefore, it will be helpful to present only one or two ways of looking at the work of Christ on the cross, and to help students proceed step by step through concrete examples of applying doctrine to daily living. Later, as they reach middle adolescence (15 to 17 or so), teenagers will be able to handle much more complexity and will be able to apply beliefs to social situations with less help. Early adolescents may seem conservative theologically; they are still learning what they believe and identify with tradition as it becomes "their own." By middle adolescence they will be ready to appreciate and critique the views of others as well as their own. A strong foundation in the Lutheran tradition along with an openness to listen to other historical and contemporary church traditions will help teens deal with issues of ecumenical understanding and dialogue.

The age range in which most students develop the ability of thinking abstractly is around 11 or 12-plus years. Some, however, will do so earlier, and some may be as late as 15. Such students simply have a different developmental timetable from others. A rule of thumb concerning the readiness of students to deal with theological thinking is their readiness to deal with abstract thinking in other subjects—for example, the skill of using symbols in algebra. If a student finds algebra incomprehensible, then he or she is also likely to struggle with catechetics. Some students "may well be embarrassed when peers laugh at their concrete attempts to deal with the theological content of the catechism. Sensitive teachers can help students move at their own pace and encourage individual work as well as group discussion, so that the slower developer has a chance to deal with the material on his or her own level."[7] Individual coaching may be needed. Often, waiting a few more months before beginning catechetical instruction will mean a much happier experience for both student and teacher. Remember that some young adolescents will not be ready for formal study of the catechisms until 14 or 15 years of age. It is essential that these teens not conclude that they will never be able to think theologically, nor that their developmental timetable will lead teachers to view them as impaired.

Early adolescents are inclined to revert to concrete thinking when tired or stressed or inundated by too much that is unfamiliar. Teachers then need to communicate in concrete terms with patience and understanding to persons who are operating at least periodically in a concrete framework. Be patient when they seem slow or reluctant to pursue theology in depth; teens easily tire of hard thinking.

Youth with abstract thinking want to know reasons why things are done or stated the way they are. They also want practice in arguing, weighing reasons, and testing their opinions. Interaction with adults whose authority they respect allows youth to have such productive, though sometimes painful, arguments over ideas and actions. Such practice in arguing can test the patience of any teacher or parent unless he or she grasps the need for youth to practice abstract thinking skills.

Exercise particular pastoral sensitivity when youth are confused as they discard previous concrete interpretations and replace them with abstract concepts. It takes time to become comfortable with new ideas. Many youth mourn the loss of the old, familiar ways of thinking.

It is essential to distinguish between cognitive grasp and devotional appropriation of content. Teaching biblical and theological content simply for information has no place in confirmation ministry. Luther's catechisms are both theological teaching and devotional aids. Good instruction in Bible and catechism understands these twin foci and never separates them. Confirmation instruction is, at its best, confession or profession—witnessing to the faith we profess, sharing the teacher's own trust in Jesus Christ as Lord, sharing the teacher's joy in the gospel.

Clearly, congregations need to recruit and train carefully those who will teach youth. They also need to surround with support and prayer those who have this critically important teaching ministry with its many joys and occasional trials. Teaching in the adolescent years is an opportunity to speak of the deepest commitments and together with students to stand in awe at the immense love and forgiveness of a merciful Savior.

Bible Content

The primary source and the norm of all Christian theology, and therefore of confirmation content, is the Bible. Scripture alone determines faith and practice (the principle of *sola scriptura*). Think back to chapter 4, which stated that the definitive written witness to the word in Christ is the Bible and that the Bible has its center in the message about the incarnate Word, a message of judgment and mercy. And so we rightly refer to the Bible as the word of God. Those who are baptized have the right and the responsibility to know this book and hear this word and also to have the Bible know them—that is, to tell them who they truly are, to name them as those who stand under judgment and promise, law and gospel.

In the Lutheran confessions, law and gospel are clearly distinguished yet deeply interrelated. The law is a message of rebuke and condemnation while the gospel is the promise of the forgiveness of sins for the sake of Christ by grace through faith. The law reveals to us our sin and shows our true state before God. It drives us toward the gospel so that we can receive the comforting good news of forgiveness. But the law is not the gospel. Salvation is through the word of grace, not the law. Youth need to reflect on their daily existence in its ever-present tension between law and gospel, sin and grace.

Youth need to read the Bible existentially; that is, it should inform their existence and speak to their existence. Help them ask of any text, "In what way is this passage law—how does it present God's demands of me? How does it drive me to my knees to ask for forgiveness? How does it remind me that I can do nothing of my own to earn God's favor?" And also to ask, "How is this text good news for me? How does it proclaim a God who freely promises forgiveness of sins and who accepts me in spite of who I am and what I have done? How does this text speak to me of God's promises? How does this text tell me of the great saving works of God who does for me what I cannot do for myself?"[8] Any text can speak the word of judgment. And any text can bring the promise of God's mercy. The same passage at one time might function as law for us and at another as gospel. What matters is what the passage does to us at any particular time, whether it convicts or comforts, kills or makes alive. Such a law-gospel hermeneutic will unlock for youth the central message of the scriptures from a Lutheran perspective.

In other words, God will use the teaching of Bible content to confirm the baptized. The Spirit will call forth faith in the young believer through the word again and again. As youth are helped to read the Bible, they will find, as Luther held, it is the cradle that bears Christ, the means of hearing that they are forgiven sinners, justified by God's grace through faith.[9]

Good biblical content will first of all give adolescents this hermeneutical key. It will teach them to read the scriptures existentially, that is, in a way that affects their existence at its roots. Confirmation instruction does not teach "about" the Bible so much as it allows the Bible to speak powerfully and personally to this generation of young people as it has done for centuries. For this reason traditionally we have a biblical overview of both Old and New Testaments, so that the word may come powerfully alive from all parts of the scriptures and so that teenagers can come to love and to listen to the word through many texts.

Such existential teaching cannot be hurried. Teens need to bring questions, experiences, and above all, their sinfulness and estrangement to the Bible, which is the answer to their needs. They need to wrestle with the text, meditate on the text, pray and sing the text in the psalms, commit the text to memory—not for the sake of memorizing but so that it is available to them as sword and shield whenever they are tempted to doubt God's promises in Christ.

Lutherans take serious account of what the church and scholars say about the scriptures. Youth need to learn sufficient background to the various books so they can read with understanding and place the writings in context. They can now appreciate sources and the editing of different strands into a whole. They need a certain amount of history and geography to be able to place events and grasp the historical and political references. Adolescents are ready to be introduced to good Bible commentaries and to regularly use concordances, atlases, and other tools that will help them in studying the Bible. A good church library will be helpful. Today's teens will appreciate technological resources and some guidelines on how to choose helpful sources versus less helpful ones. By middle adolescence youth are ready to compare passages and wrestle with different theological viewpoints of the writers while still appreciating the central message of God's revelation in Jesus Christ. But throughout all this study, youth need to read with their own situation in mind: how do these words affect me? Let them know that pastors and teachers are available to help them find answers to their questions.

In the concrete years, students may have had exposure to many Bible passages, some of whose meaning they may have misconstrued due to limitations in thinking. They will have partially formed theological ideas. Now is the opportunity to help them begin to see the theological message in passages they may have seen previously as simply stories. In the case of some passages, you may have to overcome the hurdle of familiarity in order to help teens deal anew with the text: "I know that you heard many of these parables when you were young children, but now you are ready to hear them in a mature way because of your new thinking ability. So let's look at the meaning from a point of view that children just don't have."

Teens need to hear that God's word speaks to their daily life. Encourage plenty of discussion and questions. When preparing to teach about a scriptural passage, as far as possible look for the meaning the writer had in mind, and ask how that meaning may speak to your students today.

Luther's Small Catechism

The Small Catechism cannot be taken out of the context of Luther's concern for education as a whole. Luther was concerned that education speak to service in both "kingdoms."[10] He believed that education is needed for the salvation of souls; the scriptures must be taught and interpreted correctly so the gospel will be preserved. Hence Luther's belief that the biblical languages are necessary because they are the sheath that contains the sword of the Spirit.

Luther also held that education is needed so that Christians can perform the function of the temporal government offices, of establishing law, order, and peace. As we teach youth, both concerns can be on our minds: helping youth hear the good news of the gospel for the forgiveness of sins, and also helping youth live in the world in a way that contributes to society and serves the needs of the neighbor in the various stations of family, school, community, church, peer groups, and so on.

> The promise of justification by grace through faith lies at the heart of Luther's concern for all teaching: all believers are priests who proclaim the Word, intercede for each other, bear one another's burdens, and serve each other. All Christians are called in baptism to announce the good news of justification by grace through faith. All are called to intercede for the church and the world. All are called to serve the neighbor in daily relationships and stations of life. Underlying this calling is justification. One serves because of the gospel. One prays because of the gospel. One speaks the gospel which one knows and which one is ready to communicate. The presupposition of course is that the believer has learned the good news of the gospel.[11]

Luther's horror in 1528 at the state of the Saxony churches and his passion for serious catechetical education are reflected in the preface to the Small Catechism:

> The deplorable, wretched conditions that I recently encountered while I was a visitor have constrained and compelled me to prepare this catechism, or Christian instruction, in such a brief, plain, and simple version. Dear God, what misery I beheld! The ordinary person, especially in the villages, knows absolutely nothing about the Christian faith, and unfortunately many pastors are completely unskilled and incompetent teachers. Yet they are all supposed to bear the name Christian, to be baptized, and to receive the Holy Sacrament, even though they do not know the Lord's Prayer, the Creed, or the Ten Commandments! As a result they live like simple cattle or irrational pigs, and, despite the fact that the Gospel has returned, have mastered the fine art of misusing all their freedom.[12]

Luther therefore goes on to beg that pastors and preachers take seriously the duties of their office, have pity on the people entrusted to their care, and teach the catechism to the people, especially those who are young.

Luther wrote the Small Catechism for use in households so that the young and uneducated could be instructed. He wrote the Large Catechism primarily for pastors, teachers, and adults. In the Shorter Preface to the Large Catechism, based on a sermon in May 1528, he says that the catechism's "contents represent the minimum of knowledge required of a Christian. Whoever does not possess it should not be reckoned among Christians nor admitted to a sacrament . . . For this reason young people should be thoroughly instructed in the various parts of the Catechism . . . and diligently drilled in their practice."[13]

Following the study of the Small Catechism, Luther advocated the study of a "large catechism so that the people may have a richer and fuller understanding."[14] Luther did not intend that the Small Catechism be the end of Christian learning, but rather a beginning that would lead on to more serious theological learning. So we rightly will assume that the confirmation content in this chapter will be merely the early stages of what will be expected of all Christians in lifelong learning.

Law and Gospel

Luther, of course, did not invent the major parts of the catechism. What he did was to reorder them and paraphrase them to make them clear. And he added expositions of the sacraments, so that his catechisms contain both word and sacraments. The reordering of the catechism is particularly important in teaching. Unlike medieval penitential theology, Luther begins with the law that moves toward the gospel and then to prayer, which cries out to God for his mercy.[15] "Instead of ending with the Commandments, Luther's catechisms invariably move from law to creed, prayer and sacraments (the heart of the gospel). This dying through the law and rising by faith in God's promise marks the life of each baptized Christian."[16]

We need to teach Luther's catechisms in a way that will allow them to do what they are supposed to do: help youth and adults hear about their situation of sin before God and the good news of the forgiveness of sin, the message of law and gospel. While it may be tempting to begin with the Creed or Lord's Prayer because teenagers are used to saying them regularly in worship, such a beginning is theologically and psychologically a disaster. Theologically, the move from gospel to law promotes legalism or moralism—"Now I'm forgiven, what do I have to do?" Such reasoning lands us back in the realm of salvation by works and undermines our attempts to teach the good news of God's mercy in the death and resurrection of Jesus Christ. Psychologically, adolescents are only too well aware that they do not measure up to the ideal, to perfection; standing under the law is precisely a point with which adolescents can readily identify. The teacher can help the teen move from a shallow sense of "not measuring up" to a deeper understanding of sin as unbelief, rebellion, self-centeredness, self-elevation, putting ourselves in the place of God. Then will follow the teaching of the gospel as God's merciful answer to our sinful situation.

It is important not only that the order remain true to Luther's intent, but that we follow Luther's unerring theological instinct to hold in tension law and gospel, clearly distinguishing between the two yet not separating them. To teach law without gospel leads only to despair, especially poignant in the adolescent years when cognition drives the teenager to constant introspection. To teach gospel without law is to cheapen grace and fails to recognize that the law is God's way of ordering our lives, showing us our sin, and driving us to Christ. Both law and gospel need to be held together.

Teenagers need to hear the message of law and gospel in a way that makes sense in their lives. Lutherans in recent decades have broadened the understanding of law by expressing the human situation as one of questions or questionableness. Paul Tillich, for example, analyzes the human situation of judgment as five questions (the conflicts of reason, human finitude, estrangement/sin, ambiguities of life, and ambiguities of history) to which the gospel is correlated as five answers (revelation, God's being, the New Being in Jesus as the Christ/acceptance and reconciliation, the presence of the Spirit, and the Kingdom of God).[17] Gerhard Ebeling sees the human situation as one of questionability, the experience of the absence of God, to which the gospel comes as the presence of God through word.[18] Wolfhart Pannenberg writes of "the questionableness of every phenomenon in the world of nature and of mankind [sic] that still remains open in the flow of history"[19] to which the gospel is correlated as answer of the promise of the eschatological future of God's public reign.[20] All these thinkers see the gospel of the good news of God in Jesus Christ as the answer to our deepest needs and existential questions. The teacher of adolescents is called to teach law and gospel with a similar outlook, helping teens articulate their deepest needs and questions, helping shape these needs in terms of the universal question of sin, and then helping teens see that the only answer that will truly satisfy their needs is God's merciful work of redemption in the life, death, and resurrection of Jesus Christ. The actual catechetical question-and-answer formulations become handy reminders of that which the teenager already recognizes is an accomplished fact for him or her on the cross.

The Catechism and Adolescent Thinking

Luther knew nothing of research in cognitive development as we know it today. He no doubt assumed that children were able to think much like adults. Yet, with insight, he addressed the catechisms to adults—heads of households in the case of the Small Catechism, pastors and other adults in the case of the Large Catechism. He expected the heads of households to explain the various texts to their children, but he also expected that love and understanding would accompany the parents' teaching of their children. Such love and understanding we need today as well. We now know that teaching material too abstract for an age level results at best in misunderstandings that later have to be unlearned. At worst, it results in frustrated, bored students who "act up" in class, and worst of all, may become convinced that the Christian faith is too difficult to ever hope to understand.

Probably most teenagers will be ready for the Small Catechism at about 13 or 14 years of age (roughly 8th or 9th grade). The later you begin instruction, the faster the students are likely to learn because they will have had more opportunity to practice the abstract thinking required to work well theologically. Congregations who decide to begin catechetics no earlier than grade 8 generally find much greater teacher and student satisfaction than those who begin at grade 7. Those that begin at grade 9 discover that students can deal in much greater depth with the issues in the catechism. In fact, perhaps 18 months of instruction in late grade 9 through grade 10 might be sufficient time in which to cover as much or more than three years of instruction in grades 7 through 9.

Before teaching the catechism to early adolescents, practice expressing traditional terms in language teenagers will understand. Explain the meaning of terms slowly and frequently. Progress from simpler to more complex concepts, which means that you not only need to know the catechism thoroughly, but you also need to analyze the theological concepts so that you can select the simplest and most concrete concepts to present first to teenagers.

For example, in teaching about Holy Communion, at age seven children may appreciate that communion is a time to thank God for his love, to remember Jesus and the Last Supper, to be with God and with people who love God, and to know that God is with us. By fifth grade, children's under-standing of forgiveness will have developed in a new way, because intention-ality is now taken into account in assessing wrong; no longer does the child think only of amount of damage done and amount of punishment given. So, with fifth graders you will want to emphasize the proclamation of God's for-giveness in the Lord's supper. By ages 14 or 15, you will want to add further theological insights: that communion is a proclamation of God's gracious word of mercy to sinners, a proclamation of the sacrifice once offered by Christ on the cross, a means by which Christ is truly present giving his very self to us for salvation, a strengthening for daily life lived in faith, and a fore-taste of the heavenly feast.

Similarly, in teaching the Ten Commandments one would expect that the Commandments may well come across to 10-year-olds as the civil use of the law. But 14- or 15-year-olds, now able to grasp an understanding of atone-ment, may see the Commandments primarily in terms of the second or theo-logical use of the law driving them to Christ and his forgiveness.

Content as Confession

Content and confession are inevitably intertwined in teaching the catechism. Timothy Wengert has pointed out that Martin Luther was the first Christian theologian to have witnessed the growth and development of his children while studying theology.[21] The oldest of Luther's children, little Hans, was in his third year of life when the catechism was being written. So the catechism questions reflect the true child-question, *Was ist das?*[22] And the answers are given by the adult who confesses to his or her faith. Often, we reverse the process in catechesis. We teachers ask the questions and expect long (and accurate) answers from the youth. But the catechism is more akin to the teacher confessing or professing with the youth listening rather than vice versa.[23] Such confessing of faith is more important than checking whether each teenager can accurately repeat phrases word for word. It is only too easy to turn the catechism into a cognitive exercise, in which right answers become the means to justification (or at least to church approval and acceptance). But the evangelical content of the catechism witnesses to the truth of the Christian gospel; it is confession—"I believe." The catechism is simultane-ously both content and confession for teacher as well as for student.[24]

Early adolescents are "putting it all together" theologically for the first time. This new and exciting endeavor is often accompanied by deep devotional responses and increasing commitment as God's love in Christ becomes ever more clearly apprehended. So teach students prayerfully and sensitively, knowing that counseling and worship are closely related to teaching catechetical content in the teenage years.

The catechism is, in fact, a devotional aid, a spiritual treasure. With their new thinking ability, teens can have a real sense of linkage with Christians who have used the classic catechism for so many centuries. Teach students to use the catechism as Luther did—to say each morning, and whenever else they can, the Ten Commandments, the Creed, and the Lord's Prayer. In this way, the promises of God go with youth throughout the day, and their baptism is brought to remembrance.

Many saints of the church will testify to the value of committing the catechism to memory. Rote memorizing should not be done for the sake of pleasing councils or parents, but rather for the sake of the teenager. When understanding and appropriation of the truth of the Creeds, for example, have taken place, then it makes sense to commit the phrases to memory so that in time of ritual with God's people and in time of personal need, the phrases will be readily available and helpful in recalling the mighty acts of God. Memorized phrases can be a genuine comfort and aid if understanding and emotional identification are linked with the heritage of the church.

Teachers of Content

We need to recapture the role of pastors as primary theological teachers in congregations—pastors who themselves love the catechisms and invite the baptized to study them with enthusiasm, who recruit and train congregational catechetical teachers, and who help families be the centers of Christian education as Luther had hoped. Luther's preface to the Large Catechism has some strong words concerning pastors and preachers who, either because of their "great and lofty learning" or because of their laziness, neglect the teaching of the catechism. Before teaching the catechism to others, we pastors and church leaders need to be using the catechisms ourselves. Luther urges pastors three times a day to read at least a page or two from the catechism, the Prayer Book, and the Bible, and to pray the Lord's Prayer. Of himself he says,

> As for myself, let me say that I, too, am a doctor and a preacher . . . Yet I do as a child who is being taught the Catechism. Every morning, and whenever else I have time, I read and recite word for word the Lord's Prayer, the Ten Commandments, the Creed, the Psalms, etc. I must still read and study the Catechism daily, yet I cannot master it as I wish, but must remain a child and pupil of the Catechism, and I do it gladly.[25]

He goes on to say,

> Nothing is so effectual against the devil, the world, the flesh, and all evil thoughts as to occupy oneself with the Word of God . . . For this reason alone you should eagerly read, recite, ponder, and practice the Catechism, even if the only blessing and benefit you obtain from it is to rout the devil and evil thoughts. For he cannot bear to hear God's Word . . . God himself is not ashamed to teach it daily, for he knows of nothing better to teach, and he always keeps on teaching this one thing without varying it with anything new or different. All the saints know of nothing better or different to learn, though they cannot learn it to perfection.[26]

Perhaps one of the biggest needs in Christian education in our congregations is the recovery of serious daily theological meditation by the pastors and major lay teachers. With the catechisms as a living part of the teacher's own heritage, daily reflected upon and loved, the teaching quality of the parish cannot help but improve (no matter how excellent it may be already).

In addition, we need to recover the use of the catechism in the home. Parents are the first teachers of their children. It is no accident that the baptismal service asks parents to bring their children to the services of God's house, and teach them the Lord's Prayer, the Creed, and the Ten Commandments, to place in their hands the Holy Scriptures, and to provide for their instruction in the Christian faith.[27] Luther held that parents were bishops and bishopesses in the family. Wengert notes that Luther's Small Catechism "could well be renamed 'Handbook for the Christian Household'" because it included not only the explanations to be used by parents with their children but also "the basic 'liturgy' of the household, prayers at meals, morning and evening, with instructions that these prayers be memorized. Those liturgical moments fit not the spiritual life of the monastic world, but the daily schedule of the common household: rising, eating, and sleeping."[28]

Other Age Levels

Even though confirmation includes all of the pastoral and educational ministry from baptism into young adulthood, the question often arises as to the use of Luther's Small Catechism with children under the age of 11 or 12. With children, the catechism may helpful in planning themes or topical areas for curriculum rather than as direct catechetical content to be used with students. The catechism is certainly to be used as a normative standard for writers and developers of materials. It is a tool teachers can study to ensure they bring theological sensitivity to their teaching. A good understanding of students together with such theological insights will help teachers communicate that which is age-level appropriate and theologically sound.

With older teens, the Small Catechism is clearly a valuable resource. Older youth are ready for serious theological reflection. At a time when their ideas are challenged by exploring other viewpoints through reading and discussion, the catechism can be a helpful guide against which to measure new ideas. With increasing theological sophistication older teens can examine the catechism in depth and relate their learning to their developing adult roles and responsibilities. This time is appropriate for studying the Large Catechism as well as engaging in in-depth Bible study.

Luther's catechisms are also enormously useful in teaching adults. Unfortunately, we tend largely to have lost sight of the catechisms' value for adults because of the wide use of the Small Catechism in the confirmation process with adolescents. We need to recover the catechisms' use with adults—not only those adults who are new to the Lutheran tradition, but also those who have been confirmed members for many years.

As we have seen, Luther's concern for general Christian adult education in his own day was evident. When pastors and preachers had taught the Small Catechism, Luther urged them to go on with a large catechism for a richer and fuller understanding. Such careful learning and teaching is not simply for the sake of teaching their children, but rather so that adults can worship, evangelize, serve, and relate their faith to everyday life as individuals and as members of society. Studying the catechisms gives opportunity for regular theological reflection that is important for all Christians as part of lifelong learning in the church. Congregations that offer regular adult courses on the catechisms often find that they are well attended and eagerly received. And of course youth are much more motivated to study the catechism when they know that it is something that adults do also.

Adults need more than one exposure to the catechism. Luther's concern about committing it to memory indicates that he wanted people to carry the catechism with them—have it at their fingertips—wherever they were, even when they did not have the physical document with them.

The catechism, along with the Augsburg Confession, is excellent content for new members. The Small Catechism avoids the polemics of the Large Catechism, and is particularly appropriate for those who are being introduced to the tradition.

Mission, Discipleship, and Vocation

Much of mission, discipleship, and vocation will be addressed as adolescents study the Bible and the catechism. It is impossible, for example, to teach adequately about baptism without dealing seriously with vocation, the calling in baptism to serve God and the neighbor in daily life in the various stations in which we are placed, and there to speak the word as well as serve in love the neighbor's needs.

Confirmation includes the opportunity to participate in mission and to serve, not just talk about doing so. Opportunities for mission and service abound in the congregation and the community. But youth do not necessarily perceive them or think they can participate unless encouraged to do so. Of course, sometimes youth lead the way, seeing opportunities that others of the congregation have not seen.

While love and good works flow from faith, teenagers may need help in reflecting on the way in which specific "works" may most usefully aid others in the church or in the local community. They may also need some guidance in planning and carrying out service projects.

Worship

Learning about worship and participating in worship are critically important in confirmation. In public worship youth encounter the word of forgiveness in absolution, scripture reading, preaching, and sacraments. For youth to identify with the Christian community and participate in its mission, they need regularly to participate in the assembly gathered around word and sacraments.

Some catechetical teachers encourage the taking of sermon notes, which has its points for and against. On the plus side, taking notes helps students concentrate and also gives them reference points for later reflection. On the minus side, notes can be distracting. Because most schools do not teach note-taking until grades 11 or 12, note-taking in itself may become the focus rather than attending to the message of the sermon. In addition, such notes can become a distasteful "hoop" to be jumped through or a means of earning points, rather than an aid to help youth hear the sermon as a communication of Christ. Notes may perhaps be most helpful when they are optional and the emphasis is on their aid to the hearer in remembering what is said, and least helpful when they become a legalistic exercise.

Exploring the Meaning of the Rite

Refer to chapter 4, "The Theology of Confirmation," for a discussion of the theological meaning of the rite. It is important to communicate to students what confirmation is in the ELCA—that is, a pastoral and educational ministry that helps them through word and sacraments to identify more deeply with the Christian community and participate more fully in its mission. In this sense students are already being confirmed long before they reflect on the rite.

A good time to examine the affirmation of baptism rite is following the study of baptism, or when the study of the catechism has been completed. The emphasis should be on the joy of congregation and confirmands in God's work in the death and resurrection of Jesus Christ for the forgiveness of sins, God's gift of baptism, and God's work through the congregation in pastoral and educational ministry to the baptized. Those things are worth celebrating and giving thanks for. By all means emphasize vocation, ministry in the world, and the priesthood we all share, as well as the affirmation of baptism as a lifelong process. Then teach in appropriate ways the means to carry out this process as discussed in chapter 9, "Lifelong Education and Pastoral Ministry."

Human Relationships

Studying about relationships with the diverse range of persons in God's kingdom is not nearly as important as experiencing them. Youth need opportunities to be with adults, mentors, parents, peers, children, persons who are like them, and persons who are different. So the 1993 *Report* encourages meeting the need for relationships in the congregation as follows:

> Personal identity is linked to a sense of belonging to a group. Young people need relationships with each other, with adults, and with God. Friendship-making and group decision-making skills are important. Exposure to various styles of family life, persons of different ages, and adult mentors can help young Christian feel important and needed. Youth especially need to be needed. They need to be valued as contributing members of the church, capable of being partners in the Gospel.[29]

Such relationships do not end with a rite of affirmation of baptism. They include relationships after the catechetical years, college follow-up through e-mail and care packages, and intentional relationships by the congregation with those who do not go away to college but remain instead in the community. The latter often feel lost, neither youth nor adult, and will appreciate increasing responsibility and visibility in the congregation. Mentoring may well continue into the 20s if welcomed by the individual—research shows that about half of young adults want adults as mentors as they take on increasingly independent roles in society, while the other half seem to prefer to achieve this independence on their own. Of course, it is crucial to give plenty of opportunities for learning as well as fellowship in the young adult years.

Standards

Following the 1970 commission report, guidelines suggested that between grades 7 and 10, "young people should be offered a program which meets these *minimum* standards: At least 60 hours of instruction in the Small Catechism, covering the Lord's Prayer, the Ten Commandments, the Creed, the Sacrament of the Altar, and Holy Baptism. Concurrent with their study of the catechism, at least 80 hours of instruction in the Old and New Testaments, concentrating on a comprehensive review of the Bible and salvation history. At least 20 hours, preferably toward the ninth and tenth grades, devoted to study and action projects related to the mission of the congregation and the whole church today."[30] These guidelines are not exhaustive. Some of the content areas in confirmation cannot be measured and are not on this list—worship, relationships, and so on—which does not mean they are any less important.

The guidelines are not meant to be interpreted legalistically. They should be seen more as guides for the congregation to ensure that youth will have a thoroughly serious program and not be short-changed "because there isn't enough time or teachers this year to do a decent job." In a general sense, such guidelines may also be seen as rough requirements for students but individual differences must be taken into account. Some teenagers may need more content. Some, especially students with developmental disabilities, would find such a list nothing short of an impossible burden. Pastoral sensitivity demands that each person's needs be taken into account.

Many teachers wonder whether to use exams in teaching the Bible and catechism. Arguments both for and against this practice can be made. Probably the most important negative is the danger of the students' confusing test results with God's (or the church's) assessment of the students. Student who receive an A may assume that they are approved and meritorious in God's sight; students who fail may assume that God condemns them. If you use tests, remember to say clearly that the test results are in no way related to the students' value in the sight of God. Let the students repeat often that they are baptized, and that their worth in God's sight depends on God's own action in Jesus Christ on the cross, not on any test grades.

On the other side, the good thing about tests is that they demand that material be reviewed and learned thoroughly. And that is a fine goal. So the question is, how can you best ensure thorough learning and review while avoiding the danger of cognitive works-righteousness. Perhaps these learning evaluations can be achieved by using fun quizzes without the use of formal exams. Or, you might divide the class into teams that earn aggregate marks through cooperative learning techniques. In cooperative learning all members receive praise. Or, you may choose teaching methods that are highly motivating and involve each student in active learning through projects, research, and self-selected activities. Intrinsic motivation arising from interesting material and methods results in excellent retention and a desire for continued study of the material. Carefully planned projects give feedback on learning; tests then are not necessary.

Special Needs

Much work remains to be done on the teaching of the Bible and catechisms to persons with special needs, especially those with cognitive disabilities.

Some materials exist for learning disabled persons who need adjustment in reading level. But not nearly enough has been done to develop materials for those who find difficulty in grasping concepts. As in all teaching of teenagers, begin with the simpler concepts and proceed to the more difficult. Proceed as slowly as is necessary, and do not feel guilty if the entire catechism is not covered. By all means teach as much as the student can learn, but don't pressure the student to the point where she or he becomes frustrated. Every person deserves to find study of the catechism rewarding and enjoyable.

We must challenge the gifted as well. Congregations often aim for the "middle of the road" and fail to teach either disabled or gifted persons adequately. Bear in mind that gifted students normally do not develop abstract thinking skills earlier; they develop on the same timetable as other teens but see more options and solutions. A beginning point for educating gifted students (and a strength for Christian education of all ages) is a good congregational library that youth are encouraged to use. By all means avoid labeling serious material "for adults" while helpful but somewhat shallow material is labeled "for youth." Some adolescents will outrun adults in dealing with biblical and theological content.

Planning for Continued Content

Part of confirmation is the humbling experience of realizing how little content is really covered in childhood and youth and how much more there is to go! Adolescents will be stimulated to further learning by seeing older youth and adults regularly engaged in Christian education. As students engage in Bible overview and the Small Catechism, they can plan on future study of the Large Catechism, the Augsburg Confession and other confessional documents, deeper and more serious Bible study, fuller participation in the church's mission, comparing the Lutheran view with those of other denominations, and so on. Congregations will be well advised to insist on serious learning into young adulthood before allowing persons to train in order to teach others—certainly, not before age 18. It takes years to reflect on content before one is ready to teach the word to others on behalf of the church.

Lifelong learning is an attitude that can be fostered from early years. Good teaching of Bible and catechisms will leave students with the feeling that they have only just begun and that much more stimulating content awaits them. The depths of the gospel cannot be plumbed in one lifetime. As Luther said,

"Let all Christians exercise themselves in the Catechism daily . . . Let them continue to read and teach, to learn and meditate and ponder . . . Then in due time they themselves will make the noble confession that the longer they work with the Catechism, the less they know of it and the more they have to learn."[31]

Notes

1. *The Report of the Joint Commission on the Theology and Practice of Confirmation* (1970), 29–30.

2. *Report of the Confirmation Ministry Task Force* (1993), 8–9.

3. *Confirmation in the Lutheran Churches Today,* LWF Report (1986), 5.

4. Ibid., 27.

5. See *Confirmation Ministry Study,* LWF Global Report (1995), 23, 27, 29–30, 34, 40.

6. The classic exposition of his stage theory is in Jean Piaget, *Six Psychological Studies,* trans. Anita Tenzer (London: University of London, 1968). Any major textbook on child and adolescent psychology today should have an up-to-date exposition of post-Piagetian research and description of the stages of cognitive development.

7. Margaret A. Krych, "The Catechism in Christian Education," *Word and World,* Vol. 10, no. 1 (Winter 1990): 46.

8. This section is an adaptation of a paragraph in Margaret A. Krych, *Teaching about Lutheranism,* Participant Book, Teacher Education Series (Minneapolis: Augsburg Fortress, 1993), 28.

9. See Donald R. Just, and Eugene C. Kreider, "Content Areas of Adult Education" in Rebecca Grothe, ed., *Lifelong Learning* (Minneapolis: Augsburg, 1997), 121–126. Indeed, the whole chapter, which describes content for adults, is relevant; it deals with the Bible, church history, theology, and ethics.

10. See Martin Luther, "To the Councilmen of all Cities in Germany That They Establish and Maintain Christian Schools," in Timothy Lull, ed., *Martin Luther's Basic Theological Writings* (Minneapolis: Augsburg Fortress, 1989); and "A Sermon on Keeping Children in School," *Luther's Works,* vol. 46 (Philadelphia: Fortress Press, 1967).

11. Margaret A. Krych, "The Future of the Catechisms in Teaching," *Currents in Theology and Mission,* vol. 21, no. 5 (October 1994): 336.

12. *A Contemporary Translation of Luther's Small Catechism,* trans. by Timothy J. Wengert (Minneapolis: Augsburg Fortress, 1994), 73–74.

13. *The Book of Concord,* Theodore G. Tappert, trans. and ed. (Philadelphia: Fortress Press, 1959), 362.

14. Martin Luther, Preface to the Small Catechism (Tappert, ed.), 340. The importance of catechisms for youth and adults is on the rise again, for example, Richard R. Osmer, "The Case for Catechism," *Christian Century* (April 23–30, 1997), 408–412.

15. For an excellent exposition of the development of Luther's catechisms and their use, see Timothy Wengert, "Forming the Faith Today through Luther's Catechisms," *Lutheran Quarterly,* vol. 11 (1997): 379–396, to which the author is indebted for insights.

16. Timothy J. Wengert, "What Does This Mean? Luther's Catechisms in the Parish," *Parish Practice Notebook,* no. 34, (Spring 1991): 1.

17. Paul Tillich, *Systematic Theology,* vols. 1, 2, and 3 (Chicago: University of Chicago Press, 1951, 1957, and 1963). For his method of correlating human situation and the answer of the gospel, see the introduction in vol. 1, 3–68.

18. Gerhard Ebeling, "Theology and the Evidentness of the Ethical," *Journal for Theology and the Church II* (1965): 124–5; *Word and Faith* (London: SCM Press, 1963), 347–353.

19. Wolfhart Pannenberg, *Basic Questions,* vol. 2, 232.

20. See Wolfhart Pannenberg, *Systematic Theology,* vols. 1, 2, and 3 (trans. by Geoffrey W. Bromiley (Grand Rapids: Eerdmans, 1991, 1998), for a full exposition of his eschatological theology.

21. Timothy J. Wengert, in an address to the Symposium on Confirmation, organized by the ELCA Division for Congregational Ministries, June 1998.

22. "What is this?" rather than "What does this mean?" Except, as Wengert pointed out in the address to the Symposium on Confirmation, for the question on daily bread and baptism's fourth question. Hence Luther paraphrases, rather than explains, in response.

23. Wengert (ibid.) suggested that "the catechism itself is a sterling, clear witness of Luther's confession of faith to Wittenberg's Hanses and Magdalenas."

24. Ibid.

25. Tappert, 359.

26. Ibid., 359–361.

27. Service of Holy Baptism, *Lutheran Book of Worship,* 1978, 21.

28. Timothy J. Wengert, "Forming the Faith Today," 390.

29. 1993 *Report,* 8.

30. John Stevens Kerr, *What is Confirmation Ministry?* (LCA Division for Parish Services, 1978), 12.

31. Tappert, 361.

PART 3

Confirmation Ministry: God's Work through Community

CHAPTER 6

The Congregation as Confirming Community

Norma Cook Everist

While I was an overnight guest in the home of my friend Carol, widowed a few years ago, I received my particular chapter assignment for this book. How appropriate, for it was 48 years ago that Carol's mother, Bernice, invited my then recently widowed mother, Bertha, to come and bring her two adolescent daughters to Bethlehem Lutheran Church. Bernice told her pastor about my family. He called and invited my sister and me to join confirmation class, which is where I met Carol. We would walk home from class together, memorize catechism, and talk, forming a friendship that has lasted now a generation.

Not only was my small, grieving family invited to worship services and catechism class, but, because we had no car, people regularly gave us a ride and often invited us home for Sunday dinner. The congregation discovered our gifts and equipped us for ministry. I was invited to take leadership roles in the youth group, to direct a children's choir, and to teach Sunday school. That faith community would eventually introduce me to church vocations and help me go to college. The congregation was a confirming community, loving a grieving youth into new life.

The Church as God's Confirming Gift

As we move around the country, around the world, we see congregations gathering in cathedrals or in white frame buildings in open country, in an open-air chapel on the hillside in the Philippines or in the bush of the Central African Republic. Each congregation is called to be a confirming community in its specific location. Each is also called to confirm and be confirmed by the broader church.

The church is both local and universal.[1] To be a confirming congregation means having a vision of the global and historic church, while claiming the task of being the church in a particular place. The Christian church is primarily here not to be admired nor criticized, but believed.[2] If we cannot congratulate ourselves with self-admiration, we often as not fall into self-criticism. The confirming activity of a persistently faithful God begins with belief in the gracious reality that God has been and is confirming this community of Christ in this place.

The church is a community of justified sinners, the company of those liberated by Christ, individually, but also corporately. The church is *simul justus et peccator*.[3] But that is hardly reason to justify ourselves for our unwillingness to engage vigorously in our teaching ministry. Faith in the holiness of the church can no more be a justification of its unholy condition than the justification of sinners be a justification of sin. Rather, believing that we are a forgiven, free, holy people calls us back again to confirm what God is doing among us.

The confirming congregation is a church in mission. The act of confirmation is not the mission; nor are we actually the ones creating mission. The church itself is not the mission, nor even engaged in mission. It is the mission of God that includes the church and in so doing creates a church as it goes.[4] Ephesians 4:1–16, that powerful text on equipping the saints, concludes with, "But speaking the truth in love, we must grow up in every way into him who is the head, into Christ, from whom the whole body, joined and knit together by every ligament with which it is equipped, as each part is working properly, promotes the body's growth in building itself up in love." The equipped and equipping members of the body of Christ will be in mission, and in that action of confirming the faith and reaching out to share it, Christ is himself building up the body. It is Christ's body in Christ's mission.

Christianity is something to give away. The church was not instituted to save those within, but to perform a work of service for all humanity.[5] In being a confirming congregation our primary concern is for people outside the church. This concern may seem to contradict our purpose of confirming those within. But we more fully and more adequately teach people by engaging them in ministry, not after they are taught, but as part of their being taught. Mission as service is both content and process. The pertinent question is: What is the Christian congregation to be if the one who does not yet know Christ is to receive from this congregation what God is intending to give? That question becomes a question of curriculum.

The church's vocation is as a witnessing community,[6] taken out of the world, set apart for God, but set apart in order to be sent again to the world.[7] To be a confirming congregation is to be a congregation on the move, not fleeing the world, but in being the church in all the worlds in which its members live all week long. Faith means responding to God's mighty deeds in commitment. The immediate result of God's redeeming action is the coming into being of a community of believers. The confirming congregation is always incorporating people into community. Literally by becoming part of the corpus of Christ, we become an incorporating people, no matter where we are—separate during the week, and then gathered together again for worship and education. Romans 12 and 1 Corinthians 12 powerfully describe the diverse members of the body of Christ, each absolutely necessary, together becoming a living, growing, serving community.

The body is an organic unity that cannot be divided without damage to the whole.[8] We are tempted to live in a competitive mode, either with the world, with other congregations, or within the congregation. We must remember that competitors are not what we were created and redeemed to be. God's gracious ongoing action of forgiving reconciles alienated people. We were and remain strangers, alienated and alienating. Ironically, we need to guard against too quickly turning the stranger into friend.[9] We need to honor the disparate gifts among us. The confirming congregation will realize that our task is not to meld into one like-minded people, but to believe in God's reconciling, confirming action while we are yet different from each other.

The cross is at the heart of the matter.[10] Christ's death isolates individuals; each bears each one's own guilt. In the light of the resurrection, the church of the cross is vindicated and sanctified as one in Christ. As the love of God restores communion between God and humans in Christ, so the human community, too, once again becomes a living reality of love. The Holy Spirit approaches each person in that person's singularity, making that person lonely. Each is justified and sanctified in loneliness. The Spirit places us within community so that we no longer see each other as claim, but as gift. In the cross and resurrection we become gift to one another. At any given moment we may feel as though people are claiming little pieces of us. Confirmation ministry need not be a burden or demand, but a gift that responds to our ultimate loneliness.

The church is the opposite of loneliness, which is not to say that we will not from time to time feel lonely even in community, but in its essence the church is not just a vehicle that carries the gospel. The church is gospel, good news that the alienation we experience in relation to God and among one another has been totally overcome in the reconciliation of the cross and resurrection.

The Holy Spirit takes isolated, alienated people and gathers us around the font and the table. The congregation as a confirming community is a circular image of the church.[11] The congregation also gathers in the narthex to greet and send each other forth to ministry in daily life. They gather around the word in a variety of learning experiences. The congregation's ministry from one generation to another may seem linear, but often it becomes circular in children teaching the elders. Likewise the church reaching out in witness often clarifies its own identity, as newcomers come around to witness to the established congregation. The confirming community is always in search of a round table,[12] free of unnecessary hierarchy, judgmental attitudes, and legalism, more fully incorporating those who have already been made one in the corpus of Christ.

The church is gift, good news, and it is constant. While any one congregation may disappear, the church will remain. Sometimes congregations engage desperately in confirmation ministry to save themselves. One hears: "The classes are dwindling in size." "The young people never come back after their confirmation." While not denying the figures, rather than abdicating a vigorous approach out of self-fulfilling hopelessness, we can dare to believe we are and will be the church. The church is comprised of all people and all lands, and it is gathering them as it goes. Wherever mission enters, the barriers that separate nation from nation fall.[13] Wherever it comes, it brings together what previously was far off and widely separated. The history of the church betrays an idyllic picture of the church, but herein lies the paradox:

while we are yet sinners Christ justifies us, as individuals and as congregations, and the entire church universal. Even while we are not what we were, nor what we are to become, we are called to believe the church is Christ's ongoing gospel action. To do so is ecclesiologically to be confirmed by Christ, and to become more of a confirming congregation.

Being the Confirming Church Where We Are

Over the decades I have taught and observed many and various confirmation ministry approaches. I even taught two different ones at the same time in two congregations. Wherever I have been, I have found that one central theme permeates the variety of approaches, settings, teachers, leaders, pastors. No matter how conservative, how creative, how many leaders or students, no matter the age of the church or the confirmands, the "effectiveness" of the confirmation ministry program depended on one factor: the congregation's commitment to owning their approach and carrying it out.

Congregations may use old curriculum resources extraordinarily effectively in a contemporary scene. (Likewise the newest resources and the most expensive equipment can sit idle or remain fallow as students drift away.) A congregation needs to see itself as being a confirming community.[14] Even though the following may seem like a radical promise, one could venture to say that almost any resource, any method, any setting will be appropriate and effective if the entire congregation engages itself fully, prayerfully, and thoughtfully in its corporate calling.

If each congregation is a gift to itself and the broader church, it behooves us to honor each local congregation's confirmation ministry approach and to build on the foundation they have laid[15] (no matter how shaky that foundation may have become). From time to time, it may be helpful to rethink practices that no longer seem effective, to open our minds to a fresh start. But for an individual or group to come and criticize the congregation, or for a congregation to involve itself in self-criticism in a way that negates the Spirit's past, present, and future work among the people of God in that place, is not helpful, and is a heretical ecclesiology.[16]

To begin where we are is both a pragmatic statement and a confession of belief. Christ Jesus is the foundation of the church and of each congregation. Christ's body has been at work, the Spirit has been teaching, and faithful

Christians have been carrying on their confirmation ministry as well as they were able. So the local questions are:

1. What is the history of confirmation ministry in this congregation? Seek out records, pictures. Interview parents, council members, the oldest member, and the most recently confirmed. Listen; document the stories and tell them to each other.

2. What theological and educational principles underlie various aspects of this confirmation ministry history? Look not only at what did or did not happen, but also ask "why?" Ask, what was the image of the church at work here? What was the view of the world? What was the view of human beings, particularly children and youth?

3. Assess the current situation. How different actually is it from the past? What characteristics describe this congregation and demographic area today, and what might describe them 5 or 10 years from now?

4. Gather resources. Begin first with the people. Look in unlikely places for mentors, leaders, teachers, and friends for forthcoming confirmation ministry students.

5. What are the resources of the broader parish? What does the setting itself teach? How does the context set the questions that Luther's "What does this mean?" will engage? Where in the world is this congregation?

Self-Identity as a Confirming Community

Does your congregation see itself as a confirming community?[17] Many congregations would answer, "No," even if they do some intergenerational activities. Congregations with a long history of adult education do produce older adults who see passing on the faith as their responsibility. This commitment is enhanced as a congregation evolves into a deeper community of adult faith and service. In looking at the similarities and differences among generations, congregations can begin to claim the challenge, even though they may not yet explicitly be seeing themselves as a confirming community.

Pastors invite married couples to come and talk with couples in premarital counseling sessions. Congregational members share their faith stories with confirmation classes. Confirmands visit homebound members of their congregations. To know and be known is the purpose of these visits. All of these activities build self-identity, even though its purpose has not been named as such.

The congregation probably is already a community of storytelling. Power comes in sharing one's story. Often it is the grandparents, not the parents of youth, who are most willing to tell about their own faith journeys.

When a congregation encourages youth to choose where they might use their emerging gifts to serve (perhaps as part of their confirmation ministry education), the adults serving with them—in ushering, greeting, reading scriptures—become acquainted with the youth. The elders not only accept their personal role, but also understand it to be one of training and guiding the youth who serve with them. This format may not involve formal training, but the adults "take the youth under their wing."

As more people begin serving as mentors, guides, and teachers, the congregation as a whole will begin to recognize its important role, remembering the promises they made at each baptism held within the community.

Certain committees and subgroups within the congregation may claim this self-identity, perhaps the education committee, a catechetical team, the church council, or the social concerns committee. But any individual or committee can become discouraged when they feel alone with the vision.

With encouragement, congregations gradually can claim and name themselves as confirming communities. One congregation eight years ago began using the language that parents are "partners in nurturing the faith." Each parent knew he or she would be teaching at least one class during the year. The congregation then broadened the scope so that the entire congregation began to share the nurturing role for spiritual growth. They have begun to see themselves as a congregation that lives, "knows the story, loves the story, and shares the story." As the congregation encouraged its mentors in both formal and informal ways, evangelism and outreach also began to increase.

As a baptizing community, each congregation is a confirming community, claiming the task of passing on and nurturing people in their faith. With this identity central, the community does not see itself just as caretaker of its own, thereby losing the sense of the Great Commission. One pastor said,

> One of the most beautiful ways I see the congregation claiming their role in nurturing the faith as within the baptizing community is in the way parents and grandparents teach their children to commune. When I first watched a grandfather teach his year-old grandson how to cup his hands to receive the bread, it made me cry. I was surprised and gratified to see how eagerly the elders wanted to share this gift of life with the tiny ones in our midst. I think

that the rural life, with its deep roots and long family history in one place, was prepared soil for making the Lord's table a church family table.

Developing the Confirming Community

Many congregations have no written criteria for evaluation of confirmation ministry. Informal evaluation goes on continuously in natural ways, when people compare and reminisce about past practices and their own histories. Some leaders use questionnaires for family feedback and/or meet with parents of confirmands prior to the fall program, planning and asking for comments or suggestions. These methods fall short of having an ongoing comprehensive plan and evaluative process, one that better forms the congregation into a confirming community.

In most congregations confirmation ministry has long been placed into the hands of the pastor, though frequently a board of education or church council has been willing to work together with clergy. The Lutheran church affirms the priesthood of all the baptized. All hold responsibility for nurture and mission. From the ministry of the whole body, some are called to lead.[18] Congregational boards and committees tend to focus on elementary and junior high age (attendance, classwork, memory work, tests, completion of sermon notes, and service projects), rather than holding a comprehensive view of the entire congregation as lifelong confirming community. Within or beyond the boards and committees may be a number of individuals who sound the broader call for discipleship, lifestyle, walk of faith, and adventure as Christians. These visionaries can become catalysts for developing the confirming community.

Congregations are concerned that current generations seem less biblically and faith literate. Congregations need to build a progression of catechetical lessons and projects into the entire curriculum. Congregations could build age-appropriate goals (without becoming merely grade-oriented or legalistic) to gradually develop knowledge of Bible and church teachings, growth in depth of worship and spirituality, promotion of stewardship, and involvement in ministry in daily life. Such a structure could help people move from a "graduation" mentality to a more basic meaning of that word, a gradual moving on, not away from the church, but more deeply into the faith. These goals would be guidelines for every maturing member to be reviewing and building upon.

Mutual accountability is essential. It may begin with the simple but basic sending each other forth: "Go in peace. Serve the Lord." And then the next Sunday people specifically asking each other, "Did you? How did it go? What faith questions came from your ministry in daily life?"

A congregation can gradually build the concept, not only through providing opportunities such as the ones in the preceding examples, but also through prebaptism and first communion classes, and through yearly meetings with parents that stress this concept for children and parents alike. Many congregations involve parents in meetings before the classes for their adolescent children begin. But rather than focusing only on expectations they have, parents could use this time to unpack their own stored memories. They will have brought baggage of important relationships or intimidation, of important growth in faith identity, or ridicule. The opportunity to talk about and to share their subsequent faith journeys helps them clear away the debris of expectations they may lay on their children. And it raises parents' own awareness of their ongoing role in confirming communities.

One congregation provides monthly gatherings with parents, not only to talk about their children's growth, but as a time of ongoing instruction for the adults. Each week this congregation provides a parents' lounge where they can gather (instead of driving back home, turning around, and driving back to church). Along with fresh-brewed coffee and the current newspaper are resource books on display concerning parenting and faith. One parent coordinates the communal growth opportunity.

A congregation can develop a "Growing Together in Faith Strategy," which teaches catechetical basics in elementary school years, so that confirmation instruction during the teen years can be faith dialogue. Congregations fear and yet are resigned to the young becoming less involved after the rite of affirmation. This trend in itself can become a challenge to the congregation together, not merely a sign of failure by pastors, teachers, and parents. The question the entire congregation needs to engage together creatively is: "If we teach well the dogmas of the church, but cannot be a welcoming community to the ones we teach, who have we benefited?"

A congregation can build on existing concerns. It can contract involvement of youth after their confirmation instruction years and continue to offer opportunities to grow in grace and service.

A congregation can build on individual pastoral interviews with students before they are confirmed and make this activity more of a communal one, not just evaluation of one's personal knowledge.

Involvement in the Confirming Community

Many individuals beyond the typical confirmation age are involved in confirmation ministry. In too many congregations, however, laity expect their pastor to be solely responsible for confirmation instruction, and lay leaders for evaluating their pastor's performance. When congregations are not connected to the confirmation program, they have little actual input and support for it.[19] This general apathy is quite frustrating to most pastors, who remain amazed at how concerned parents are with schedules for extracurricular activities and yet do not give any priority to Christian instruction. Sadly some congregations are satisfied with keeping the confirmation system heavy-handed and full of legalism and moralism, the rationale being "We went through this, and you should too."

Some congregations still do not perceive confirmation as a ministry, and one's affirmation of baptism as a lifelong journey. Young people sense when the congregation is telling them with words that confirmation is important, while confirming for them with their actions that it really is not. Why spend precious time affirming something that doesn't really matter? It is essential that confirmands and the entire congregation as lifelong confirmands be continuously engaged in active communal learning.

A growing number of people are serving as lay catechists, small group leaders, and mentors. In some large congregations more than 100 parents and mentors (in addition to education staff) help teach confirmation modules or Sunday morning classes throughout the year. Roles include teaching, leading activities, adding lectionary-based curriculum, serving as prayer partners, and listening to student's faith statements. Usually congregations select people who are firm in their faith and can relate to students. One student selected his own grandfather to be his mentor (although family member selection was not recommended), and their relationship grew from the normal familial pattern into one of mutual confidant and mentor.

Some congregations may not have mentors in the "assigned" sense of the word, but rather wise guides on the journey. Low-level involvement may include adults hearing memory work, coming in to share on a certain lesson or issue, or accompanying youth on retreat.

Even one evening of such simple guidance can be memorable. In one case, guides interviewed and were interviewed by confirmation students. Both groups were given a series of questions in advance and invited to answer any or all. Samples included: What is/was confirmation like for you? What have you remembered from your time in confirmation instruction? What was/is important to you from that time? What do/did you do in school? Who did/do you look up to?

Without some such connection, students who spend two years or more of intensive study are not really known by the faithful of a congregation. Nor do their wonderfully gifted elders seem to find avenues to pass along the communal story. The "elders of a village" concept holds much promise in an alienated and segregated, mobile, hectic society.[20]

The most powerful examples are parents who have taken seriously their own role as teacher/mentor for their child's faith. One congregation invites parents to participate in a Bible study that coincides with confirmation lessons. It's a joy to hear the stories of those parents who took this role seriously, and whose monthly guided dialogue of faith opened up conversation at home. The lifelong confirming community concept does not replace parents, but enhances, supports and broadens relationships among many adults and children. In this spirit, an 83-year-old woman gave generously to the congregation campership fund to send students to camp. In the same congregation fourth graders received their own Bible and read the Gospel of Mark with their parents.

For many, the most successful use of mentors is in 9th or 10th grade. One congregation completes the year with a mentor banquet. After dinner several students and mentors tell their mentoring stories and even do musical numbers together. "We laugh a lot and cry some because many stories are quite touching. No one wants to miss the Mentor Banquet."

A small percentage of confirmed students, almost always gifted, go on to become Sunday school teachers. Sometimes confirmands are involved in "pre-catechism" work with fifth or sixth graders. Youth themselves become mentors and so the church continues to be involving community.

Raising Up Mentors

Role models and mentors already play significant parts in the Christian community. Throughout the history of God and God's people, we have learned from one another simply by watching each other walk the journey of faith. Unlike the "good example" concept, which too easily leaves open the charge of hypocrisy, a role model shows us his or her life as both saint and sinner, including problems and pain. We watch and learn—sometimes what to do and where to walk, and sometimes what not to do and how we might avoid a pitfall.

One has many role models in life, some appropriate and some not. All members of the community continue throughout their lifetimes to observe others on the journey: elders, peers, and those younger. We form decisive images, concepts, and judgments, whether or not we are cognizant of the process. God provides such role models and the opportunities to learn from them. We may not know their names, nor they ours. We may glean just one example from a simple encounter or episode, or someone may serve as a role model over the course of many years. Leaders can make such learnings explicit by inviting people to think about those whose lives have influenced their own.

When 10-year-old Mark was asked, "Who do you watch in the congregation?" he surprised his questioner by mentioning not teacher or pastor or parent, but a man who quietly sat near the rear of the nave on Sundays. Mark didn't know his name, but he knew (at least when asked to think about it) that he had been seeing in this man some characteristics he wanted to claim as his own. Such noticing, naming, and evaluating of a role model can enhance learning, reduce disappointment, and perhaps build relationships that will continue to confirm us in the faith of the community, one by one.

Mentors, however, are different from role models. Whereas one may have many role models for the different aspects of one's life, one has selectively few mentors. A role model may be a leader one never knows personally, or a saint from another century, or an anonymous member of the community, but one knows and is known by one's mentor. The relationship is chosen, or needs to be. A community may facilitate mentoring relationships, and even suggest matches, but one cannot actually assign someone a true mentor.

One looks to a mentor for guidance; the mentor must also look to the student and want to know, appreciate, spend time with, and see potential in this junior partner. The relationship is real and, while not equal, reciprocal. Appropriate boundaries, role clarity, and guidance are necessary to make and keep it a healthy growth experience.

We do select for ourselves and are selected to be in mentoring relationships. Who among us has not relished the potential of being noticed by someone we admire, invited to learn in one-on-one ways with that person? Likewise one enjoys being selected by someone who chooses to learn specific things from us in a cherished relationship. We need to be careful not to idolize the mentor, literally make him or her our god, nor to play God by trying to shape someone in our own image. Mentoring relationships can be fraught with domination or disappointment if the ties frazzle or bind too tightly. Healthy relationships require prayer, introspection, wisdom, clarity of expectation, and guidance.

At some point, one may grow out of a mentoring relationship, or at least the intensity of time commitment lessens. Celebrating what was, then letting go, is as important as having spent time together. Mentorship may turn into friendship or peership, or may simply stop, leaving both with memories, but free for new investments of time. The Christian learning community needs to develop ways to equip and support its guides and mentors. Without such intentional guidance, support, and accountability, relationships may be spotty or problematic.

Pastors, church council, or the youth or education committee may invite people whom they feel to be potentially wise mentors to consider this calling. Both the leaders and those less visible in the congregation may have good gifts for relating one on one. A person should never be coerced into this ministry, and should understand clearly its roles, responsibilities, and boundaries. Training, support, and mutual accountability must be provided. Often a student will be invited to select a mentor from a list provided, or to generate possible mentors. The confirmation ministry team should know about and guide this selection to avoid problematic relationships and disappointment.

Some congregations have mentor training sessions during which respected mentors give encouragement to new mentors. A helpful training tool is sharing stories related to past and present mentor experiences. Some mentors or guides check in once a month to talk about how it's going.

Youth committee members often act informally as mentors. One congregation uses church council members to conduct informal interviews with confirmands. They meet with the confirmands for an hour and a half about three weeks before the class is confirmed. All have questions and statements to use selectively during the interview as a guide for conversation. Sometimes the conversations are held over a meal. The pastor is not present.[21] Some congregations foster prayer partnerships with confirmands. Adult catechumenates may have a spiritual mentor. Sometimes an adult mentor works with one Sunday school or confirmation ministry class for a year, meeting individually or in small groups. This format works well in earlier grades, beginning perhaps in third grade. By seventh grade these young people may be ready to select their own mentor.

One woman reported: "I really wanted to say 'No' when you asked me to be a mentor. I didn't think I had anything to share. But now I am so glad I did. The young person and I became closer and closer. I think we will always be sisters in the faith."

Leadership

Leaders need to begin where a congregation is and help it grow toward what it can become, trusting that God has already created, forgiven, and recreated this people to be the people of God in mission. The challenge is to become what we already are in Jesus Christ.

Pastors talk about their frustration and even shock at how little the congregation knows about the basics of our faith.[22] They grow discouraged, but they also speak about their passion for young people, for confirmation ministry. They talk hopefully about lifelong confirmation ministry, and developing more fully the concept of the entire congregation being and becoming a confirming community.

All expressions of the church, from the smallest local task force to the broadest ecumenical coalition, are partners and resources for the task. The essence, however, remains the basic concept that curriculum is God and God's people in this time and place. All else—and that includes much—is resource. The confirming community needs to be its own curriculum.

A confirming community will realize it is both rooted in the past (historical) and living into God's promised future (eschatological). Leaders realize that many methods that once worked are ineffectual today. Still they can honor and learn from the past, even as they promote more relational and experiential learning. Foolish leaders may either dismiss new tools out of hand, or rush toward them without knowing whether anyone is following. A confirming community enters God's future welcoming new people, resources, tools, and challenges, trusting God's ability to incorporate them.

What do people remember from their confirmation experience? Most can't remember "what" they learned, but remember events and people: "the time the pastor slammed down his book, swore at us, and stormed out of the room"; "the friends that I made." Of course, people do remember some of the content they acquired, even though they are unable to articulate it. It impressed and formed them for life, was incorporated into their very being, became the basis upon which later learnings are built. We are a confirming community whether we know it or not, shaped by the cumulation of relationships, continuing to impact the whole body of Christ as our circles change and expand. Wise leaders invite people to reflect on the past, and make such memories accessible. Such rehearsal and "unpacking" may call for forgiveness, but this sharing of experience will also revive and open us all to new learnings.

Leaders need to consider the neighborhood parish as context, mission, source, and resource for the confirming congregation.[23] One pastor reported, "When we study baptism, I take them all to the community pool. When we talk about life and death, we tour the funeral home. We always begin each session by talking about their week and we end each class with prayer aimed at how God will be with them in the coming week." Confirmands gather from and return to worlds in the parish.

Involvement beyond the classroom may be as simple as a scavenger hunt around the church to learn about church symbols and the community at worship. It may stretch confirmands through a 36-hour retreat with the goal of learning a theological method of ethical decision making. A wonderful (but underused) method is for young people to learn from visiting faithful members of the congregation on the job and hearing about how they live out the faith in the workplace.

Wise leadership is liturgical leadership. Baptismal hymns, sung often, whether or not a baby's head gets wet, remind parents, sponsors, teachers, and everyone of the promises we made and the promises made to us. Affirmation of baptism is a lifelong promise encompassing all of our life together in the body of Christ. We are joined in his baptism, as Jesus' baptism was the entrance into his ministry for and among us.[24]

A confirming community approach will be comprehensive. One congregation designed and implemented a program for children, which integrated worship, nurture, witness, fellowship, and service. A "step-up program" for youth included worship, music, service, teaching, camping, and fellowship. Crucial to that design was calling a director of education ministry and a part-time program support person. After eight years, the post-confirmation retention rate is nearly 50 percent, with youth involved in education classes, youth group, congregation committee leadership, music ministry; and as assisting ministers, lectors, communion assistants, teaching assistants, and ushers.[25]

Leaders will help congregations move toward new methods, experiences, and programs, careful not to jolt them nor negate their past. Pastors and catechists may move gradually from lecture toward a dialogical approach, remembering that presentation is still an efficient use of time. Hands-on learning, servant events, and intergenerational activities all have their place. No one learning method is ever sufficient to meet the varied learning styles of the members; no one resource will "save the program" any more than one leader alone will be able to carry out a comprehensive confirming community model.

Barriers to a Confirming Community Perspective

Congregations tend to see themselves as a "confirmed community" as well as a "confirming community." It's been said that the only things a person can be sure of in this life are death and taxes. Most pastors would probably add, "the abrupt disappearance of confirmands and their parents after confirmation day."

Barriers are real. It is worth noting a few (not in order of prevalence or seriousness). Readers with their congregations will want to construct their own lists.

- Failure to call forth the giftedness of God's people, to involve them in the body of Christ for edification of the church.

- A long history of pastors controlling aspects of confirmation ministry, coupled with a congregation's expectation, even insistence, the pastor alone will "take care of it."

- Lack of empowerment of the saints for ministry in daily life, which would stimulate their awareness of the need for ongoing communal growth in faith.

- Confirmation viewed as a social rite of passage rather than a communal process of ongoing faith growth and development.

- Confirmation viewed as an incontestable right of all baptized members regardless of their participation and commitment.[26]

- Confirmation expected to "keep my kids out of trouble and teach them good behavior."

- Perception of confirmation as secondary "fire insurance" coverage. Baptism is primary but confirmation is "just in case," to "make sure we're saved."

- Little commitment to youth ministry and adult educational ministry.[27]

- Hesitancy to "meddle" in the lives of others in calling all in the congregation to growth in faith.

- A fear of, if not an antipathy toward, adolescents; parents' own struggles with their youth in regard to discipline and respect.

- The privatization of faith at the expense of a healthy ecclesiology.

- An increasingly post-Constantinian church in an increasingly secularized society and the resulting compartmentalization of church and life in the world.

- Lack of faith conversation, devotional life, and rituals in the home.[28]

- The stress of congregations trying to maintain wholeness when families are being torn apart in their midst.

- Pastors and teachers who are more willing to adopt a new model or curriculum resource than to reveal their own personal spirituality and faith.

- Lack of time, amazingly overloaded schedules, and people's resulting stress.

- Fear of change.

- Lack of congregational vision.

The reader's list may be much longer. But even the barriers can become turning points toward commitment. One pastor recalls his own confirmation many years ago:

As the day approached I, along with the other confirmands, was invited to an interview with the senior pastor. As we came to the end of the interview (read, monologue), he asked if I had any questions. I suspect he was wondering if I wanted to know where to walk or what to say, but I asked, "Why is it that all the Hindus and Buddhists will go to hell?" I was told, "Well, you are not old enough to understand it now, but when you grow up you will." It just confirmed what I had spent two years learning, that my questions would continue to be dismissed and that my concerns had no voice in the church.

In this example was, of course, a half truth—he would understand more as he grew older, but the dismissal, so strongly felt and long remembered, has been converted to this pastor's passion for youth and confirmation ministry.

No matter how long-standing or all-encompassing these barriers are, when removed, amazing things can happen. Acknowledging them and working to remove them are congregational responsibilities.

The Vocation of the Confirming Community

Barriers to becoming a fully confirming community could be overwhelming were we not to realize the goal of the congregation is not to save itself by shoring up its confirmation program. A church cannot protect its own future, even through growth. Christ has already done that in the cross and resurrection. The Christian community, rooted and grounded in grace, is freed for servanthood beyond its own self.[29] As it is giving itself away, participating in God's mission, the church experiences Christ's guidance, nurturing, challenging, empowering, strengthening, confirming the community. This is the vocation of the confirming community.

For Luther, vocation is rooted in the forgiveness of sins.[30] God comes to each Christian, each local congregation, and lifts us up from our daily preoccupation with survival, forgiving us our lack of fearing, loving, and trusting God above all things. The difficulty is believing that these struggling people are the church. But freed from self-searching, we are placed back into our context, into our daily lives and our life together. There we find the call to vocation. Confirmation ministry is all about call, about God's call in baptism, about calling people together to know God's grace more fully, and about calling us forth to ministry in daily life. The confirming community is always a sending forth and a gathering people.[31] Even and especially when God's people go forth to diverse ministries all week long, gathered once again at the cross, this community is confirmed to be who they were created, forgiven, and Spirit-filled to be and to become.

The confirming community will teach, and they will send forth a forgiven, free people:

- *Freed from alienation for reconciliation:* the estranged mother, encouraged by a small group Bible class, telephones her adult children.

- *Freed from shame for righteousness:* the self-conscious teenager, noticed and admired by an adult congregation mentor, becomes an advocate for the class outcast.

- *Freed from rebellion for restoration:* the angry young adult who missed his chance for a choice job assignment, in a Connections adult study sorts out his feelings and his options and eventually changes his career.

- *Freed from brokenness for wholeness:* the woman who has lost most of her hearing in older adulthood is invited to read aloud in her Sunday morning Bible study group, because the community realizes that in sharing abilities as well as disabilities the community is whole.

- *Freed from fear for security:* the young child who lives in an abusive family relationship is surrounded by a caring community that intervenes, thereby confirming the reality of a trustworthy God in her life and theirs.

- *Freed from death for life:* the young widower, who is despondent in grief and unable to cope with the needs of three motherless preschool children, is supported in his immediate needs and discovers new potential for relationship and joy in the community.

- *Freed from guilt for action:* the education class that spent most of its time judging leadership and lamenting global problems moved beyond mere guilt by becoming actively engaged in the parish neighborhood, building coalitions for change.

Grounded in grace, the confirming community's vocation is open to ever-widening potential for ministry.[32]

The Confirming Community and Mission

This chapter title assumes an inward task. The congregation is intended to be a confirming community in mission within the entire parish neighborhood.

Even in "overchurched" areas, a great many people are in no faith community. Many have never been to church at all and do not know about Jesus Christ. We need to focus on the kind of confirming community that goes beyond offering a good Lutheran service to its own, and find new ways to lead people into a relationship with Christ.[33] Christians confirm their faith primarily by living that faith and sharing that relationship. At its best, confirmation is the playing out of one's faith beyond the boundary of one's church community in ways that testify to the redeeming and renewing power of Christ. The confirming community needs to become love in action.

A confirming community is all about relationships. Youth who are in sustaining relationships in the faith community will invite other youth to come along. When they do, a congregation has the opportunity to become acquainted with a new family and develop a relationship with them. Mission is built around relationships; it's what Jesus did.

Spiritual growth and nurture at any age involve witness and service. Servant projects have become regular components of confirmation ministry. Some have a servant-trip project for youth in the summer, or periodic projects during the year. Others have started neighborhood tutoring programs. But in order for this attitude to be sustained and skills continually developed, the entire congregation needs to be committed to service. A service component of confirmation programming can also help lead the congregation to more service in the community.

Countless stories describe congregations in mission through confirmation ministry. A seventh grader invited her friend to attend. After a session or two she asked if she could join officially. After a few discussions, her pastor realized the girl had not been baptized. They began instruction and she was baptized on Maundy Thursday. The class became this young woman's sponsors. The renewal of the catechumenate corresponds with a renewal of outreach. It has been going on in many ways in many places, as one by one people reach out and the community supports, instructs, and celebrates, whether at Easter Vigil or any other time.

Another congregation has four unbaptized youth whose parents are not members of the congregation. One is in eighth grade and also a felon who stole a car and vandalized the post office. The congregation hopes these young people will come to live a baptized life through confirmation ministry.

Most congregations recognize they have much room to grow in being fully engaged in mission. Congregations with an undeniable situation for mission at their doorstep may provide the clearest view of confirmation mission.

One such inner-city congregation opened an ELCA Urban Outreach Center, supported in varying degrees by six other congregation partners. Three years ago they began a summer work program for neighborhood youth. Young people worked for the elderly and infirm in the community at no cost. They received a small stipend that was kept in a bank account until the end of the summer, and then presented to them for the purchase of school supplies.

The Center's activities have grown into an afterschool program for more than 60 youth, a clothes closet, a women's support group, a summer basketball program for 7th through 12th graders, and the only basketball program for adult men in the region. Congregation members volunteer in all these mission outreach activities, plus they serve a Thanksgiving Day meal for almost 200 people. Neighborhood people also participate, helping cook and distribute the meal.

This congregation is known as a church that reaches out to neighbors, and neighborhood people are joining. Sandy, a parent, started a small group for other new members, most of whom she brought to the church. They have subsequently become the mainstay of volunteers in service. A confirming community is open, and in turn, the new people confirm others, the entire congregation is confirmed in faith, and all grow in their commitment to being in mission.

Another congregation has created a summer confirmation program (three hours each Saturday morning) for high school and older youth who missed catechetical instruction, who recently moved, or who otherwise fell through the cracks. It focuses on the catechism (with biblical connections) and is particularly geared for people who say, "I don't know anything about religion, Bible, or the faith, and I have not been confirmed."

They go to visit a hospital chaplain, a nursing home resident, and a soup kitchen in a nearby city. The field trips (along with classwork) are the subject of conversation in the car, as students reflect on the church's calling and their own. These youth are often from families not active in the church and are themselves isolated from church youth activity. Of those who have completed this outreach approach, 50 percent have become and remained active in the congregation.

Mission is not an add-on. Relevancy, as well as relationship, is key. Youth (and people of all ages) are craving caring conversation about essential matters. A dynamic confirmation ministry that meets people where they are, and tackles the issues with which they struggle, can be an excellent tool for outreach. The congregation needs to be an open place for visitors. When people feel they are heard and belong, they will enjoy being there; they will come back and invite their friends.

The confirming community does not draw in on itself like wagons encircling the camp. It does not assume a "Christ against culture" mode, but dares to listen to other faith communities and to dialogue with the daily news.[34] As individual people deeply engage in diverse daily ministry and in communal service and works of justice, they will know more clearly who they are. They will become less threatened by change and more empowered for partnership in a pluralistic world striving for peace.

The Diversity of Confirming Communities

Although linked in the body of Christ, each congregation will be contextually diverse from its partner congregations. They will vary in demographics, leadership, history, style, vision and much more; we illustrate with four. (Readers are encouraged to picture their own context.)

The first congregation is only a few years out of "mission" status, small but growing rapidly. Set in the most rapidly growing county of a midwestern state (about an hour's drive from a major U.S. trade center), it is comprised almost completely of people engaged in middle to upper management white-collar positions. The membership is highly mobile; the average age is 37 years. Most adult members hold bachelor's degrees, and many have graduate degrees. Although some people were raised in the Lutheran tradition, many are from other church backgrounds, and quite a few have come to this congregation as their first faith community.

The second congregation is large, with more than 1,200 members, established approximately 75 years ago. Originally at the edge of suburbia near a city dominated by the automobile industry, now it is an increasingly urban arena. It was founded and is maintained by people from long-standing Lutheran traditions. The average age of membership is 65. Most graduated from high school, although some left schooling early to work in the factories.

Their strong traditions were rooted in Lutheran practice, particularly in the areas of worship and confirmation.

The third congregation is rural with about 500 members. Farming and agriculture-related businesses are the primary work for most members. Most have high school diplomas, some college degrees, and a few master's degrees. The congregation is well over 100 years old. The average age of membership is over 70. Founders of the congregation were first- and second-generation German immigrants. Most members have two or three generations of history here. Most are interrelated to one another. The question is not who is related to whom but who is more closely related to whom. The traditions are long term, and (with only two exceptions) the congregation has been served by pastors steeped in the German Lutheran tradition.

All three congregations are overwhelmingly Northern European in ethnic heritage with little ethnic diversity.

The fourth congregation is located in the inner city of a moderately large metropolitan area on the East Coast. Although a Lutheran congregation had been at this location for decades, at one point that congregation moved. The building was purchased by the judicatory, and eventually a new mission began, with specific goals of outreach to the African American and Hispanic neighborhood population. The present pastor has been here for 13 years, gradually gathering grade school and high school youth. Eventually they were able to incorporate as a congregation. It is comprised of and led almost entirely by youth and young adults who have grown up in this reborn congregation. While the ministry struggles, particularly financially (a mirror image of the neighborhood itself), it is sustained by individual and congregation mission partners. Some youth now attend college, a formerly unattainable goal, and serve as leaders in the congregation's confirmation and youth ministry programs.

FOR REFLECTION

1. What are the demographics of your congregation? How has the "church local," located in this specific place, been faithfully and uniquely the church? How has this congregation thereby learned from and contributed to the church universal?

2. Dare to discuss together eras of difficulty, moments of pain, or crisis that are part of your congregation's history or present. How does the concept

of church as *simul justus et peccator* give perspective? Help each other sort out the situation and the memories for clarity and challenge.

3. Involve youth and adults in discovering your parish neighborhood. How is it changing? Help them interview longtime members of the congregation, as well as people in the parish who are part of other faith communities or of none. Incorporate these contextual realities into confirmation ministry.

4. Look seriously at the patterns of leadership. Brainstorm a broader base of people to be involved in a variety of ways in vision, planning, leadership, and support of your congregation's confirmation ministry.

Models of Confirming Communities

One is hesitant to provide models, because a model contradicts the premise that each congregation is already the gifted people of God they need to be. But stories of actual models stimulate each faith community to learn from its own history, to look around and see the grace-filled people already engaged in confirming ministries, and to envision together God's promised future for them.

A LOGOS PROGRAM MODEL

In this model, 35 to 40 youth and about 70 adults sit around dinner tables. For three hours they share food, Bible study, worship time, and fun time.[35] One older widow who was a "table parent" developed a special relationship with a seventh grader who is having problems in school and his personal life. He waited by the phone each week for Mary to call him and brags to the rest of the family that Mary called. They shared a common interest in hunting and talked and talked and talked. The Logos program uses mentors, and the confirmation students also meet with the pastor during part of the three-hour time. Youth are encouraged to bring friends and they do. As new youth come, their parents are asked to join and help, and they often do.

A LIFE QUESTIONS MODEL

A class of 17 sophomores—eight boys and nine girls—meet without text or work manual. Their assignment over three months is for each student to bring a faith question one week, present it to the group, and ask the group to respond. No restrictions have been placed on the faith questions. The group simply needs to honor the question of the presenter. The questions range from, "How do we know that God hears our prayers?" to "Why do we say the creed every Sunday?" to "When a person commits suicide, do they go to hell?" Two of the young men had experiences that drew forth the latter question. One youth's father had taken his own life, and another's good friend shot himself a year before. Through much discussion and many tears, the class struggled with the questions and were a confirming community to one another.[36]

MARKS OF THE CHURCH MODEL

Each year 3rd to 10th grade students deal with one *mark of the church*: word of God, baptism, the Lord's supper, Office of the Keys, office ministry, public prayer, praise and thanksgiving, suffering (the cross), service. The pastor meets with each grade for one month on Wednesdays after school, but their study is also incorporated throughout the year in the community's life together. For instance, 4th graders help with baptisms throughout the year and at Easter Vigil. Occasionally the whole congregation works together on these marks, as at their Advent workshop and their Epiphany tree burning. At an affirmation of baptism service for 7th and 10th graders each year on Reformation Sunday, the 10th graders speak on biblical passages related to each mark.[37] The young people bring friends; they express regret when their month is over.

FOR REFLECTION

1. Gather a history of the various approaches to confirmation ministry that have been used in your congregation over the past years. Invite the congregation at a special meeting, in small groups, or at the regular council and committee meetings to tell their own stories and experiences with confirmation in this congregation and in others to which they belonged. Simply listen, inquire more deeply about what made them effective or ineffective. Celebrate the past.

2. Gather many models of confirmation ministry and assess each for potential for involving the entire congregation.[38] Without losing the images gleaned in number 1, envision new possibilities for your context, more fully explore resources among this people in this time and place.

3. Make plans that might be implemented to build on the past as you move toward God's promised future. Give thanks for the church you have been, and support one another in more fully becoming the confirming community you have been called to be and become.

A Ministry of Grace

A confirming community at its core will see its ministry as a ministry of grace. Without resorting to backup legalism and moralism, its grace-filled ministry itself teaches powerfully.

Most Lutheran congregations understand that being in relationship with Christ means being connected to divine grace, but how they define grace is another matter. So much fundamentalist "evangelical" theology has to do with surviving judgment day and getting into heaven; it depends on decision theology. People need to know that having a relationship with Christ affects our lives here and now. This impact happens personally, but never just privately, always in relationship to the entire body of Christ, joined with him for all eternity, yet already at work in the world today. People need the assurance that Christ cares deeply about them and what they are experiencing in this lifetime.

Many Lutheran congregations are beginning to more fully claim their mission to people of all backgrounds, but they are afraid they will lose members if they open their doors to diversity. Forgiveness and grace lie at the heart of their faith, but they see the more legalistic churches in the community growing more rapidly. One paradigm for being a grace-filled confirming community is to be a sanctuary for people, a place and a relationship that is safe, understanding, and radically communal in an alienating and privatized world.

One congregation named Grace believes that their outreach ministry has led them to claim more fully a grace-filled ministry. Most members support and welcome the neighborhood people into their midst. In some cases that kind of action is difficult, because the image of what this church was 50 years ago still lingers. But it's a different place today, and they need to be reminded that they have changed. They had built an addition and stayed to do ministry where they were, while other churches moved away. Now Grace continues to be an exciting, evolving, grace-filled confirming congregation engaged in outreach ministry.

Some congregations remain locked in guilt and judgment, mired in conflict, and frustrated by new challenges. Their attitude toward confirmation ministry may be expressed as: "When I was in confirmation, we had to memorize the whole catechism and be questioned before the congregation!" When asked, "Did you like that?" they almost always answer, "No!" The next question then is, "Why do you then think that we should do that to our youth?"

Confirmation should be challenging, but not demeaning or intimidating. Today's youth will refuse to participate in the old legalistic models of confirmation. It doesn't mean they don't want to learn, but that they also want to be valued and nurtured in their faith. Some congregations are youth unfriendly. Their leaders need to work diligently to celebrate what it means to be different together across generations. When a community loses its passion to see confirmation as grace, when they care little about how the faith is passed on, when they experience intergenerational hostility, a congregation will become a dying congregation.

Thus, confirmation ministry needs to be a high priority for a congregation, one in which all members play an active part. They nurture faith in each other by knowing the story, by loving the story, and by sharing the story from their own unique perspective. Most congregations have not tapped into all the talents that lie within them.

Each new venture doesn't need to be a success. If we adopt an emerging approach that builds on the congregation's history, moving toward God's future, no one endeavor is ever the final measure. We can bless even our creative failures and move on to yet another venture, allowing ourselves the freedom of God's grace, in the continuing adventure of communicating the faith itself.

One can see grace—touch, hear, taste, and smell it. A pastor who has been serving a congregation for 11 years (and says he hopes to serve there 11 more) says he constantly preaches grace, but that it was a pretty graceful community before he arrived: "I think it really started with the first pastor, who was a wonderful man of grace." This congregation is especially supportive of its youth. The people make space for children to make noise and not be perfectly behaved during worship. A couple that tragically lost their own son have said that anytime the church needs money for youth ministry, to let them know.

The congregation as confirming community is a concept that doesn't simply mean everything we do is confirmation. It does mean that all we do confirms us in the faith. The question is, which faith: one of trust in an active and vital God, or one of self-serving self-justification?

When the confirming community is trusting God to be at work among all of them, it will result in integrated communal life that uses the gifts of all. God's grace becomes Christ's love in action.

Listening to the Individual Members of the Body

By grace Jesus Christ becomes incarnate in this out-of-the-way place among these people. By grace Christ takes each individual part of the body, incorporating them all into one living body. Listen to the stories of five such individual members; then listen to the lives of people, especially alienated people, in your congregation and neighborhood parish, who might think, "Because I am not a hand I do not belong to the body" (1 Corinthians 12:15a).

Kenny is 13 years old. His parents are long divorced, and his father lives in another state and is involved with drugs. His mother has four other children, from two marriages and one liaison, and is currently living with yet another man. Kenny is rebellious, has been in trouble at school, and generally does not get along with his siblings or parental figures. The household is at the poverty level. Kenny and his family have been in the area for about three years and have become active in the Lutheran church. Kenny still has some rough edges, but he is (by his own choice) coming to confirmation class. One of the differences for him is that at this church people express genuine interest in him, taking time to notice and affirm his artistic talent. In turn, he is quite good with smaller children and assists in the nursery.

Sabrina is an exchange student from Germany. She is staying with relatives but has no emotional attachment to her aunt and uncle. Coming to the United States was her parents' idea. Curiously, she refuses to call her hosts by name, even when asked to do so. To give someone a name confers identity and some implied value. When the name or identity is shared, a bond of relationship may be established and a feeling of belonging arises. Confirmation works in much the same way. In our shared faith, in the bond of baptism, in our common name of Christ, our relationships are affirmed. As we share the mission of the church, we learn to respect each other's gifts and to depend on each other as partners, even as brothers and sisters. The power is in naming and in learning to trust—to know and be known by name.

Wendy was raised in a Lutheran congregation but fell away, had an "evangelical" experience for a while, and now has returned to the Lutheran church as an adult. The current congregation doesn't know quite what to do with her. She gets up in church every Sunday and challenges the people with their responsibility to spread the gospel. She affirms the privilege we have as people of faith. She personally has brought five people into the church in the year she's been a member. She has seen to it that six of her eight grandchildren have been baptized and she brings them to Sunday school each week. The majority of the members think "she's forgotten what it means to be a Lutheran."

Steve was a youth who for two years was present in body only. He and his family rarely attended worship. He never completed any work, and the pastor was soon faced with the dilemma of whether to confirm him. His older sister was dying from ovarian cancer. In the month prior to the rite, the pastor met with him and his parents to discuss the pastor's hesitation to confirm Steve. What the pastor anticipated might be a confrontational meeting turned out to be a grace-filled discussion about Steve's faith and struggles with his sister's cancer. Steve was confirmed. In the months to come the sister died, and the family saw the church as a place of support and comfort. Their participation in the life of the congregation grew. What would have happened had the congregation held to a more narrow gate? Steve may not have passed exams, nor completed the required work, but he did demonstrate a living faith in Jesus Christ.

Brian is in second grade. He is an usher in church. He didn't ask permission of anyone to serve. He is a mature child who simply loves to help. No one questioned whether it was appropriate for him to be involved. Everyone smiles a little as the two-and-a-half feet of him walks down the aisle with the adults. He guides people to their pew and hands them a bulletin. He is a quiet, powerful witness that faith and service are for everyone and anyone.

Each of these people—and legions more in your locale—already was created, loved, and cherished by God. The Holy Spirit makes us lonely for each other. We through grace are gift, "grace" to each other. In God's sight the community and the individual are present at the same moment and rest in one another.[39] "Now you are the body of Christ and individual members of it" (1 Cor. 12:27). Each congregation in designing its confirmation ministry curriculum will need to begin with God and God's people in this time and place, thinking long term, lifelong.

The Lifelong Confirming Community

Not many people in congregations think of affirmation of baptism as a journey. They may use the terms *discipleship*, *relationship with Christ*, or perhaps *life of faith*. The congregation may be well grounded in Lutheran theology but not be able to articulate it in terms of their present life passage.

Congregations may recognize faith passages through ordinary life transitions such as of affirmation of faith, or commissioning services for those who teach or serve in caring ministries. They may recognize life achievements and the passages of high school graduation,[40] first job, occupational or relationship transitions, and retirement.[41] And for many, grace comes through loud and clear at these critical points of life. Just then, something from confirmation days "sticks" and rings clear in a new way.

If a congregation is to fully claim its role as a lifelong confirming community, it must not only hear repeated words, but engage in being a continuously confirming congregation though multidimensional activities.[42] Confirmation ministry is a continuous, communal ministry. An eighth grade girl didn't feel ready for affirmation of baptism at the expected time. The pastor became her advocate against parental and grandparental pressure; he confirmed her two years later. A young adult, who for various reasons did not "complete" confirmation as an adolescent, responded to a campus ministry initiative to affirm his baptism through education and ritual.

Some congregations invite youth to bring their baptismal candles to the affirmation of baptism services and to add this date to the candle. Baptismal candles and banners for each child, or a congregational banner with the Greek letters, alpha and omega, symbolize God's never-ending presence on the journey. Some add "I have called you by name, you are mine" with the name of each person to the communal banner. Even in a mobile society, to have one's name on a congregation's banner helps instill the communal nature of the church. Perhaps particularly now, to be named and remembered in one place (while moving about the larger world and church) helps sustain the communal realities and the connected nature of the entire church.

One woman late in life decided she didn't wish to wait until her death to celebrate her life. So she, together with her pastor, arranged a party—she announced it as a "wake"—with music and a brief worship service. She invited the congregation. It was a joyful event. She died suddenly a few months later.

Challenges for the Confirming Community

Christian congregations, by God's grace, have always been confirming communities intricately bound together as the church. Each in its own way has responded to its local context, being mentors and models for people on the way.[43] And as the historical and universal church, God has been confirming God's mission, creating the church along the way.

Confirmation ministry should be viewed as both a distributed and an intentional work of the congregation. It is distributed through teaching in Sunday school, participation in worship, involvement in service, and integration into the faith life of community. Intentionality is needed in the formal confirmation years to bring together fragmented pieces into one's individual faith.

But what if this people of God in its particular place took even more seriously its challenge and its promise to be grace-filled people whom God is creating into a new people? What might that look like?

- How might members reach out to one another, not only in times of crisis, but weekly, inquiring about their ministries in daily life, equipping one another to speak the good news in the languages of the workplace?

- How might older adults be confirmed in their faith as they ask critical questions about the meaning of life, retirement, leisure, health, death?

- How might people in transitions of vocation be sustained, educated in small groups to search out the scriptures, to pray, to assess their gifts and to respond to God's new challenges?

- In what new ways might all members of the congregation see themselves as catechists and as continually being stretched in ongoing catechetical instruction?

- How might the catechisms come to life at each stage of the life cycle, and how might Christian educators design appropriate learning experiences so that each person in the parish has at least two educational opportunities a week to grow in his or her faith?

- Who in the parish neighborhood is asking the basic questions of faith? How might each member of the congregation be equipped to be a teacher of the faith in their encounters with friends, work associates, community contacts?

- How might the entire congregation corporately become more visibly active in being a faith community that loves and supports each other and is open to being in mission in the broader pluralistic community?

The confirming community by God's grace will be open to these and more new challenges as they move confidently, confirmed in Jesus Christ, into God's promised future.

Notes

1. H. Richard Niebuhr, *The Purpose of the Church and Its Ministry* (New York: Harper and Row, 1956).

2. Hans Küng, *The Church* (New York: Sheed and Ward, 1967).

3. Jurgen Moltmann, *The Church in the Power of the Spirit* (New York: Harper and Row, 1977), 22.

4. Ibid., 64.

5. Juan Luis Segundo, *The Community Called Church* (Maryknoll, NY: Orbis, 1973).

6. The term *community* to many people refers merely to the municipality in which they reside. In a much deeper sense community means being bound together in ways that connect, give identity, value, and meaning to life.

7. Suzanne de Dietrich, *The Witnessing Community* (Philadelphia: The Westminster Press, 1958).

8. First Corinthians 12:14-20 emphasizes that even when a member feels or is made to feel he or she does not belong, that does not keep that one from being part of the body.

9. Parker Palmer, *The Company of Strangers* (New York: The Crossroads Publishing Co., 1981).

10. Dietrich Bonhoeffer, *The Communion of Saints: A Dogmatic Inquiry into the Sociology of the Church* (New York: Harper and Row, 1963). Bonhoeffer's dissertation was presented in 1927 at the age of 21. This sociological theology of the church serves as a basis for understanding his later works, notably the well-known *Life Together*.

11. Letty M. Russell, *Church in the Round* (Louisville, KY: Westminster/John Knox Press, 1993).

12. Christine Grumm, "In Search of a Round Table" in Musimbi R. Z. Kanyoro, *In Search of a Round Table* (Geneva: World Council of Churches Publications, 1997), 28–39.

13. Wilhelm Loehe, *Three Books About the Church,* trans. by James L. Schaaf (Philadelphia: Fortress Press, 1969).

14. The Evangelical Lutheran Church in America's *Confirmation Ministry Task Force Report* (Chicago: ELCA's Division for Congregational Ministries, 1993), 1, asks the basic question, "What is the role of the congregation in affirming youth in Christian faithfulness with an emphasis on lifelong learning and discipleship?"

15. Ibid. Central to the 1970 *Report of the Joint Commission on the Theology and Practice of Confirmation* was the idea of the church as a confirming community: "Confirmation ministry is a pastoral and educational ministry of the church that helps the baptized through Word and Sacrament to identify more deeply with the Christian community and participate more fully in its mission."

16. A healthy theology of the church precludes denying another expression of the church as part of Christ's body (1 Corinthians 12). However, we as member churches together do need to call each other to biblical and confessional faithfulness.

17. "Congregation as Confirming Community" was the theme of an initiative of the Division for Life and Mission in the Congregation of the former American Lutheran Church in the early 1980s. As part of that strategy they published a folder of "Congregational Stories" of models and approaches.

18. At ordination a pastor is set apart to the office of word and sacrament in the one holy catholic church by laying on of hands and by prayer. The pastor promises to be diligent in the study of the Holy Scriptures and the use of the means of grace, to pray for God's people, to nourish them with the word and holy sacraments, and to lead them in faithful service and holy living (Service of Ordination, *Occasional Services*, 192ff.). The constitution of the Evangelical Lutheran Church in America "affirms the universal priesthood of all its baptized members and commits itself to the equipping and supporting of all its members for their ministries in the world and in this church. It is within this context of ministry that this church calls or appoints some of its baptized members for specific ministries in this church" (ELCA Constitution 10:11).

19. See Samuel Torvend and Lani Willis, eds., *Welcome to Christ: A Lutheran Introduction to the Catechumenate* (Minneapolis: Augsburg Fortress, 1997), 26ff. Although the catechumenate emphasizes adult seekers preparing for baptism, its renewal today challenges the entire congregation to ongoing commitment. All the baptized are involved while certain gifted and willing people are responsible for specific leadership (for example, catechumenal coordinator, pastor, catechist, sponsor, catechumen).

20. See Hillary Rodham Clinton, *It Takes a Village* (New York: Simon & Schuster, 1996), 12–13. The author in choosing this African proverb for her title reminds the reader that youth thrive only if their families thrive and if the whole of society cares enough to provide for them. Today the horizons of the contemporary village extend well beyond a small geographic place, as far as the impersonal global village technology and mobility have created. Still needed is the network of values and relationships that support lives.

21. The church council/confirmation interview questions from Zion Lutheran Church, Beloit, Kansas: (1) Why should you go to church? (2) What are ways God comes to you with gifts of love? (3) Share your understanding of baptism. (4) Why read the Bible? (5) What role does the Holy Spirit play in our life? (6) What is your call as a Christian? (7) Share your understanding of Holy Communion. (8) What does confirmation mean to you? (9) How are you going to continually live out your confirmation? (10) What does the church mean to you? What does it offer? What do I have to offer the church?

22. Martin Luther grew frustrated too. In 1531, looking back on the situation he had found in Saxon churches, he described it thus: "No one knew the real meaning of the

gospel, Christ, baptism, confession, the Sacrament of the Altar, faith, Spirit, flesh, good works, the Ten Commandments, the Our Father, prayer, suffering, comfort, temporal government, the state of matrimony, parents, children, masters, manservant, mistress, maidservant, devils, angels, world, life, death, sin, justice, forgiveness, God, bishop, pastor, church, a Christian, or the cross. In brief, we were totally ignorant about all that is necessary for a Christian to know." From Martin Luther's "Warning to His Dear German People," *Luther's Works*, vol. 47 (Philadelphia: Fortress Press, 1971), 52.

23. *Parish* is used here to designate the geographic neighborhood, whether that be a town, rural township, part of a county, a few city blocks, or a suburban subdivision. All people, institutions, and events are parish resources.

24. See Mark 1:1–12.

25. Susan B. Sheffer-Meyer, pastor, Madison, Wisconsin, describing her former congregation, Cross of Life, in Brookfield, Wisconsin.

26. Martin Luther, "Letter to the Mayors and Alderman of all the Cities of Germany in Behalf of Christian Schools" in F. V. N. Painter, *Luther on Education*. (St. Louis: Concordia Publishing House, 1889), 176. Luther's urgency to provide Christian education is expressed: "Gather the harvest while the sun shines and the weather is fair; use the grace and Word of God while they are near. For know this, that the Word and grace of God are like a passing shower, which does not return where it has once been . . . And the German people should not think that they will always have it; for ingratitude and neglect will banish it. Therefore seize it and hold it fast."

27. *Ibid*, 178. "In my judgment here is no other outward offense that in the sight of God so heavily burdens the world, and deserves such heavy chastisement as the neglect to educate children."

28. Martin Luther, sermon on "The Duty of Sending Children to School" in F. V. N. Painter, *Luther on Education*. (St. Louis: Concordia Publishing House, 1889), 248. Luther insisted that education was not just for monks, priests, and nuns, but for all in their daily callings. "It is a shameful contempt of God that you do not bring up your children to such an excellent and divinely appointed calling, and that you strengthen them only in the service of appetite and avarice, teaching them nothing but to provide for the stomach, like a hog with its nose always in filth and do not bring them up to this worthy station and office. You must either be insensible creatures, or else you do not love your children."

29. Martin Luther, "A Treatise on Christian Liberty," published in Martin Luther, *Three Treatises* (Philadelphia: The Muhlenberg Press,1947), 249–290. Luther says that a Christian is a perfectly free lord of all, subject to none and that a Christian is a perfectly dutiful servant of all, subject to all. In this paradox is the freedom for a vocation of servanthood.

30. Einar Billing, *Our Calling* (Rock Island, Ill.: Augustana Press, 1988), 6. "When it began to dawn on Luther that just as certainly as the call to God's kingdom lifts us infinitely above everything that our everyday duties by themselves could give us, just that certainly the call does not take us away from those duties but more deeply into them."

31. See Paul Nelson, Frank Stoldt, Scott Weidler, Lani Willis, eds., *Welcome to Christ: Lutheran Rites for the Catechumenate* (Minneapolis: Augsburg Fortress, 1997), 59–60, for a

service of "Affirmation of the Vocation of the Baptized in the World," set within the service of Holy Communion following baptism. This service signifies liturgically that "through Holy Baptism we have been made members of the priesthood we share in Christ Jesus that we may be freed to bear God's creative and redeeming word to all the world." It sends people forth in different directions for service, invoking God's gifts for courage, patience, vision and strength for vocation, trusting that by the power of the Spirit God has "knit these servants into the one body" of Christ.

32. F. V. N. Painter, *Luther on Education* (St Louis: Concordia Publishing House, 1889), 64. "Religion is not a thing apart from our daily labors, but a spirit sanctifying our whole life, and ennobling the lowliest service."

33. Nelson et al., *Welcome to Christ: Lutheran Rites for the Catechumenate* (Minneapolis: Augsburg Fortress, 1997), 9–15. A service of "Welcome of Inquirers to the Catechumenate" begins at the door before the Entrance Hymn stressing that the entire congregation meets people where they are, inviting them into the community of faith in Jesus Christ.

34. H. Richard Niebuhr, *Christ and Culture* (New York: Harper and Brothers, 1951). Niebuhr outlines five types of relationships between Christians and their world. The typical Lutheran "Christ and Culture in Paradox" worldview recognizes that the tension between the two exists outside and inside the church.

35. David Pederson, Trinity Lutheran, Dallas, Oregon. Logos was started by a Presbyterian who wanted to develop a congregation-based program. The program was adapted by Pederson for use at Trinity Lutheran.

36. What happened throughout that adolescent class was no different than what would happen with adults in the church, if only a safe arena were available. The best material lies within the confirming community, drawing on the tenets of the faith, scriptures, catechisms, and creeds.

37. Althea Sondahl, pastor, Good Hope, Gifford, Idaho, and Faith, Kamiah, Idaho. Future plans include parents receiving Large Catechisms. In preparing this "Marks of the Church" approach the education committee studied the history of confirmation in this congregation, which led to a change in their constitution so that all baptized members, regarded as already confirmed in their faith by Christ, may be communed. The congregation has so claimed their own role that when interviewing for a new co-pastor, they asked that the new pastor be committed to their approach.

38. See Ken Smith, *Six Models of Confirmation Ministry* (Chicago: Evangelical Lutheran Church in America, 1993).

39. Dietrich Bonhoeffer, *The Communion of Saints: A Dogmatic Inquiry into the Sociology of the Church* (New York: Harper and Row, 1963), 22–48. Bonhoeffer wrote that God does not desire a history of the individual, but the history of the community. Nor does God desire a community that absorbs the individual into itself. God creates us interdependent with one another.

40. One congregation provides handmade quilts to each graduating high school student with a handwritten label sewn in stating, "Given to you, *(name),* to honor your high school graduation and to remind you that you are wrapped in God's love forever."

41. See Norma Cook Everist and Nelvin Vos, *Connections: Faith and Life* (Chicago: Evangelical Lutheran Church in America, 1997). This four-unit, 24-session adult study is based on Martin Luther's Large Catechism and is appropriate for use throughout adulthood in small groups for lifelong Lutherans and for adults preparing for baptism and affirmation of baptism.

42. Ibid. Leader Guide, Unit 4, Session 6, 27–29. Young adulthood is a prime time for affirmation of faith tied to public commitments. Middle adulthood in a time to incorporate personally claimed beliefs with the perspectives of others during life's transitions and changing responsibilities. Older adulthood is a time to struggle with the realities of a deep faith as one moves between despair and shalom. See also Robert L. Browning and Roy A. Reed, *Models of Confirmation and Baptismal Affirmation* (Birmingham, Ala.: Religious Education Press, 1995), 161–195.

43. The nineteen pastors and one associate in ministry who shared their stories, passions, and challenges with the author in preparation of this chapter are: Beverly-Jo Arnold, Florissant, Missouri; Michael G. Clark, Beloit, Kansas; Ruth Drews, New Haven, Connecticut; Frank Ehling, Fargo, North Dakota; Randal Fett, Spearfish, South Dakota; Paul H. Geye, Turlock, California; Kenneth Gibson, Chassell, Michigan; Jeffrey Jacobs, Verona, Wisconsin; Patricia Johnson, Kenosha, Wisconsin; Michael D. Peck, Overland Park, Kansas; David A. Pederson, Dallas, Oregon; Wayne Pfannkuch, McCallsburg, Iowa; Carolyn Pflibsen, AIM, Hawkeye, Iowa; Scott Postlewait, Seattle, Washington; Fred Rilling, Prairie du Sac, Wisconsin; Susan B. Sheffer-Meyer, Madison, Wisconsin; C. Althea Sondahl, Nezperce, Idaho; Craig A. Swenson, Minonk, Illinois; Stephen D. Van Gilder, Hamilton, Montana; Kristin Wee, Austin, Minnesota. Our sincere thanks for their help in this writing project so that this chapter was not simply an individual process, but a communal activity.

CHAPTER 7

Living in the Spirit

Robert L. Conrad

How do you stay alive in faith? Stay within earshot and eyeshot of the Spirit. It's that simple. The Spirit brings you to faith and keeps you alive in faith. But the Spirit doesn't come to you out of the blue. The Spirit uses words and water and bread and wine. The Spirit uses people to bring us words and water and bread and wine. The words are God's word. The word is heard. The water is baptism. Bread and wine are the stuff of Holy Communion. The sacraments are seen. You need to stay within earshot of the word and eyeshot of the sacraments. Staying alive in faith means staying where the Spirit is present. The whole purpose of this chapter is to explore the times and places in which the Spirit is present.

We could simply list the times and places of the Spirit's presence and assume that you would put yourself in the picture. However, it is more interesting to follow Christine and Christopher in their journey of faith. Christine and Christopher are the twin children of Elizabeth and John. The family belongs to the Lutheran Church of the Holy Spirit. You are present at the baptism of the twins. You watch them pray. You listen as they read the Bible. You go to church with them for worship, confession, and forgiveness. You kneel with them at their first communion. You celebrate their affirmation of baptism. You participate with them in a life of devotion to God and service to people. Throughout this journey they, and you, are surrounded by Spirit-bearing sounds and sights that keep you alive in faith.

The Spirit in Baptism

Life in the Spirit begins for Christine and Christopher in their baptism. Elizabeth and John bring them to the font. It is not the twins' first bath but it is the most extraordinary. An ordinary bath is just water, but baptism is water and the word of God. The presence of the word and the water means the presence of the Spirit. The spoken word brings the Spirit along with the poured water. Word and water have great spiritual power. Elizabeth and John, along with the whole congregation, believe that God is acting here.[1] God acts to begin life in the Spirit for Christopher and Christine.

The Five Meanings of Baptism

Baptism is a beautiful star! It is a five-pointed star that shines with God's saving love. The five points of the star are: gift of the Spirit; death and resurrection; conversion, pardoning and cleansing; incorporation into the body of Christ; and sign of the reign of God.[2] Each facet is important to Christine and Christopher.

GIFT OF THE SPIRIT

As water is poured over the heads of the twins, they are given the gift of the Spirit. They take part in the baptisms of the first Pentecost. When the people asked Peter what they should do he said to them, "Repent, and be baptized every one of you in the name of Jesus Christ so that your sins may be forgiven; and you will receive the gift of the Holy Spirit" (Acts 2:38).[3] The gift of the Spirit brings the fullness of God: Father, Son, and Spirit. First, baptism brings the gift of the Son, Jesus. Jesus promised the Spirit when he ascended so that he could be present more intensely than ever with people. The Spirit is not a substitute for an absent Jesus but an intensification of the presence of Jesus. Secondly, because Jesus and the Father are one, the gift of the Spirit means the Father is given. What a wonderful gift for the twins! The gift of the

God who is within them, the God who walks beside them, and the God who beckons them on toward home. The gift of the Spirit is a powerful gift for Christine and Christopher. The Spirit not only calls them in baptism but enlightens them with God's gifts, sanctifies, and keeps them in faith.

DEATH AND RESURRECTION

At baptism, Christine and Christopher went under water and came up again. Being under water (even in sprinkling) is going down into the death of Jesus Christ and rising again to new life. Paul says, "Do you not know that all of us who have been baptized into Christ Jesus were baptized into his death? Therefore we have been buried with him by baptism into death, so that, just as Christ was raised from the dead by the glory of the Father, so we too might walk in newness of life" (Rom. 6:3-4). Christians raised with Christ are not to go on living in sin. They live a new life. Luther, building on Romans 6, says in the Small Catechism that baptizing with water signifies that the old sinful person in us, together with all sins and evil lusts, should be drowned by daily sorrow and repentance and be put to death. A new person should come forth daily and rise up, cleansed and righteous, to live forever in God's presence.[4] Repentance and coming forth means that Christine and Christopher confess their sins and ask God for forgiveness daily in their prayers. They also participate in the confession of sins and hear the words of God's forgiveness in every service of worship. Living in the Spirit is a constant return to baptism in daily devotions and weekly worship.

CONVERSION, PARDON, AND CLEANSING

Conversion, pardon, and cleansing are closely related to death and resurrection in baptism. Death to sin is an about-face from living in sin. Paul, in Jerusalem, addressed the crowd and said, "And now why do you delay? Get up, be baptized, and have your sins washed away" (Acts 22:16). In baptism past sins are forgiven to make possible new beginnings. Jesus said, "The one who believes and is baptized will be saved" (Mark 16:16). A new life in Christ begins with baptism, a new life cleansed of past sins and present failures. It means living with a clear conscience. Baptism is not removal of dirt from the body but a good conscience through Jesus Christ, says 1 Peter (3:21). Hebrews says baptism sprinkles clean an evil conscience (10:22). A clear conscience is the mark of a life moving in a new direction, a direction of hope for the future rather than despair over the past. In Titus Paul says, "[God] saved us . . . through the water of rebirth and renewal by the Holy Spirit. This Spirit he poured out on us richly through Jesus Christ our Savior, so that, having been justified by his grace, we might become heirs according to the hope of eternal life" (3:5-7). Christine and Christopher can live in hope even in times of despair by remembering their baptism and the Spirit's promises.

INCORPORATION INTO THE BODY OF CHRIST

Before their baptism, Christine and Christopher belonged only to the family of Elizabeth and John. Now they belong to the larger family of God. They have become members of the body of Christ. The body of Christ is a powerful image. The twins are related to a group of people who care for them until they are mature enough to become caregivers themselves. The twins have gifts to contribute to the welfare of the body even though their contributions may not seem like much. At the same time they value the gifts of others in the body regardless of their seeming worth. They accept a variety of people and work together for the common good.

Paul speaks of all these aspects. In Ephesians Paul emphasizes the unity of Christians in one body, one Spirit, one Lord, one faith, one baptism, one God and Father of all. The gifts of members are used to minister to one another and help each other grow from childhood to maturity. In Romans Paul emphasizes humility about one's own gifts and urges respect for what others contribute. In 1 Corinthians he speaks even more forcefully of honoring the Spirit-given gifts of others and recognizing their contributions to the common good. What have Christine and Christopher gotten into? Others will have to minister to them for a long time until they can become ministers themselves. It will be years before they fully realize that their baptism calls them into ministry in the body of Christ and in the world. But right from the start, they can experience the high regard that other members of the body have for them and begin to contribute to the common good in whatever way they can.

SIGN OF THE REIGN OF GOD

Christine and Christopher do not realize it yet but they are part of the universal and timeless work of God's reign. God is at work in the world through the members of the body of Christ, the Christian community. The reign of God has a veil about it in the present that will be lifted at the end of time. The reign of God is "already-but-not-yet." The twins, along with every other Christian, enlisted in a never-ending ministry to make the reign of God evident. God's reign has the qualities Paul speaks of in his final words to the Christians at Philippi. "Finally, beloved, whatever is true, whatever is honorable, whatever is just, whatever is pure, whatever is pleasing, whatever is commendable . . . think about these things" (Phil. 4:8). Still, Christians work to make these qualities more and more evident until God's reign comes in its fullness.

Growing into Baptism

To help Christine and Christopher grow into their baptism their parents and the congregation do a number of things to remind them of baptism. For example, their baptismal birthday is remembered each year. Since baptisms usually occur on a Sunday, they celebrate their baptismal birthday on the Sunday of the church year on which they were baptized. The family and the congregation celebrate their baptism on that date. The Church of the Holy Spirit lists baptismal birthdays in its monthly newsletter. The newsletter features an explanation of a different point of baptism along with the list. The Church of the Holy Spirit also publishes a booklet that is given to parents in preparation for the baptism of their children. The booklet's contents are discussed with parents in small groups or individually. The booklet contains an explanation of the five facets of baptism, the way in which baptism is celebrated in the congregation, preparations for the child's baptism, and further resources for understanding baptism and its implications.[5] The adult booklet is the basis for another booklet written for the children that explains baptism and includes artwork appropriate for young children. Parents can use this booklet with their children, especially on the anniversary of baptism. The booklet contains a short liturgy of remembrance of baptism. The liturgy includes the lighting of the candle given at baptism and the sign of the cross as remembrance of the Father, Son, and Holy Spirit in whose name the child was baptized.

The Spirit in Community

The Family

Robert Coles graphically describes the way in which children search for the meaning of their lives. In *The Spiritual Life of Children* he writes of the experience he had with a group of fifth graders in Lawrence, Massachusetts. He asked them to say or draw something about who they saw themselves to be. After several hours with the children he said, "I found myself, finally, looking at these children in a new light, one they provided, actually, as young pilgrims just setting out on a journey, getting ready to 'march through life.'"[6] He mused that we all are pilgrims marching through life.

> So it is we connect with one another, move in and out of one another's lives, teach and heal and affirm one another, across space and time—all of us wanderers, explorers, adventurers, stragglers and ramblers, even fugitives, but now and then pilgrims; as children, as parents, as old ones about to take the final step, to enter that territory whose character none of us ever knows. Yet how young we are when we start wondering about it all, the nature of the journey and of the final destination.[7]

Christine and Christopher's parents help their pilgrim children learn about the nature of the journey and its final destination. The Spirit uses them and their words and deeds to convey God's grace to the children. The Spirit moves pilgrims to pray. Elizabeth and John give words to the impulses of prayer. They teach simple prayers of praise and thanks and forgiveness and protection. As the twins grow in their ability to say more complicated prayers, they include the aspects of adoration, confession, thanksgiving, and supplication (ACTS). God is praised, sins confessed and forgiveness sought, thanks given for God's goodness; and requests made for help and healing. They are taught the greatest of all prayers, the Lord's Prayer. This model for all prayers acknowledges the Holy One from whom all things come and whose gracious will is to be obeyed everywhere. It asks for daily food, forgiveness, and protection from evil. It ends in adoration of the One who is able to answer prayer. Luther has high praise for the Lord's Prayer. He says:

> We should be encouraged and drawn to pray because God takes the initiative and puts into our mouths the very words we are to use. Thus we see how sincerely he is concerned over our needs, and we shall never doubt that our prayer pleases him and will assuredly be heard. So this prayer is far superior to all others that we might ourselves devise.[8]

Prayer in the words of the Lord or in the words of a child is the Spirit's work. Paul states that plainly when he says, "When we cry, 'Abba! Father!' it is that very Spirit bearing witness with our spirit that we are children of God" (Rom. 8:15-16). The Spirit helps God's children when words fail them.

"Likewise the Spirit helps us in our weakness; for we do not know how to pray as we ought, but that very Spirit intercedes with sighs too deep for words. And God, who searches the heart, knows what is in the mind of the Spirit, because the Spirit intercedes for the saints according to the will of God" (Rom. 8:26-27). The form of the prayers of Christine and Christopher matters little but it matters much that Elizabeth and John teach them to pray.

The Congregation

As they grow Christine and Christopher participate more and more in the community of believers. Just as the Spirit calls them by the gospel, enlightens them with gifts, sanctifies and keeps them in true faith, so the Spirit calls, gathers, enlightens, and sanctifies the whole Christian church on earth and preserves it in union with Jesus Christ in true faith. The Spirit uses the members of the church to sustain, encourage, and support one another with the audible words (the gospel) and the visible words (the sacraments) by which each of them were called.

The community shares with one another the primary word, the Bible. The Church of the Holy Spirit introduces young children to the Bible and helps them begin to read it. The congregation uses the approach of Kennith Smith.[9] Pastor Martin sends an invitation to parents of all children who have completed first through third grade. The children are to come once a week for an hour to read stories in the Bible with the pastor or another person. The children read the Bible for a period of months under the guidance of the adult leader. Sometimes they read stories they have selected and other times the leader suggests stories important to the fuller scope of God's story in the Bible. The children talk about the stories and their meanings with the leader. When they have completed the agreed-on length of time for reading the Bible, the congregation recognizes the new Bible readers in one of the worship services of the congregation. The children receive a special edition of the Bible for their very own. They participate as readers in the service. In addition to Smith's suggestions, the Church of the Holy Spirit includes a little liturgy of affirmation of baptism and the faith into which the children were baptized. The liturgy helps all recognize the continuing presence of the Spirit of God in the children's lives through the reading of scripture.

Christine and Christopher, in your baptism, Jesus received you and made you members of God's people. At your baptism your parents and sponsors promised to bring you to God's house and give you God's scriptures so that you grow in the Christian faith. In your Bible reading sessions you have learned God's word and God's loving purpose for you and all creation. You have been nourished in faith by the Spirit through the scriptures. We join with you now in affirming the faith in which you were baptized.

The congregation and the children join in the Apostles' Creed followed by a prayer.

O God, for Jesus' sake, stir up in these young people the gift of the Holy Spirit; confirm their faith, guide their lives, empower them in their serving, give them patience in suffering, and bring them to everlasting life. Amen

After the special service of recognition and affirmation the new readers participate in the reading of scripture in other worship services.

Christine and Christopher participate more and more in the worship of their congregation. They are continually gathered, enlightened, sanctified, and preserved in faith. They return to their baptism in confession and absolution in every service. Luther placed his section on confession and absolution immediately after that on baptism in the Small Catechism.[10] He says that confession consists of two parts. The one is that we confess our sins, and the other is that we receive absolution or forgiveness from the confessor as from God. He exhorts Christians to firmly believe that their sins are actually forgiven by those words. Luther does not dwell on confession but on absolution, because the gospel *is* forgiveness. "The Word or absolution, I say, is what you should concentrate on, magnifying and cherishing it as a great and wonderful treasure to be accepted with all praise and gratitude."[11] Christopher and Christine grow in an understanding of the power of words in the Brief Order for Confession and Forgiveness in *Lutheran Book of Worship*.[12] The members of the congregation say:

Most merciful God, we confess that we are in bondage to sin and cannot free ourselves. We have sinned against you in thought, word, and deed, by what we have done and by what we have left undone. We have not loved you with our whole heart; we have not loved our neighbors as ourselves. For the sake of your Son, Jesus Christ, have mercy on us. Forgive us, renew us, and lead us, so that we may delight in your will and walk in your ways, to the glory of your holy name. Amen

The pastor is bold enough to say the following words, words that do what they proclaim.

Almighty God, in his mercy, has given the Son to die for us and, for his sake, forgives us all our sins. As a called and ordained minister of the Church of Christ, and by his authority, I therefore declare to you the entire forgiveness of all your sins, in the name of the Father, and of the Son, and of the Holy Spirit. Amen

Robert Jenson writes of the power of words spoken by human beings but used by the Spirit to actually do what they proclaim. Leaders in worship, for instance, are to "so speak of Christ and the lives of your hearers, that our lives' meaning in Christ is made visible."[13] Leaders of worship speak, not about the gospel, but the gospel itself so that lives are transformed. Confession and absolution are an example.

When the confessor says, "You have confessed cheating and coveting. Now I forgive all your sins, in Jesus' name," these words do not seek to stimulate conversion as an event external to their being said. Rather, this utterance *is* a conversion of the penitent's life, from a situation in which the word he or she hears and must live by is "You are a cheat and a coveter," to one in which the word he or she hears and must live by is "You are Jesus' beloved."[14]

Corporate confession in the worshiping community is not the only type of confession. Luther tells of two other kinds, confessing to God alone or to our neighbor alone.[15] He finds these two expressed in the Lord's Prayer. When Christians pray, "Forgive us our sins as we forgive those who sin against us," we are confessing to God what we have done and begging for God's forgiveness. We can be certain that God hears and forgives. When we confess to our neighbors that we have wronged them and ask forgiveness and are forgiven, God forgives as we are forgiven. Luther also mentions a third kind, the confession that takes place before a single brother or sister. When a brother or sister speaks the word of forgiveness it is as if God has spoken and sins are forgiven.[16] Christopher and Christine know that their confession in prayer to God alone brings forgiveness just as they know that a fellow Christian speaks a word of forgiveness when the burden of sin becomes so great it must be confessed. Likewise, they speak a word of forgiveness to parents or brothers or sisters or friends, and it is God's forgiveness.

The Spirit gathers, enlightens, sanctifies, and preserves faith in worship in many other ways. The Spirit works through hymns, prayers, readings, sermons, and sacraments. Christopher and Christine participate, along with all the other children in the Christian community. Many congregations do not do well in inviting the participation of children, say the authors of the Children in Worship study project conducted by a team from Concordia University, River Forest, Illinois. Shirley K. Morgenthaler directs the study, assisted by Gary Bertels and Peter Becker, which involves a team of researchers who visited 100 Lutheran congregations from The Lutheran Church—Missouri Synod, ELCA, and the Wisconsin Evangelical Lutheran Synod in order to determine the worship environment of the congregation, the worship practices of the congregation, and the way in which worship leaders took children into account when planning worship.[17] The impetus for the project is the work of John Westerhoff. Westerhoff says eight aspects of communal life contribute to and influence the practices and experiences necessary for spiritual formation: (1) communal rites, (2) environment, (3) time, (4) communal life, (5) discipline, (6) social interaction, (7) role models, and (8) language.[18] Westerhoff contends that children are formed spiritually by the extent of their involvement in the worship of the church.

Congregations that do not welcome children into worship and do not make it possible for them to participate in worship fail to help children in their spiritual growth. Though the study is not yet complete, the leaders summarize their findings to this point in terms of the power of ritual, environment, and planning.[19] The power of ritual is the power of liturgy. Ritual repeatedly tells the faith story so that all understand. Children need elements of sameness and structure. Children need to participate in prayers by folding hands and kneeling, greeting others in the sharing of the peace, and other repeated practices of the liturgy.

The authors of the study recommend using predictable elements of the liturgy in which children participate each week: prayers and prayer postures; the exchange of peace in which children are intentionally greeted; the sign of the cross made by the congregation as well as the clergy; specific addresses to children in the sermon of the day; and responsive liturgy, which is repeatedly present so that it will be learned by the children. When a children's sermon is part of the service it should be addressed to children, not the adults who are listening in. The children's sermon can include explanations to children at their level of the meaning of the liturgy, the symbols in the church, and the use of paraments.

The environment has power to teach. Children, especially preschoolers, learn about worship through the signs and symbols in the church. They learn about faith and worship from visual elements. They learn from objects they touch, sounds they hear, and aromas they smell. Children also learn whether they are welcome by arrangements in the worship environment. How well can children see and hear in worship? Do parents with young children have a special place to sit where all can participate? Recommendations regarding the environment include banners that communicate the faith story to young children; physical provisions for children such as booster seats and church bags with activities for children; explanations of the liturgy; references to changes in the liturgical environment so that children understand their meaning; and seating arrangements that assure that children can see the focus of worship and participate more fully.

Planning has power. Worship planners either include or exclude children from worship by the way they plan. Planners need to cultivate a "child's eye" view so that children are intentionally included in worship. The study recommends that worship planning include intentional planning for frequent participation of preconfirmation children in worship activities; messages of welcome, both verbal and nonverbal to families with young children; use of school-age children as acolytes and assistant ushers; providing role models of varying ages, genders, and ethnic backgrounds in worship leadership; and bulletins and/or newsletter inserts that sensitize congregational members to the children in worship.

The research team concluded that most congregations do not strongly consider the perspective of children in worship. Such congregations are missing a great opportunity to play an important part in the growth in faith of children.

Growing in Worship

To involve children effectively in worship, the Church of the Holy Spirit offers a workshop for worship planners, parents, and children, which makes worship more welcoming and meaningful to children and their parents. The congregations use Elizabeth Caldwell's *Come Unto Me: Rethinking the Sacraments for Children* as a resource for a workshop for young children to prepare them for worship. This one-session workshop involves the children and their parents. The children learn the elements of worship and the ways in which they can participate in the service.[20] The workshop includes worship planners. They get a "child's eye" view of worship and take that point of view back to the worship and music committee. The congregation also puts together a booklet called, "Come Unto Me—Children in the Life of This Congregation." It is given to parents of small children and newcomers. The content includes children in worship, church school for children, children as stewards, children in service and mission, special opportunities for children, learning and celebrating with others, and the children's library.[21]

The Spirit in First Communion

At the age of 10 Christine and Christopher celebrated their first communion at the Church of the Holy Spirit. They and their parents attended a first communion class and learned the meaning of Holy Communion. They learned that, just as baptism has many meanings, so does Holy Communion. It is a beautiful gem with six facets that sparkles with the beauty of God's presence![22] The six facets are invocation of the Spirit, remembrance of Christ, forgiveness of sins, thanksgiving to God, communion of the faithful, and meal of the reign of God.

Invocation of the Spirit

The World Council of Churches document *Baptism, Eucharist and Ministry* sees "the role of the Holy Spirit as that of the One who makes the historical words of Jesus present and alive . . . The Church prays to the Father for the gift of the Holy Spirit in order that the eucharistic event may be a reality."[23] The communion liturgy in *Lutheran Book of Worship* speaks of the role of the Spirit in a little different manner. "Send now, we pray, your Holy Spirit, the spirit of our Lord and of his resurrection, that we who receive the Lord's body and blood may live to the praise of your glory and receive our inheritance with all your saints in light."[24] The Spirit empowers the communicants to live lives of praise and hope. *Baptism, Eucharist and Ministry* echoes this petition when it says, "The Church, as the community of the new covenant, confidently invokes the Spirit, in order that it may be sanctified and renewed, led into all justice, truth and unity, and empowered to fulfill its mission in the world."[25] As Christine and Christopher commune, Christ comes to them through the Spirit. They have power to fulfill his mission in the world.

Remembrance of Christ

Jesus said that Christians celebrate Holy Communion "in remembrance of me." But the sacrament does more than remember Christ, it brings the living presence of Jesus. Lutherans confess in Article X of the Augsburg Confession, "It is taught among us that the true body and blood of Christ are really present in the Supper of our Lord under the form of bread and wine and are there distributed and received."[26] And in the Small Catechism Luther says that the Sacrament of the Altar is the true body and blood of our Lord Jesus Christ, under the bread and wine, given for us Christians to eat and drink.[27] The Spirit of God makes that presence possible. When the celebrant says, "The body of Christ, given for you," and "The blood of Christ, shed for you," Christ is really present to the communicants. The bread and wine make Christ's presence visible. The twins experience the presence of Jesus as they faithfully take the bread and wine. As they first learned to pray, "Come, Lord Jesus, be our guest," now they pray, "Come, Lord Jesus, be our host." In faith they believe Jesus to be present, which is all that's necessary. When Luther speaks of who are the worthy ones to receive the sacrament, he says they are the ones who believe the words, "for you," and "for the forgiveness of sins."[28] The Spirit who makes faith possible is the one who nourishes that faith through bread and wine.

Forgiveness of Sins

Lutherans have traditionally stressed forgiveness of sins almost to the exclusion of other facets of Holy Communion. Jesus himself stresses this aspect of Holy Communion when he says in Matthew 26:27-28, "Drink from it, all of you; for this is my blood of the covenant, which is poured out for many for the forgiveness of sins." In the Small Catechism Luther asks, "What is the benefit of such eating and drinking?" He answers: "We are told in the words 'for you' and 'for the forgiveness of sins.' By these words the forgiveness of sins, life and salvation are given to us in the sacrament, for where there is forgiveness of sins, there is also life and salvation."[29] The forgiveness begun in baptism continues in Holy Communion. The twins need forgiveness for their journey of life.

Thanksgiving to God

Another name for Holy Communion is Eucharist. The word *eucharist* comes from the Greek word for *thanksgiving*. The name highlights the thanksgiving offered to God for all the gifts given in creation, redemption, and sanctification, which God continues to give till the end of time. In the biblical accounts of the Lord's supper, Jesus gives thanks when he takes the bread or the cup (Matt. 26, Mark 14, Luke 22). The words of Jesus are echoed in the communion liturgy. In *Lutheran Book of Worship* the celebrant says, "Let us give thanks to the Lord our God," and the congregation responds, "It is right to give him thanks and praise."[30] The celebrant also says, "We give thanks to you for the salvation you have prepared for us through Jesus Christ."[31] Holy communion invites us to a time of celebration and thanksgiving. It is not a time of sadness and solemnity. It is a time of joy.

Communion of the Faithful

When Christine and Christopher come to communion with their parents and their friends they participate in an event that makes them one with Christ and with all other Christians. Paul speaks of this unity with God and others in 1 Corinthians. "The cup of blessing that we bless, is it not a sharing of the blood of Christ? The bread that we break, is it not a sharing in the body of Christ? Because there is one bread, we who are many are one body, for we all partake of the one bread"(1 Cor. 10:16-17). The twins realize that they are reconciled not only to God but to all others who share the body and blood of Christ with them. Unity with others goes beyond sex and age and color and temperament. They are reconciled with Bobby who torments them, Mrs. Johnson who scowls at them, Mr. Smith who has no patience with children, and Mr. Pulaski who looks different and speaks with an accent.

Meal of the Reign of God

This facet emphasizes the present and ongoing reign of God as it breaks in upon the world. Signs of God's reign are here, but Christians look forward to its coming in fullness when they will celebrate with Christ in the Father's presence. Jesus says in Matthew 26 that he will drink the fruit of the vine with his disciples in the Father's presence. In *Lutheran Book of Worship* the celebrant says, "And, believing the witness of his resurrection, we await his coming in power to share with us the great and promised feast."[32] The twins leave the celebration of Holy Communion with strength to do the work of God's reign in the world while looking forward to God's coming again.

The Spirit in Affirmation of Baptism

At the Church of the Holy Spirit, the rite of affirmation of baptism takes place at the age of 13. Christine and Christopher go once a week for catechetical sessions and celebrate their affirmation of baptism on Pentecost. The rite of affirmation of baptism recalls their baptism and God's promises. The rite is not a completion of baptism as if their baptisms were incomplete. Neither is their affirmation a confirmation in the historic sense. In the ancient rite of baptism, confirmation occurred after baptism. The bishop confirmed the gift of the Spirit to the baptized through prayer and the laying on of hands. Then the newly baptized participated in Holy Communion for the first time. As time went on the bishop could not be present for baptisms, delaying the confirmation of the gift of the Spirit until such time as the bishop could be present. This delay over a period of years evolved into the pattern that has been part of the experience of children in some churches until late in the twentieth century.

Recent studies into the meaning of confirmation have produced the present rite of affirmation of baptism. In that rite children remember their baptism and affirm the faith in which they were baptized. The Holy Spirit has not been absent from the lives of the twins since their baptism, so the rite does not assume or say that the Spirit is being given for the first time. Instead, the pastor lays hands on Christine and says, "Father in heaven, for Jesus' sake, stir up in Christine the gift of your Holy Spirit; confirm her faith, guide her life, empower her in her serving, give her patience in suffering, and bring her to everlasting life."[33] The Spirit has been present in her confirmation ministry through the word spoken and shared in scripture in Sunday school and through the words of the catechist and the other members of the class. The rite of affirmation of baptism is not the first nor should it be the last time the twins affirm their baptism and the faith into which they have been baptized.

Living in the Spirit

Affirming Baptism at Special Times in Life

The twins affirm their baptism and faith on many occasions in life. The education committee of the Church of the Holy Spirit uses the work of Mark Winkler as a resource for families in the congregation. Winkler has written a series of celebrations for *Family Milestones and Celebrations*.[34] The outline for each milestone celebration includes an introduction, Bible perspectives, family time, family worship, and servants in action. Winkler's celebration for "First Job/New Job" begins with an introduction addressed to the young person about the importance and consequences of the first job. The *Biblical perspectives* portion features the varieties of gifts the Spirit has given young people and how those gifts can be used in the new job. In *family time* the members of the family talk of the jobs each of them has and how important they are. The jobs range from family tasks to wage-earning occupations. *Family worship* includes a litany based on Psalm 16, a reading of 1 Corinthians 12, a discussion of the meaning of "priesthood of all believers" and a prayer. *Servants in action* points to living the Christian calling at work. The education committee of Holy Spirit added an affirmation of baptism and faith to the celebration because baptism is a calling to ministry. The baptized use their gifts on the job. The family worship includes this liturgy:

> Christopher, in your baptism Jesus received you and made you a member of God's people. In the community of God's people, you have learned from God's word what God's loving purpose is for you and all creation. God has given you gifts and abilities to be used for the good of other people both within the Christian community and outside of it. God's Spirit goes with you to help you use your gifts to serve others. We join together now to affirm the faith into which you were baptized. (See *Lutheran Book of Worship*, p. 199.)

The family joins in the Apostles' Creed followed by a prayer.

> O God, for Jesus' sake, stir up in Christopher the gift of the Holy Spirit; confirm his faith, guide his life, empower him in his serving in this new task, give him patience in suffering, and bring him to everlasting life. Amen (See *LBW*, p. 201.)

The education committee also uses the work of Kennith Smith in producing materials for affirming baptism at special times in life. Smith has a strategy based on the ancient catechumenate. The strategy has four phases: an *invitation* to reflect on the meaning of the special time, a period of *preparation* in which learning takes place, followed by a ceremony or ritual or *worship* experience. After the worship experience comes opportunity for *continuing* in what has been learned. The special times that Smith plans for are learning to read the Bible, first communion, confirmation ministry, preparation for marriage, the baptism of children in the congregation, and becoming a member of the congregation. He has a list of other possibilities such as going to Sunday school for the first time; getting one's driver's license; consideration of an engagement; work or vocational transition; graduation; retirement, living alone again after a divorce or a death; adult baptism; and becoming a grandparent.[35]

Preparation for marriage is one of Smith's strategies used by Holy Spirit congregation. Pastor Martin sends an *invitation* to prepare for marriage to couples contemplating marriage. The workshop is a one-day event on Saturday beginning at 9:00 A.M. and continuing until early afternoon. The *preparation* sessions include assisting couples in the consideration of their relationship through a series of exercises and assisting couples in planning their wedding as a service of worship. The wedding service of *worship* includes the following affirmation of baptism and faith in those instances where both members of the couple are baptized Christians.

> Joanne and George, in your baptisms Jesus received you and made you members of God's people. In the community of God's people, you have learned from God's word what God's loving purpose is for you and all creation. God's Spirit has given you gifts to be used for the good of each other. You are to treasure the differing gifts each of you bring to this union. In that way, you treasure each other. We join with you in affirming the faith in which both of you were baptized. (See *LBW*, p. 199.)

The congregation joins in the Apostles' Creed followed by a prayer.

> O God, for Jesus' sake, stir up in Joanne and George the gift of the Holy Spirit; confirm their faith, guide their lives, empower them in their service

and love to one another, give them patience in suffering, and bring them to everlasting life. Amen (See *LBW,* p. 201.)

The presence of the Spirit begun in baptism continues in the new life with each other. *Continuing* possibilities are many. The couple is invited to participate in a group for young married persons. A mentor couple is assigned to the newlyweds. The congregation invites the couple to an annual service for the renewal of wedding vows.

Making Use of the Gifts of the Spirit

Christopher and Christine's baptism calls them to minister by using their gifts in everyday life. Pastor Martin of the Church of the Holy Spirit offers a workshop on gifts of the Spirit for students in confirmation ministry, teens, and adults. He uses the book *LifeKeys* as a basic resource.[36] The workshop is offered as a weekend retreat from Friday evening till late Saturday afternoon. The themes of the workshop are Discovering Life Gifts, Determining Spiritual Gifts, Writing a Mission Statement, and Setting Priorities. The first session on Life Gifts focuses on discovering the kinds of gifts useful in all areas of daily life. Each person has life gifts, chosen by God to fit with an overall design. Pastor Martin uses a questionnaire adapted from *LifeKeys* to guide participants to discovery of their gifts in six areas: realistic gifts (Let's roll up our sleeves and get it done); investigative gifts (Let's figure out this situation); artistic gifts (Let's create); social gifts (Let's work on it together); enterprising gifts (Let's get going); and conventional gifts (Let's be dependable).[37] The session on spiritual gifts begins with a study of 1 Corinthians 12. Paul stresses three crucial points: (1) all believers have been given spiritual gifts by the Holy Spirit; (2) God distributes the gifts among believers according to God's will, not because of some effort on our part; (3) in the body of Christ each of us has something to contribute. Spiritual gifts are different from life gifts because they are given to carry out God's purposes. However, definite overlap joins spiritual gifts with life gifts. The life gift of speaking can be used as the spiritual gift of evangelism. Teaching as a life gift can be the spiritual gift of teaching God's word and will. The spiritual gifts are administration, apostleship, discernment, encouragement/counseling, evangelism, faith, giving, healing, helps, hospitality, knowledge, leadership, mercy, miracles, pastoring/shepherding, prophecy, teaching, tongues, interpretation of tongues, and wisdom.[38]

After discussion of the meaning of each spiritual gift, participants fill out a questionnaire to discover their personal spiritual gifts. Next, each person writes a personal mission statement. The statement incorporates personal life and spiritual gifts. Each participant prioritizes life choices as the final step of the retreat. The principles for prioritizing are (1) put first things first—seek the kingdom of God; (2) know your mission—a mission statement helps; (3) know your limits; and (4) simplify—aim for balance in your life.[39] The participants leave the retreat with their list of priorities as a guide for daily life. Christopher and Christine cannot know the fullness of their gifts at a young age but periodic reassessment of their gifts will give depth to their lives.

Spiritual Life

Christine and Christopher exhibit the Spirit's presence and stay alive in the Spirit through a life of daily prayer. The twins express their spirituality in different ways. Pastor Martin helps Christine and Christopher understand their spiritual style and the best way to express it in daily life. During confirmation ministry leading to affirmation of baptism the pastor uses Allan Sager's *Gospel-Centered Spirituality* as a tool.[40] Sager describes four types of spirituality. The most prevalent type in America is the spirituality of *personal renewal.* People with this style of spirituality believe that scripture is important but the primary way a person relates to God is with the heart, not the mind. The Spirit of God moves the heart. The Spirit may move people in ways that do not necessarily depend on scripture and the sacraments of the church. People with this spiritual type tend to be suspicious of doctrinal formalism. They prefer heartfelt emotion to creedal or theological statements. They cherish music that expresses feelings for God more than music that expresses what a person is to believe about God. A spirituality of personal renewal does not mean persons withdraw from society. They want to transform society. The goal of transformation is change of heart. People with changed hearts work to change society. Evangelical churches in the United States stress this kind of spirituality. Many Americans find this spiritual style appealing and join churches exhibiting the style of personal renewal.

The second type of spirituality is *theological renewal*. People who prefer ②
this type of spirituality focus on the mind rather than the heart. God is
known through scripture and the creeds. God is best understood through the
mind. These people prefer sermons that explain God. Studies of scripture and
doctrinal statements are appreciated. The Spirit uses the word to explain
Christ. Faith is response to the word. Many believe Luther to be a person who
had this type of spirituality. Certainly, most followers of Luther prefer this
style of spirituality. Theological renewal people prefer study, reflection, journaling, and meditation on the word.

Spirituality of the *inner life* is a third type. Persons with this style believe ③
God cannot be known directly through words and statements. God is best
known intuitively, not rationally. These people see Christians on a pilgrimage
toward God. They value contemplation on the nature of human existence
and one's relation to God. God is more and more present in moments of con-
templative silence. Persons of the inner life prize spiritual disciplines such as
solitude, fasting, and spiritual direction as they stress the inner life. They are
attracted to asceticism and monasticism.

The spiritual type with the fewest adherents in America is that of *social* ④
action. People of this type "just know" what the mind of God is and what
needs to be done to transform society. They seem to have an intuitive sense
of the call of justice. They claim to see what others cannot see, that this world
has a cosmic destiny that cannot be realized unless the forces of evil are overcome. True destiny can only be achieved with change in the social structure.
Individual transformation is not enough. Systemic evil must be overcome so
society is transformed. The prophets of old and the political activists of the
present are examples of a spirituality of social action.

The pastor of the Church of the Holy Spirit offers a workshop in spirituality as part of confirmation ministry. Adults and older youth are also invited
to participate. The four-session workshop is called, "Habits of Discipleship:
Finding a Rhythm of Spirituality." The purpose of the workshop is to help
participants explore ways of reading, meditation, prayer, and silence that are
suitable for their spiritual styles. The four sessions are: "The Spiritual Rhythm
of My Life" (current personal devotional activities); "Spiritual Habits for a
Life of Faith" (various ways to develop habits of spirituality); "Resources for
Prayer and Meditation" (printed and other resources); and "Habits of
Discipleship" (selection of a spiritual discipline).[41]

Surrounded by the Spirit

God has blessed Christine and Christopher with parents like Elizabeth and John who care enough to bring them into the Spirit's presence and surround them with many opportunities to keep the Spirit alive. But Elizabeth and John could not accomplish the task by themselves. Members of the Church of the Holy Spirit become coworkers in the work of the Spirit. The Spirit calls them all through the gospel, gathers, enlightens, and preserves them in faith. So they make certain that Christine and Christopher are called, enlightened, sanctified and preserved in faith through baptism, prayer, scripture, worship, confession and forgiveness, communion, and affirmation of baptism. In their pilgrimage through life, Christopher and Christine are accompanied by the Spirit within them, the Son beside them, and the Father who beckons them on toward home. May it be so for all baptized children of God.

Notes

1. *The Book of Concord: The Confessions of the Evangelical Lutheran Church,* trans. by Theodore G. Tappert (Philadelphia: Fortress Press, 1959) Small Catechism, Part II, paragraph 6. Hereafter references to *The Book of Concord* will be abbreviated as follows: *BC,* SC, II, 6.

2. *Baptism, Eucharist and Ministry* (Geneva: World Council of Churches, 1982), 2–3.

3. All scripture quotations are from the NRSV.

4. *BC,* SC, IV, 12.

5. Elizabeth Francis Caldwell, *Come Unto Me: Rethinking the Sacraments for Children* (Cleveland: United Church Press, 1996), 27.

6. Robert Coles, *The Spiritual Life of Children.* (Boston: Houghton Mifflin, 1990), 320.

7. Ibid., 335.

8. *BC,* LC, III, 22.

9. Kennith Smith, *Learning at the Special Times of Life* (Columbus, Ohio: Center for Educational Ministry in the Parish, Trinity Lutheran Seminary, review draft, 1998).

10. *BC,* SC, V, 16.

11. *BC,* LC, Confession, 22.

12. *Lutheran Book of Worship* (Minneapolis: Augsburg Publishing House; Philadelphia: Board of Publication, Lutheran Church in America, 1978), 56.

13. *Christian Dogmatics,* Vol. II (Philadelphia: Fortress Press, 1984), 133.

14. Ibid., 134.

15. *BC,* LC, Confession, 8.

16. *BC,* LC, Confession, 13.

17. Report of the study appears in five issues of *Lutheran Education* from September 1997 to June 1998, vol. 133, nos. 1–5.

18. "The School of the Church: Fashioning Christians in Our Day," in S. A. Hauerwas and J. H. Westerhoff, eds., *Schooling Christians: "Holy Experiments" in American Education* (Grand Rapids: Eerdmans, 1992), 262–281.

19. *Lutheran Education,* vol. 133, no. 5, 262–281.

20. Caldwell, 38–40.

21. Ibid., 26–27.

22. *Baptism, Eucharist and Ministry* has five facets but Lutherans add a sixth: the forgiveness of sins.

23. Ibid., 13.

24. *Lutheran Book of Worship,* 70.

25. *Baptism, Eucharist and Ministry,* 13.

26. *BC,* AC, X, 1–2.

27. *BC,* SC, VI, 1–2.

28. *BC,* SC, VI, 9–10.

29. *BC,* SC, VI, 5–6.

30. *Lutheran Book of Worship,* 68.

31. Ibid., 70.

32. Ibid.

33. *Lutheran Book of Worship,* 201.

34. Mark Winkler, unpublished D. Min. thesis, (Chicago: Lutheran School of Theology, 1998).

35. Smith, 5.

36. Jane A. G. Kise, David Stark, and Sandra Krebs, *LifeKeys: Discovering Who You Are, Why You're Here, What You Do Best* (Minneapolis: Bethany House Publishers, 1996).

37. Ibid., 38–48.

38. Ibid., 70–71.

39. Ibid., 215–217.

40. Allan H. Sager, *Gospel-Centered Spirituality* (Minneapolis: Augsburg, 1990).

41. Caldwell, 99–103.

CHAPTER 8

Adolescent Development

Diane J. Hymans

Confirmation ministry, at its very core, is about real, living, breathing young people who come to us with all of the hopes and dreams, hurts and fears that go with being a teenager. When they walk through our doors, they embody all the issues and concerns that are a part of being an adolescent in today's complex, often bewildering world. How we adults who are their leaders feel about these young people and the way in which we relate to them may be as important as anything else we do during their confirmation experience. In this chapter we will consider the young people themselves and where they are in the process of developing into mature adults—mature Christian adults, we hope. We will also explore the world in which they live. Because part of that world consists of their interaction with adults, we will first look at ourselves, adults who are concerned about young people, and our attitudes toward the young people.

The cover of a recent magazine asked, "Are Americans afraid of teens?" The question is disturbing. Our first reaction may be, "Surely not." But, what the accompanying article had to say may give us pause to reflect on how we in the church really do view the youth within our midst. It quotes from a recent report, "Kids These Days: What Americans Really Think about the Next Generation":

> Americans are convinced that today's adolescents face a crisis—not only in their economic or physical well-being but in their values and morals. Most Americans look at today's teenagers with misgiving and trepidation, viewing them as undisciplined, disrespectful, and unfriendly.[1]

Fear may be too strong a word to describe how many adults in the church feel about teenagers including, and perhaps especially, those who attend our confirmation classes. But, it is probably not an exaggeration to say that many adults, among them pastors and teachers, are uncomfortable around young people. The adults in our churches may simply reflect cultural attitudes about youth, and the message that culture sends about teenagers is mixed at best. The media each evening presents a picture of American adolescents on our television screens. It is all too often a scene dominated by images of gangs, automatic weapons, drugs, teenage pregnancy, and hard rock. While most church members are pretty certain that their young people (at least most of them) are not involved in this kind of behavior (at least not in their extreme forms), many adults are still uneasy in the world of adolescents. Teenagers often do seem loud, boisterous, and unmanageable. Their music is foreign to adult ears and their style of dress is strange. Adults wonder how to talk to a teenager. What do they really think?

When working with groups of adults, I often ask them to suggest adjectives that they would use to describe young people. Every group immediately suggests words such as *disrespectful, irresponsible*, and *spoiled*. These adults are representative of the larger population. A Search Institute survey discovered that two-thirds of the adults polled think that youth no longer respect adults and that they get into more trouble today than did youth years ago.[2] After a while, the adults with whom I speak usually become uncomfortable with the picture they have painted and begin to describe particular young people they know in more complimentary terms. These adults reflect the ambivalent attitude that much of our culture holds in relation to teenagers. Although we may know particular teenagers who we love and appreciate, as a group we are not so sure about them. We envy and admire their youthful energy, and yet we are wary about what they are up to and what their futures will be. We are not sure whether they are children or adults. Youth often have to pay adult prices by age 12 in order to see a movie, but they are not allowed to see many movies until they are 17 or 18. Many states have raised the ages at which young people can drink alcohol or obtain a driver's license in order to protect them from danger. Yet, many young people themselves seem dangerous to us. Indeed too many youth in our culture are engaged in dangerous activities. So, in an effort that we believe will protect us from these young people, we enact laws that lower the age at which youth can be tried as adults. For many adults in our culture, adolescence seems like a disease that will be cured only when youth finally reach their 20s.

If our understanding of adolescence is shaped at least in part by cultural images of this period in the life span, we must remember that adolescence as we know it is a twentieth-century phenomenon. The notion that individuals travel through a particular period of life between childhood and adulthood that brings with it special needs and interests is a fairly recent development. One important influence on this movement was the book *Adolescence* by psychologist G. Stanley Hall, published in 1904.[3] Hall believed adolescence to be a time separate from either childhood or adulthood, characterized by emotional turmoil that was often exhibited in adolescent behavior. He saw these adolescent foibles as normal outgrowths of biological maturation that should be allowed free rein to play themselves out. Hall's theory influenced all kinds of people who worked with young people in the early part of the century, including educators and adults within the church.[4] Much of what he believed has since been discredited. However, his influence is still apparent in how we view young people and this period in the life span today. Every time someone makes a reference to "raging hormones," we hear a slight echo of Hall's ideas. And we still do understand adolescence to be a time set apart for the purpose of preparing to move from childhood into adult responsibilities.

The role of young people in society has changed significantly in this century in part because of Hall's influence, and in part because of increasing enrollment of adolescents in public high schools in the early decades of the twentieth century. Prior to that time, most young people spent much of their time working alongside adults on farms or in factories and apprenticeships. Today most adolescents spend most of their time with their peers in age-segregated settings. The adults with whom they come in contact serve primarily in supervisory roles. At one time in our history, most young people would have followed in the footsteps of their parents. Young men would work on the family farm, or might follow their fathers into business or a profession. Young women would grow up to become wives and mothers. Today our young people have an unprecedented number of alternatives from which to choose, not only in relation to occupation, but also in relation to religious and moral values, and even family life. For instance, it is now possible for couples and even individuals to choose whether to have children and how many they wish to have. Finding one's way into adulthood is more complex than it was for the grandparents and great-grandparents of today's teenagers, and in many ways it is more challenging than it was for their parents as well. And young people are having to make this journey with far less input from adults than in previous generations.

In this chapter, we will explore the world in which today's adolescents seek to find meaning, and we will consider the psychological and developmental dynamics that affect the young people themselves. Adolescence as a phase in the human life span presents distinct challenges and opportunities. The youth who engage in confirmation ministry are entering a process that we pray will be an important step as they move from childhood toward a mature Christian adulthood. During this period of their lives, they must struggle with matters of sexual identity, vocational possibilities, and the need to construct for themselves a coherent system of beliefs and values that will sustain them throughout life. We will examine the particular developmental tasks that come with adolescence and discuss the emerging cognitive abilities that support those tasks. We will explore the interplay of culture and developmental issues in order to better understand the powerful impact of culture on how youth view themselves. Finally, our discussion will include consideration of where faith fits into the entire process and what role the church can play, particularly through its confirmation ministry. We begin with a look at where youth are developmentally and the implications for our ministry with them in the church.

The Task of Adolescence

In our culture, we define the period of life that we call adolescence by referring to both biological and social factors. Generally, the onset of puberty and its accompanying physical changes are the accepted indicator of the beginning of adolescence. For most girls, this change occurs about the age of 9 or 10, for boys about two years later. It happens earlier now than it did as recently as the 1950s. Of course, significant individual variations are common, with many young people beginning earlier and others at a later age. Individual young people can be developing physically well before they are socially and emotionally moving into adolescence. For others the reverse may be true. Their physical development may be behind social and emotional growth. Either situation can cause emotional turmoil in the individual. These variations will be apparent in the young people in our confirmation classes. While biology signals the beginning of puberty, we tend to use social markers to indicate when it ends. Events such as marriage, joining the permanent workforce, or becoming financially independent usually mark the movement of young men and women into the world of adults.[5]

Thanks in large part to G. Stanley Hall, adolescence is now seen as a distinct stage in the human life span. Individuals are no longer children, but neither are they yet adults. Our culture has come to view this period as a time set aside for youth to become mature physically, sexually, and socially; to acquire the skills needed to assume adult roles; to gain autonomy from parents and family; and to develop healthy relationships with members of the same and opposite sexes.[6] But, none of this happens in a vacuum. The understanding of themselves and of the role they will play in the world is shaped in powerful ways by their interaction with the social world around them. As we will discuss later in this chapter, that world is different for adolescents today than it was for previous generations of young people.

As we have come to understand more about this age group, we have identified particular developmental tasks that characterize the period of adolescence and the emerging abilities that support those tasks. Perhaps the primary task of adolescence in terms of healthy social and emotional development is that of forming a coherent personal identity, one that will provide a sense of continuity between who the young person was in childhood and the adult they hope to become. By identity we mean an internal, self-constructed structure of abilities, beliefs, attitudes, and individual history that provides young people with a sense of both their own uniqueness and their similarity to others. A healthy identity gives them a picture of their own strengths and weaknesses as they seek to make their way in the world. Young people whose sense of identity is less developed seem to struggle more to discover how they are distinct from others, and may rely more on external sources such as peers to provide a measure of how they are doing.[7]

Our understanding of this process of identity formation is a result of the work of Erik Erikson who incorporated it into a larger theory of sociopsychological development. Erikson was the first person to propose a life-span theory of development that encompasses the entire life cycle from birth to death.[8] This chapter has not nearly enough space for a complete discussion of Erikson's theory, but it may be sufficient to say that he understood persons to move through a series of stages, each of which is distinguished by a particular crisis that needs to be resolved in a satisfactory way in order for the individual to grow into a psychologically healthy person. Though the word *crisis* suggests something akin to impending catastrophe, Erikson states that it should be understood as "designating a necessary turning point, a crucial moment, when development must move one way or another."[9] These moments could easily be called opportunities or challenges rather than crises. These opportunities are a result of the interaction of biological maturity and social forces in the life of the developing individual. For example, during infancy, the first of Erikson's stages, the crisis a child must resolve is to develop a healthy sense of trust rather than an attitude of mistrust. It includes acquiring a sense of trust toward others in the world and a sense of one's own trustworthiness. The biological need here is to be fed and cared for. The social context that is critical is the nature of the love and care given by parents or other primary caregivers. Children learn to trust when they are cared for in a dependable fashion by loving adults.[10]

Erikson termed the crisis particular to adolescence as "identity versus identity confusion." The challenge here for young people is to find an identity that will connect who they were in childhood with who they will become as adults. During this period of life, each adolescent must answer the questions: "Who am I?" "Where am I going?" "What am I to become?"[11] The particular task for the young person is to find a way to answer these questions that will preserve a sense of sameness of self in spite of all the changes they are undergoing during this period of life. This sense of sameness must remain constant over time and in differing contexts and when playing different roles in the social order.

The achievement of a clear sense of personal identity has several implications for the developing adolescent. First, failure to achieve an identity may result in what Erikson has called *identity diffusion* or *identity confusion*. Young people in this state may seem aimless and uncommitted to a system of values and beliefs. Often they are open to outside influences, which may or may not be healthy ones. These youth may identify strongly with heroes or heroines or cliques to the point where they lose their own individuality.[12] Virtually all youth experience some period of identity diffusion during adolescence. We need be concerned only if the situation shows no resolution, or if young people exhibit more extreme forms of the characteristics mentioned.

Further, in Erikson's larger theory, the healthy resolution of each stage is necessary for the individual to successfully navigate the next one. In this case, a clear sense of personal identity is a prerequisite for the stage that follows, which is the challenge of intimacy versus isolation. In order to move into healthy intimate relationships, particularly those leading to marriage, each person must have a clear sense of self to bring to the relationship.

This challenge to find one's identity is triggered by aspects of adolescence related to the normal growth process. During this time of rapid physical growth, the young person must adjust to a changing body that may not fit with his or her mental sense of who he or she is. This change is most noted by society in relation to the physical changes they are undergoing in relation to sexual maturity. Also, the cognitive abilities of young people are developing in a manner that allows them to think in ways that were not possible when they were still children. We will explore the cognitive abilities of adolescents more in a bit. For now, we can say that a dimension of these new abilities is that youth can imagine possibilities for themselves and their world that they could not previously. They can see beyond the restrictions of time and place and situate themselves in roles and contexts that open up all kinds of new possibilities for them to consider for their futures. Finally, the expectations of the social order in which young people live is changing. Because adults now see young people as moving closer to adulthood themselves, they are expected to assume more responsibility for their own behavior. At the same time, youth are usually allowed more freedom to make their own decisions than they were as children.

Young persons learn about who they might become and the roles they might play by observing others. At the same time, they watch others watching them try out ways of being and behaving.[13] The process is one of simultaneous reflection and observation. Consequently, the role played by peers is critical. Peers provide both role models and personal feedback to young people as they try out various roles to see how they fit. Peers become a sounding board for adolescents during a time of continuing physical and social change. When one's identity is not yet fully achieved, the safety of conformity to group standards and norms provides a certain amount of self-defense against losing oneself. In fact, youth during this time are often preoccupied with what others think of them in a way that seems self-centered to adults.

They seem to assume that everyone around them is as concerned about them as they are about themselves. Psychologist David Elkind refers to this phenomenon as the *imaginary audience*.[14] Teenagers believe that they are on stage, that everyone is always watching them to judge their appearance and behavior. The idea of an imaginary audience helps to account for the extreme self-consciousness we see especially in younger adolescents. The normal desire to want to conform to one's peer group becomes a danger only when it causes a dependency in which an individual is too ready to accept the opinions of others without really meeting the question of a personal identity head-on.

Several aspects of youth's search for identity can be frustrating for parents and other adults who work with youth, and have implications for confirmation ministry. This effort is actually a process that extends over a period of several years, and not every young person's experience is the same. It is a time of real experimentation, often resulting in what may appear to adults to be inconsistent, irresponsible behavior as the loyalties and commitments of young people seem to shift with the wind. As they work to develop unique identities by which to define themselves, youth may reject, temporarily or permanently, the values and convictions of their parents or other authorities.[15] This necessary part of the growing process comes as youth separate themselves from parents and families in order to establish their own identity. But, it can be a difficult time when parents, teachers, and other youth workers may wonder what they have done to generate what often seems to be a great deal of hostility.

This quest for identity focuses on three particular areas of life, which are of special interest to those of us who work with young people within the context of the church. Each of the three may provide a possible focus for some aspect of confirmation ministry. They are (1) becoming comfortable with one's sexual identity, (2) finding a vocation, and (3) constructing an ideology, a system of beliefs and values that will provide direction in life. The focus on sexuality involves more than simply dealing with the physical aspects of sexual behavior. It includes discovering one's identity as a male or female in the context of what society teaches about these matters.

The vocational search can be complicated for young people today because of the enormous number of choices available to them. It is made more difficult by the fact that many early and middle adolescents hold highly idealized, even glamorized conceptions of vocational roles that are likely beyond their reach—models, actors, rock musicians, athletes, and so on.[16] This issue presents the church with a real opportunity to engage young people in theological reflection on the meaning of vocation.

Finally, the search for an ideology is one in which the church will naturally take a particular interest. As young people work to construct a system of beliefs and values, we want to make sure that we provide many opportunities to help them consider how the faith into which they were baptized can provide the foundation for such a system. We need to make sure that as we engage them in a study of the Bible and catechism in confirmation classes and in other settings, we do so in a way that allows them to reflect on the significance of what we believe for the living of life. Youth need to discover from adults how what the church teaches can provide guidance in making choices about behavior and values. But we need to handle this process gently. While we need to present clearly the challenge of the gospel, we need to do so in a manner that provides room for young people to find their own way.

Erikson suggested that the process of identity formation follows a fairly predictable path. First, the adolescent experiences what he called *identity diffusion* in which the adolescent has no coherent sense of self. This diffusion stage is followed by a period marked by experimentation, which we have already described. Erikson called it the moratorium period and believed it to be a necessary part of the process of identity formation. Finally, the process culminates when the young person achieves identity formation involving choice, commitment, and consolidation.[17]

James Marcia worked with this formulation of the process in his empirical research on what he called *identity statuses*. Marcia's research identified a number of patterns and issues that are present in youth who are working through the identity formation process. He determined two criteria that indicate the presence of a mature identity in an individual, both based on variables already identified by Erikson—crisis/exploration and commitment. Crisis/exploration refers to the period of adolescence when a young person is actively exploring options and identity issues; when he or she actively questions the goals, values, and beliefs of parents and other authority figures, such as the church; and when she or he begins the search for a system of beliefs and values that are personally satisfying and appropriate. Commitment, on the other hand, refers to the degree of personal investment in and allegiance to such a system that is self-chosen.[18]

By applying these two criteria to the process of identity formation through the extensive use of interviews with adolescents, Marcia identified four identity statuses or modes: identity achievement, foreclosure, identity diffusion or confusion, and moratorium. Identity achievement refers to individuals who have gone through a period of crisis or exploration and who have resolved identity issues on their own terms. They hold beliefs and values that are self-chosen rather than simply adopting those of their parents, and they are pursuing their own goals. Persons in foreclosure are also committed to a set of goals and beliefs, but they tend to be identical to those of their parents or other authorities. Their values are a result of socialization or even indoctrination into a system sanctioned by others. Even though they show commitment, they have not gone through a process of exploration and choice. Young people experiencing identify diffusion or confusion are those for whom identity issues are not yet a significant issue or for whom, if they were an issue, they were not resolved. They have not made any commitment to vocation or to a set of beliefs and values. *Moratorium* is a word Erikson used and one that Marcia borrowed to indicate the status of an individual who is actively searching for a vocation and a system of values to claim for his or her own. Young people in moratorium may be actively experimenting with alternative roles or beliefs, but they have not yet made a commitment.[19]

Several aspects of the process of identity formation deserve attention. First, this process is not easy for young people. It may involve saying "no" to elements from childhood that are familiar and comfortable. Identity formation may mean claiming for oneself many of the values and beliefs that were acquired in childhood from family and community after a period of exploration and experimentation. But the process also may mean affirming and choosing new elements that represent the unknown.[20] These elements may include occupational choices that go against a parent's preferences or expanded understandings of God, the church, or the Bible, which are different from those with which one has been brought up. Secondly, this process is not one that can be neatly resolved once and for all. None of the four identity statuses should be understood in rigid terms. Each is in itself an ongoing process. Although the process of identity formation may be understood as a progression through the four statuses, no one status should be viewed as a necessary and predictable stepping-stone for another. Moratorium is the only one that Marcia argues is an essential prerequisite for the achievement of a healthy personal identity. However, no one's identity is permanent. Changes in our circumstances or roles throughout life may cause identity issues to reemerge. As a consequence, an individual may revisit one or more of the stages in the process of reestablishing an identity.[21] And even during adolescence, an individual may resolve different identity issues at differing times. A young woman, for example, may have made a decision about occupation even though she may still be struggling with questions of belief.

Identity achievement usually does not occur until late adolescence.[22] Because most of the youth who are part of confirmation ministry are in the period of early adolescence, they will likely be experiencing either identity confusion or foreclosure. Identity confusion, as we mentioned earlier, is characterized by lack of commitment. This confusion is fairly normal, usually temporary, and perhaps even developmentally necessary in early adolescence.[23] *Foreclosure* is also common in early adolescence, but introduces a different set of issues. To recall, young people in foreclosure have made commitments, but without going through a process of exploration so that their choices may be more a reflection of the wishes of others rather than their own. A simple example might be the case of the young person who, when asked what she wants to be, responds, "A teacher." When asked why, she may say, "Because my mom is a teacher." The issue in foreclosure is not the choices themselves, but the way in which they are made.

The danger in foreclosure is that a young person never achieves a fully formed personal identity based on freely chosen values and beliefs. Even though some individuals may go through life in this way quite contentedly, many others may have cut themselves off from potentially rewarding opportunities and experiences. Early foreclosure becomes a problem for a person when some external crisis arises, calling into question the values and beliefs that the individual has always assumed. Foreclosed persons may lack the inner resources to examine and reconsider their belief system in order to arrive at one that is more adequate for changing life circumstances.

Foreclosure presents certain dangers for adults who work with young people in confirmation ministry as well. Many junior high–aged young people come to us having achieved a kind of temporary foreclosure. Because of where they are in their cognitive development, they are still comfortable espousing the beliefs and values they learned from parents and at church without question. But, because these young people say the things we want to hear, adults are often too willing to simply affirm them. Foreclosed youth often fit our image of what we want youth in the church to be. We like them. But, if our concern is to help them grow into mature Christian adulthood, we may not be helping them if we allow them to stay where they are. Our task is surely not to destroy the faith of young people. But, we may be called to invite them to explore options they may not have yet considered.

This task of guiding calls for us to walk a delicate line. Because the process of identity formation is one that involves exploration and the trying on of roles, adults in the church must seek a balance between giving young people room to grow and experiment, and outlining borders defined by who we understand ourselves to be as the church of Jesus Christ. In actuality this balance is important in our work with all youth, not just those in premature foreclosure. Youth need to know that adults care about them and are willing to create space in which they can explore themselves and the world around them while being assured of a safety net to fall back on when needed.

As mentioned earlier, young people today are faced with more choices than ever before in regard to almost every aspect of life, including sexuality and sexual behavior, vocation, and belief systems. Although their cognitive abilities are growing, many of them still have little sense about how to go about making these important decisions. In spite of the important role that peers play in the process and their need to separate from their parents, most young people still long for relationships with significant adults in their lives who will serve as sounding boards for their emerging ideas and values. They need adults who can listen without being shocked (at least visibly) and who can share openly and honestly their own life experience in return. Young people need what William Myers has called *guarantors*.

> A guarantor is someone who is appropriately anchored in adulthood but who will walk with youth on their journey. Guarantors share the burden of the journey, help read the road maps and offer encouragement. They incarnate "adultness" in ways that encourage young people to grow. In this way they "guarantee" the fact that adulthood will be a good place to be. A guarantor who stands within the Christian tradition knows that Jesus Christ is the perfect guarantor.[24]

Adolescent Thinking and Identity Formation

The process of forming a solid personal identity is made possible in adolescence in part because of other developmental processes that are occurring at the same time. Not the least of these processes is the significant change taking place in the way young people think. Teenagers are able to engage in what Swiss psychologist Jean Piaget called *formal operations,* that is, they are able to think abstractly or theoretically.[25] What is most significant about this change—some would call it a revolution—is that youth are able to engage in thinking about possibilities, about what might be, and not just what is.

We can understand formal operational thinking more clearly by contrasting it with the concrete thinking of childhood. The thinking of the elementary-aged child, while logical, is bound by concrete reality. If we ask a child of this age to imagine that the grass is blue, he or she might respond, "But grass is green." "Green" is the concrete reality of grass. An adolescent, however, has no problem in engaging this contrary-to-fact proposition and reasoning in a logical fashion from that point. Elementary-aged children tend to engage the world as it is given to them. Adolescents are able to imagine a world that might be. Psychologist Robert Kegan offers an eloquent description of this newly acquired power:

> This rebalancing, often the hallmark of adolescence, unhinges the concrete world. Where before the "actual" was everything, it falls away like the flats of a theater set, and a whole new world, a world the person never knew existed, is revealed. The actual becomes but one instance (and often one not very interesting instance) of the infinite array of the "possible" . . . The formal thinker can ponder about situations contrary to fact; accept assumptions for the sake of argument; make hypotheses that can be expressed in terms of propositions and tested; leave the tangible, finite, and familiar for the infinitely large or the infinitely small; invent imaginary systems; become conscious of her own thinking; and reflect on her thinking in order to provide logical justifications.[26]

One result of the emergence of formal operations is the idealism so characteristic of youth. The ability to imagine things that might be allows teenagers to envision a more perfect world, or church, or family. When you can imagine an ideal, the actual all too often comes up short. This perceived shortcoming in turn leads to the critical attitude young people so often exhibit toward all things familiar, including their family and the church. Parents, pastors, and other adult authorities are measured against an abstract standard. On one level, young people are also measuring themselves against others in their world to see how they stack up. As trying as this stage can be for adults, it is part of the learning process in which young people begin to see people as both flawed and gifted, which is necessary for the development of healthy adult relationships.[27]

Another aspect of the adolescent's new thinking ability that can be frustrating for adults is the tendency to become argumentative. As they become able to engage in abstract thinking, they want to practice it. Teenagers are now able to gather facts and ideas together to make a case for some cause or issue of importance to them. Things are no longer simply black and white; they can discern shades of gray. Rightness and wrongness now come in degrees. Youth are less willing to accept matters just because an adult says it is so. They readily engage in what appears to adults as arguing for the sake of arguing. To a great degree, it is exactly what is happening. They are practicing a newfound skill. Part of our role is to help them learn to argue on the basis of logic or principle, not simply on emotion. As adults we also need to learn to leave our emotions behind in these situations in order to help our youth grow.

Because most of the youth we work with in confirmation ministry are early adolescents, their abilities relating to formal operational thinking are just emerging. Their newfound ability to imagine alternatives too often results in a kind of unconstrained quality to their thinking. In early adolescence, the real world can easily become lost in the ideal. As adults, we have a responsibility to help young people test their ideas against reality in ways that are supportive. The self-consciousness of adolescence mentioned earlier reminds us that we must be careful not to embarrass them in the process. By middle and later adolescence, youth have had more opportunity to test out their newly reasoned ideas against the real world, and more balanced thought returns.[28]

The implications here color our work with adolescents in confirmation ministry. First and foremost, we are called to take their emerging cognitive abilities seriously. The ability to engage in abstract thinking means that our young people can begin to reflect on theological questions at a deeper level than they could as children. We must be ready to hear their questions and to help them explore ways in which to answer them rather than simply handing easy answers to them. Why are there so many hypocrites in the church? Why did God let that child die? Will my friend who is not a Christian go to heaven? Why do we sing such dull music in church? Many of their questions reflect their immaturity and their limited life experience, but at the same time, for the young people themselves, they are serious matters and represent their attempts to use their new cognitive powers.

We may also need to raise questions they haven't considered, to challenge their thinking when it is fuzzy, and to question their logic, which is not infallible even though they may think it is. This particular task is contrary to how we often view our role in working with youth in the church. Too often we worry that we should not let youth think too freely because they may just think the "wrong" things. We are quick to "talk at" teenagers, to give them answers that we hope will come to mind when they are needed. Several problems emerge here. First, we are not taking seriously the young people themselves and their developing ability to love God with their minds. Secondly, we are ignoring their need to develop their own faith identity by exploring what they believe and why. And finally, we are not developing what has been called a "thinking climate" in our ministry with youth, which research from the Search Institute has shown to be one of the strongest factors leading to faith maturity, even more than a climate that is warm and accepting. A thinking climate is one that encourages youth to ask tough questions about the world, themselves, and who God is. It encourages thoughtful study, though not necessarily using the traditional lecture-oriented approaches typical of too many confirmation programs. A thinking climate is one in which youth are encouraged to grow and think for themselves.[29]

The Impact of Culture

The process of identity formation is one that involves the interplay of developmental factors in the individual and the cultural context in which the individual lives. Culture is a primary teacher in relation to all issues of adolescent identity: vocation, sexuality, and a belief and value system. Those of us who work with young people must pay attention to what culture is teaching, particularly popular culture, so that we are aware of its influence and can enter into conversation with youth about what they are seeing and hearing.

One cultural teacher deserves particular attention because of its pervasive influence in all of our lives, especially the lives of adolescents. The world of youth today, perhaps more than in any previous era, is shaped in powerful ways by popular electronic media. Media provide young people with influential messages about who they are to be and how they are to look and behave to make it in the world. These same media give adults their picture of what today's generation of young people are like. All of us today are surrounded by a variety of media, from newspapers and magazines to billboards to movies and music. But, youth particularly tune in to music, radio, television, and most recently computers and the Internet to an amazing degree.

Young people in this country wake in the morning to the sounds of their favorite music on their clock radios. While dressing, they may continue to listen to the radio or to a tape or CD on the stereo system in their rooms. They walk or ride to and from school listening to that same music on their stereo headphones. And later that evening, they may meet with friends and listen again, or watch TV, go to a movie, or "surf the Net." No matter where a teenager lives, no matter what his or her ethnic, racial, or religious background, young people around the globe have access to this electronic culture with significant consequences.

> Day in and day out, contemporary youth live simultaneously in the world of their parents and in a separate generational enclave created by the electronic media. Of course, they have daily contact with nearby friends and relatives, but electronic communications technologies tie them to millions of other young people whom they will never know personally . . . New communications media do much more than enable masses of young people to absorb the same entertainment simultaneously. They also isolate youth from the more traditional worlds of previous generations, including the daily lives of their own parents.[30]

The authors of the book *Dancing in the Dark* argue that electronic media have become a major socializing force in our culture, especially in relation to adolescents. We now have in place vast electronic systems of mass communication through television and increasingly, the Internet, that allow us to communicate across continents in a matter of seconds. This electronic transformation of space has brought into being a national youth culture, which in many instances plays a more powerful role in the lives of young people than do the people and institutions that make up their local communities. In fact, these authors suggest that the strong relationship between youth and the electronic media has taken on a symbiotic quality.

> The media need the youth market, as it is called, for their own economic survival. Youth, in turn, need the media for guidance and nurture in a society where other social institutions, such as the family and the school, do not shape the youth culture as powerfully as they once did.[31]

The media do not have complete control over young people, of course. Because their intention is to sell their products to youth, they must pay attention to their wants and interests, even their needs. The persons who shape the media have learned to be especially adept at helping young people discover how to fulfill their needs for identity and intimacy by offering a wealth of information and role models.[32] Unfortunately, this information is not always healthy for developing adolescents.

The primacy of media in the lives of youth presents particular challenges to those of us in the church. For one thing, media tend to exacerbate the distance between generations. The corporations that control media are experts at giving youth the means to demonstrate their difference from older people by providing them with their own music, clothing, movies, TV programs, and radio stations through generational marketing. One consequence has been the acceleration of change in popular culture beyond the point where most adults are able to keep up. If young people do not like what they are seeing on television or hearing on the radio, media producers are able to pick up on that information quickly and change what is being offered. Music, clothing styles, and movies all change in a matter of months, even weeks. It is easy for adults, even those of us in the church, to feel quickly outdated. We worry a great deal about being "relevant" and too often believe that in order to be "successful," we must find younger adults to work with youth who are more in touch with their world.[33]

The development of a worldwide, rapidly changing youth culture created in large part by the media raises another issue with which we must struggle in the church. Many youth are not nearly as interested in local or traditional ways of life as they are in the newest fads and trends presented to them on MTV or the World Wide Web.[34] Although the electronic media offer youth, and all of us, access to a much wider range of cultural options and information, they also tend to cut us off from the people and issues that concern our neighborhoods and communities. And ironically, while media give the appearance of offering youth a wider, more exciting international community that frees them from the options presented by parents or church, in reality they only give young people a different set of cultural expectations with which to conform.

If adults in the church give in to these challenges presented by the media, we will only contribute to the problem. Other adults are more than willing to take over on our behalf—the producers and celebrities involved in the creation and delivery of media entertainment. Schultze and fellow writers of *Dancing in the Dark* argue that this reality has already happened to a far greater degree than we would like. The result has been a crisis of authority. They suggest that we now live in what anthropologist Margaret Mead has called a *cofigurative* culture. Young people today learn more about life from their peers than they do from their elders. The general communication pattern through which knowledge and information is transferred operates more horizontally within generations than vertically across generations. As traditional local institutions, including churches and schools, and adults such as parents, teachers, and pastors feel more and more irrelevant, we tend to pull back. Youth look elsewhere for guidance, and the media are ready to move in to fill the gap.

The picture presented here may be more stark than necessary. Media are a powerful force shaping our culture and influencing us in ways of which we are not always aware. But the situation is not hopeless. We do not have to allow ourselves to be simply passive consumers of this culture. We can become active agents who contribute to the creation of culture and invite our youth to join us. I am convinced more and more that in the church we must begin to take seriously the reality of media in our lives and to teach our youth how to become critical consumers of media. The solution is not simply to tell them to turn off their TVs and radios, which is not a realistic step in our world. We are called to enter into conversation with them about what they are seeing and hearing, to help them understand how media works through the power of images that play on our emotions, to question the assumptions and values implied in what they find on TV and in the movies, and to become media literate. We need to reclaim our local communities as alternative sources of meaning and value by bringing youth into contact with committed, caring adults who can articulate the meaning of the gospel and are making a difference in the world.

If we are going to engage our youth in this manner, we adults must pay some attention to the media world in which our young people live. Most of us will never be able to keep up entirely with the many forms of popular culture that our young people enjoy. But this area is where we can invite them to become our teachers. We can ask them what TV programs they like to watch, what music they are listening to, what movies they are going to see. And we can watch and listen with them, asking for help with the words when the music seems too loud and inviting them to tell us what they find interesting or appealing in the movies they watch. Rather than ridiculing us for being "out of it," many young people welcome the opportunity to tell adults about their world as long as they believe that we genuinely want to hear what they have to say and are not simply waiting for an opportunity to preach to them about how "bad" things are. It is imperative that we begin to help our youth become astute readers of culture so that they will be able to hear what messages it is offering and make healthy choices about whether they agree.

We also want to help youth to discern those occasions when the holy appears in media culture, those moments of grace that do occur, often unexpectedly. They are there if we watch for them, and they can provide wonderful opportunities to talk about matters of faith. Culture is a powerful teacher, but we do not have to passively accept what it has to teach us. We can choose how we wish to respond. We can question and even influence the culture we live in. Young people need to know of this power. But we have to earn the right to be heard by being willing listeners and learners of what they have to tell us.

Finally, one more concern begs awareness. Because media are a form of culture that instructs while it entertains, we must not let ourselves be seduced into thinking that we have to compete, or that all of what we do with young people must be equally entertaining. In the first place, we cannot compete on an equal basis because we simply do not have enough money or access to the kind of technology needed. And secondly, youth need something different from the church. Their challenge to forge an identity characterized by mature Christian adulthood is not one encouraged by media. Indeed, the media do not encourage any kind of adulthood. The view of life presented in most forms of media is markedly immature. Most research shows that youth actually want something more. They long for significant relationships with adults, including their parents, who will take them seriously and serve as mentors and guides on the road to maturity. These relationships are what our confirmation ministry needs to offer—significant contact with the "saints" of the church who can model Christian adulthood and who can serve as guarantors that adulthood is a good place to be.

Special Concerns

The influence of culture in the process of identity formation raises special concerns in particular areas. Our culture sends powerful messages today about how we view women and men, and about the place of persons of color in our society. Young people face distinct challenges in sorting out their femininity and masculinity in the midst of the ideal presented in popular culture. And youth who belong to racial and ethnic minority groups must deal with a range of issues all their own. It is impossible in the space available here to do justice to each of these issues. But, because of the importance of each, they must be mentioned. Readers are encouraged to explore more deeply on their own.

A number of years ago, through the work of Carol Gilligan,[35] Mary Pipher,[36] and others, we became aware of the fact that adolescence, especially early adolescence, is a critical time for girls. They must find their way through a thicket of social and cultural dynamics that may have an important impact on their sense of self-esteem and how they view themselves as women. Gilligan has focused much of her work in human development on the differences between men and women. She has discovered that while men forge their identities through separation from others, women define themselves through their relationships and their ability to maintain them.[37] Through her extensive work with adolescent girls, Gilligan has discovered that this need to maintain relationships reaches a developmental crisis in early adolescence. Using the image of "voice" to mean both the way in which we reveal our true selves and the way in which we make connections with others in relationship, Gilligan's work revealed that in early adolescence, girls begin to stifle their voices in order to maintain relationship. That is to say, they mask their true opinions and feelings in order to do what they think necessary to stay connected to others.[38]

Psychotherapist Mary Pipher made a similar discovery in her work with adolescent girls. In her book, *Reviving Ophelia: Saving the Selves of Adolescent Girls*, she discusses the dramatic differences she found between how these girls view themselves in elementary school and their self-image as they move into adolescence:

> Just as planes and ships disappear mysteriously into the Bermuda Triangle, so do the selves of girls go down in droves. They crash and burn in a social and developmental Bermuda Triangle . . . Studies show that girls' IQ scores drop and their math and science scores plummet. They lose their resiliency and optimism and become less curious and inclined to take risks. They lose their assertive, energetic and "tomboyish" personalities and become more deferential, self-critical and depressed. They report great unhappiness with their own bodies.[39]

Adolescence is a time when individual and developmental factors interact with forces of massive cultural indoctrination to produce results that are often devastating. Too many girls in this age group find themselves dealing with eating disorders, addiction problems, the aftermath of sexual or physical assaults, sexually transmitted diseases, and attempted suicides, just to name a few.[40] These problems may seem surprising considering the real progress women have made in education and in the workplace. But, our culture, especially through the popular media, sends a different message. There, more than ever, women are sexualized and objectified in order to increase ratings and to sell everything from automobiles to deodorant. By early adolescence, most young girls are in a rigorous training course to prepare them to take on what society understands to be an acceptable female role. They learn the code of "goodness," and its rules are clear: "be attractive, be a lady, be unselfish and of service, make relationships work and be competent without complaint."[41] And girls know what the cost of breaking the rules can be. Girls who speak their minds freely are frequently labeled as bitches, and girls who are unattractive are ostracized. Carol Hess argues that we live in a culture in which male traits are generally valued more highly than female traits, which puts girls in a real predicament. Competency and femininity are perceived as incompatible. "If women are successful, they are unfeminine. If they are feminine, they are perceived incompetent."[42]

Not anymore...

These still-existing pressures of sexism and appearance are a minefield for young girls to navigate at a time when they are especially vulnerable because of the developmental factors we have been discussing. So much in their lives is changing. They are developing new bodies about which they are extremely self-conscious. The way they think about everything is new and different. And they are wrestling with basic human questions: What does my life mean? What is my place in the universe? What is more, our society pushes young people to begin the move away from parents just when they may need their parents' support more than ever. To make up for this loss, they look instead to their peers.[43]

Our culture, argues Pipher, allows room for girls to make use of only a small portion of their gifts. In the face of this pressure, girls can choose to conform or withdraw. Many become angry or depressed. Far too often, our adolescent girls learn to be nice rather than honest. Many girls discover that it is safer to split themselves in two, separating the authentic selves whom they know themselves to be deep inside from the false selves that they reveal publicly. They allow themselves to become what the culture wants them to be and not what they themselves want to become.

According to Pipher, part of the problem facing adolescent girls lies in the way in which our society defines "manhood." She argues that we need to find new ways to teach boys what it means to be men.[44] Others are beginning to take up that call. Recently, research has shown that adolescent males have their own issues to deal with in adolescence that have a similar effect on their understanding of themselves and their masculinity.

Our culture has taught young girls that they must find their identities through relationships. Boys, in contrast, are taught that they become men by separating themselves from relationships with those whom they care about most and learning to stand on their own two feet. The most critical time for this "separation" in young boys is in childhood. For example, when little boys begin school, they are taught implicitly and explicitly that it is not good to show any emotion in this process of separating from their mothers. Even at this young age, boys learn that men do not cry even when they are hurting.

Boys are taught what William Pollack describes as the "Boy Code." In his book *Real Boys: Rescuing Our Sons from the Myths of Boyhood*, Pollack identifies the four stereotypes of male behavior at the heart of this code.[45] First, boys and men are to be like "sturdy oaks." They should always remain stoic, stable, and independent, never showing weakness or revealing pain. Second is the "Give 'em hell" mandate. The implication here is that boys are somehow "biologically wired to act like macho, high-energy, even violent supermen."[46] Third, men and boys are charged to achieve power, dominance, and status by acting like the "big wheel." No matter what, they are to avoid shame by always acting as though everything is under control even though it may not be. Finally, "no sissy stuff" is allowed. Boys are not allowed to reveal any feelings or tendencies such as dependence, warmth, or empathy that might be seen as "feminine."[47]

Just as young girls are implicitly taught to mask their more assertive, individual selves, boys are taught to mask their feeling, empathetic selves. Girls do it in order to maintain connections with others. Boys, on the other hand, must demonstrate that they separated from others, that they are independent and capable of standing on their own. And just as this behavior presents a cost for girls, a comparable one is visited on boys. Pollack argues that in contrast to much popular opinion, boys are not doing well in our culture, especially in the academic realm. From elementary school through high school, boys' grades are consistently lower than girls'. In junior high school, boys are 50 percent more likely than girls to be held back. And by high school, boys make up two-thirds of the students in special education classes.[48]

Adolescence brings a new crisis of separation for boys as they move away from their families in the process of establishing their own identities. At this time, Pollack argues, they also begin to experience a new double standard that society imposes on men. While on the one hand they are to be confident and independent, at the same time they are to be egalitarian in their relationships with girls, sensitive, and willing to openly share their feelings.[49] This double standard plays itself out especially in the arena of sexuality. While most of the cultural messages to young boys tell them that to act like a man means to be sexually active, they are receiving a different message from parents, teachers, and the church. Here they are told that they are to respect girls, to consider their feelings, and to focus more on developing the emotional, loving relationship necessary for a permanent commitment. Pollack argues that boys feel more insecure about their sexuality than they do about any other area of development, which leads them to compensate by exhibiting a bravado they do not feel, by engaging in "locker-room talk," reducing girls to sexual objects, and bragging about their sexual conquests.[50] We are much more sympathetic to the pressures girls feel related to sexuality than we are to those of boys, Pollack suggests. While we tend to sympathize with girls, boys are blamed for causing the problem. "The attitude seems to be that boys don't have their own confusion, as if they're sexual machines, poised and ready to go at all times."[51]

Boys react to these cultural pressures in a manner similar to that of girls. They mask their true selves and their feelings and assume an external persona that does not always fit who they understand themselves to be. As I read both Pipher and Pollack, it strikes me that the solutions suggested for both boys and girls contain many of the same elements. Girls are taught that to assert their true selves, to use their "voices" to speak who they really are is selfish and may damage their connections to others. Boys learn from an early age that to show feelings of warmth and caring in order to foster connection is shameful and not masculine. We need to help both boys and girls discover that growing up into healthy adults does not require separation, that one can be one's self and still be connected.[52] For girls, it will mean learning to claim a self that is strong and assertive with a voice of its own. For boys, it will mean discovering that showing warmth and emotions in relationships with friends and family is not a risk to one's masculinity.

In order to maintain a sense of their true selves and to grow into healthy women and men, Pipher and Pollack suggest that boys and girls need a number of similar things. First, they need the support and encouragement of parents. In their struggle for identity, youth may push against, and even away, from parents. Both Pipher and Pollack argue, however, that we should not interpret that pushing to mean that they want to sever ties with their families completely.[53] Most teenagers want to be close to their parents, to know that they can talk to parents about all they are feeling and experiencing, and to know that they can count on parental support. Teenagers do not want their parents to try to control their behavior, or to treat them in the same way they did as children. But they do still care about their parents and want to know that they will always be welcome at home. Both authors provide evidence that adolescents who maintain strong ties with parents and families fare much better than those who do not.[54] This finding suggests that confirmation ministry must seek healthy, helpful ways to include parents. It may also suggest that we need to explore ways to minister to parents as part of confirmation ministry to help them understand what their children are coping with during adolescence and to provide them with skills to maintain healthy relationships with their young people.

Secondly, both Pipher and Pollack suggest the need to provide safe places for adolescents where they can feel free to show their true selves. Homes especially need to provide asylum from cultural pressures to be a certain kind of man or woman. Pipher calls for parents to provide a home that offers both protection and challenge, affection and structure for girls.[55] And Pollack urges parents to create a safe space in which boys can explore their emotions and allow themselves to be vulnerable without shame or ridicule.[56] Although she is writing specifically about girls and women, Carol Lakey Hess suggests that communities of faith must provide this kind of "safe house" as well. She states, "They [communities of faith] can invite all girls to honestly offer their voices and listen to them, making it clear that assertion will not break the relationship. They can also provide a free enough atmosphere so that girls can be both assertive and flexible; their voices can be respected while allowed to change and grow."[57] Can we do the same for boys? Can we provide them a safe space that offers the freedom to relearn how to connect in warm and caring relationships with adults and peers? This challenge is one for the church.

In confirmation ministry, we are in a unique position to support young girls and boys in their efforts to maintain their authentic selves in spite of what the culture tells them. The early adolescents who participate in confirmation ministry are most vulnerable in relation to these issues. We must connect them with adults who can model forms of masculinity and femininity that empower rather than constrict. We must take great care to avoid language and behavior that inadvertently reinforce the harmful message youth are receiving from the culture around us. We can challenge our young people to develop all the gifts God has given them. Communities of faith must become safe places for our young people, making sure they know that as part of the church of Jesus Christ they are loved and accepted just as they are.

Adolescents of color have additional identity issues with which they must struggle. For these young people, adolescence is when they begin to explore their racial identity. Once again, this complex topic is much too large to explore in depth here. However, the issue is too important to ignore completely, so we will introduce the issue and encourage readers to do more exploration on their own.

In her helpful book, *"Why Are All the Black Kids Sitting Together in the Cafeteria?" and Other Conversations about Race,*[58] psychologist Beverly Daniel Tatum suggests that for young people of color, racial identity is a much more significant issue than it is for most white young people.[59] Because white is the dominant culture in our society, racial identity can be simply assumed. Who white people experience themselves to be is reflected back to them by others so that they have to pay little attention to this aspect of their identity. For people of color, such reflection is not the case. Their experience is more one of dissonance between who they understand themselves to be and the image that culture reflects of who they are. Because the culture "pays attention" to their identity, they must do so as well.[60] Young African Americans, for instance, think about themselves in terms of race because that is the way the rest of the world thinks about them.

This issue tends to come to the fore for African American adolescents when they enter junior high or middle school, the age at which they might also enter a confirmation program. Tatum notes that it is not at all uncommon in racially mixed elementary schools to see children of racially diverse groups interacting in all sorts of ways—playing together, eating together, working together—with an ease that seems to disappear in adolescence. The search for a personal identity that begins in adolescence raises the question of racial identity for young people of color in new and powerful ways. This identity issue is not to say that younger children do not notice racial differences. Even preschool children are aware that people have different skin colors. But, younger children have not yet begun to grasp the personal and social significance of one's membership in a particular racial group.[61]

The process usually begins when a young person has an encounter that forces him or her to acknowledge the impact of racism in a personal way. Children who previously played across racial lines, for example, may discover that interracial dating is not looked on as favorably.[62] Because it is difficult even for caring white youth to understand what their African American peers are experiencing, it is often difficult for them to be supportive. Consequently, African American youth turn to each other as they struggle to answer questions such as, "What does it mean to be a young African American person?"[63] The feelings of anger and resentment that often arise from their growing awareness of racism in our society may lead to the development of an "oppositional social identity" on the part of many young people of color in which they begin to keep their distance from whites. Styles of speech, dress, and behavior that are believed to be authentically African American are valued, while anything white is viewed negatively.[64]

While we have been looking primarily at the experience of African American youth, young people from other racial groups must struggle with similar issues. Again, this volume simply does not provide room to explore the specific needs and concerns of Hispanic, Asian American, or Native American youth. They too must go through a process of actively defining for themselves what it means to be a member of their own racial or ethnic group.[65] Our hope is that these young people will be able to find their way through this complicated personal and cultural maze and emerge on the other side with a strong, secure, positive sense of their own racial and ethnic identity. In confirmation ministry, it is important again that we provide support and room for young people in this process, and that we help them to discover strong role models who can serve as guides.

Developing a Faith Identity

This chapter focused on the adolescent task of identity formation and a number of dynamics and issues that play into this process. As we think about identity formation and its relationship to confirmation ministry, we remind ourselves that identity formation is not our primary goal. Developmental processes do not set our agenda for confirmation ministry, but they do offer a tool we can use to make that ministry more effective. We engage in ministry with young people in the context of larger developmental issues taking place in their lives. We do not help the young people or ourselves by ignoring them. An understanding of adolescent development can help us to make sense out of the attitudes and behaviors we encounter in our relationships with youth. What is more, we do care about what kind of identity they forge for themselves, and especially about how faith fits into that identity. So, knowing something about identity formation can help us to design experiences and to foster relationships that are supportive of adolescents in this task. Most of the young people with whom we work in confirmation ministry will be just beginning the process. Not all that we have said here will apply directly to them. But a larger view can help us appreciate the greater challenge facing them and can provide clues to the kind of foundation we want to lay for what lies ahead.

The adolescent's search for identity is ultimately a search for meaning. Our prayer is that our young people will find that meaning in the call of Jesus to a life of discipleship. In our work with youth, we need to be clear about who we are as the church of Jesus Christ with all its flaws, even as we make room for youth to question what we say.

We need to challenge our young people to become part of what theologian Stanley Hauerwas has called a *worthy adventure*.[66] Richard Osmer, who borrowed this term from Hauerwas, argues that perhaps the reason many young people are dissatisfied with the church is that we have not offered them a vision big enough to satisfy their hunger to participate in a venture larger than themselves. We have focused too much on keeping young people safe from the seductions of the larger world, asking nothing more of them than that they be "good" people. Osmer argues that we need to push youth to move beyond wholesome friendships, regular church attendance, and even worthwhile service projects—though these are all good things—to discover that the gospel calls them not so much to do something as to be something. We need to give them a vision of what they can be that is bigger than what most of us have settled for, something big enough to capture and stretch their idealism. We need to challenge them to commit themselves to some One who will ask everything of them—and give everything in return.[67]

Biblical scholar and religious educator Robin Maas suggests that too often the faith with which we hope to challenge youth is presented to them in terms of obedience, which they translate as a list of rules to be obeyed. Even though this to-do list may seem heretical to Lutherans who are keenly conscious of the heresy of "works righteousness," I suspect that too often it may be true. Maas tells about a student of hers who reported that as an adolescent he found no particular challenge in the Ten Commandments. He had no plans to steal anything; he had plenty of things and did not really envy what others had; because he was not married, adultery was not an issue; and he certainly was not about to murder anyone. Obedience was no big deal.[68] As adults, we know that things are usually much more complicated and that the meaning of the Commandments goes much deeper than this young man's simple understanding. But, the issue is not how we see the matter, but what adolescents see. Maas challenges us to help our youth understand that what they are being asked to do is to abandon themselves completely, not to a set of rules, but to a person; not to conform their behavior to a standard imposed by others, but to risk "an act of real recklessness," to make a decision entirely for love.[69] The question for young people, says Maas, must not be, "Are you going to obey these rules?" but rather "Do you love me enough to give up everything for my sake?" This approach may offer an adventure worthy enough to capture the imagination of our youth, an adventure to offer them an identity for a lifetime. And perhaps in the process, it is an adventure that may capture adult imaginations as well.

Notes

1. Kathleen Kimbell-Baker and Eugene C. Roehlkepartain, "Are Americans Afraid of Teens?" *Assets*, vol. 3, no. 2 (Summer 1998).

2. Ibid., 7–8.

3. See Joseph F. Kett, *Rites of Passage: Adolescence in America 1790 to the Present* (New York: Basic Books, Inc., 1977), for a more complete discussion of the impact of Hall's book on our understanding of adolescence.

4. Kett, 217–218.

5. Glen R. Elliott and S. Shirley Feldman, "Capturing the Adolescent Experience," in *At the Threshold: The Developing Adolescent*, S. Shirley Feldman and Glen R. Elliott, eds. (Cambridge, Mass: Harvard University Press, 1990), 3.

6. Ibid.

7. James E. Marcia, "Identity in Adolescence," in *Handbook of Adolescent Psychology*, Joseph Adelson, ed. (New York: John Wiley & Sons, 1980), 159.

8. Rolf E. Muus, *Theories of Adolescence,* 6th ed. (New York: McGraw-Hill, 1996), 43.

9. Erik H. Erikson, *Identity: Youth and Crisis* (New York: W. W. Norton & Company, Inc., 1968), 16.

10. Ibid., 47. For a thorough discussion of Erikson's theory, see his *Childhood and Society,* 2nd ed. (New York: Norton, 1963).

11. Muus, 54.

12. Erikson (1968), 132.

13. Erikson (1968), 22.

14. David Elkind, *All Grown Up and No Place to Go* (Reading, Mass.: Addison-Wesley Publishing Company, 1984), 33.

15. Erik H. Erikson, "Youth: Fidelity and Diversity," *The Challenge of Youth* (Garden City, N.Y.: Anchor Books, 1965), 15.

16. Muus, 53.

17. Susan Harter, "Self and Identity Development," *At the Threshold: The Developing Adolescent*, (Cambridge: Harvard University Press, 1990), 377.

18. Muus, 59.

19. Marcia, 161; Muus, 59–60.

20. Marcia, 160.

21. Muus, 60–61.

22. Marcia, 169.

23. Ibid., 63.

24. William Myers, *Theological Themes of Youth Ministry* (New York: The Pilgrim Press, 1987), 35.

25. Those who want to read Piaget's own description of his theory might find his book *Six Psychological Studies* helpful (New York: Vintage Books, 1967).

26. Robert Kegan, *The Evolving Self: Problem and Process in Human Development* (Cambridge, Mass.: Harvard University Press, 1982), 38.

27. Elkind, 28–31.

28. John W. Santrock, *Adolescence: An Introduction*, 6th ed. (Dubuque, Iowa: Brown & Benchmark Publishers), 109.

29. Eugene C. Roehlkepartain, "The Thinking Climate: A Missing Ingredient in Youth Ministry?" *Christian Education Journal*, vol. 15, no. 1, 54–55.

30. Quentin J. Schultze, et al., *Dancing in the Dark: Youth, Popular Culture, and the Electronic Media* (Grand Rapids, Mich.: William B. Eerdmans Publishing Company, 1991), 47.

31. Ibid., 11–12.

32. Ibid.

33. Ibid., 3–4.

34. Ibid., 52–53.

35. See Carol Gilligan, *In a Different Voice: Psychological Theory and Women's Development* (Cambridge, Mass.: Harvard University Press, 1982) and Lyn Mikel Brown and Carol Gilligan, *Meeting at the Crossroads* (New York: Ballantine Books, 1992).

36. Mary Pipher, *Reviving Ophelia: Saving the Selves of Adolescent Girls* (New York: Grosset-Putnam, 1994).

37. For a complete discussion of Gilligan's theory, see *In a Different Voice*, especially chapters 1 and 2.

38. Brown and Gilligan, *Meeting at the Crossroads*, 6–7, 20–21.

39. Ibid., 19.

40. Ibid., 27.

41. Ibid., 39.

42. Carol Lakey Hess, *Caretakers of Our Common House: Women's Development in Communities of Faith* (Nashville: Abingdon Press, 1997), 125.

43. Pipher, 23.

44. Ibid., 290.

45. William Pollack, *Real Boys: Rescuing Our Sons from the Myths of Boyhood* (New York: Random House, 1998), 23–24.

46. Ibid., 24.

47. Ibid.

48. Ibid., 15.

49. Ibid., 146.

50. Ibid., 149–150.

51. Ibid., 151.

52. See Hess, *Caretakers of Our Common House,* for an extended discussion of this matter.

53. Pipher, 65; Pollack, 173.

54. Pipher, 284; Pollack, 174.

55. Pipher, 284.

56. Pollack, 180.

57. Hess, 146.

58. Beverly Daniel Tatum, *"Why Are All the Black Kids Sitting Together in the Cafeteria?" and Other Conversations About Race* (New York: Basic Books, 1997).

59. We still wrestle with questions of language in referring to the various racial and ethnic groups that make up our society. I have chosen to use the language that Tatum herself uses. For her discussion of the issues involved, see Tatum, 15–17.

60. Ibid., 21.

61. Ibid., 55.

62. Ibid., 57–58.

63. Ibid., 60.

64. Ibid., 60–61.

65. See Tatum, 131–166, for her discussion of this important matter.

66. Richard Osmer uses this term in an article titled "Challenges to Youth Ministry in the Mainline Churches: Thought Provokers," *Affirmation*, vol. 2, no. 1 (Spring 1989), 6.

67. Osmer, 6.

68. Robin Maas, "Christ and the Adolescent: A Decision for Love," *Christ and the Adolescent: A Theological Approach to Youth Ministry* (The 1996 Princeton Lectures on Youth, Church, and Culture), 54.

69. Ibid.

CHAPTER 9

Lifelong Education and Pastoral Ministry

Nelson T. Strobert

Each year I read papers from students in courses entitled "Christian Initiation" and "Confirmation and Adult Trends in Christian Education." The students interview adolescents in catechetical programs, senior high youth, and adults who have a history of involvement in congregational life. Each year I am faced with the surprise of students who are themselves surprised by the responses. The students note that many of those interviewed have difficulty remembering or identifying what seminarians assume are common terms in the language of the church: grace, law and gospel, salvation, justification, and so on. Some of the respondents have recently completed confirmation ministry classes in their congregations. Others are a number of years from the rite of affirmation of baptism but are lifelong Lutherans in "typical" congregations. While the commentary and analysis of the students include surprise, shock, and disappointment, the respondents' comments indicate the need and responsibility of the Christian community to provide ongoing engagement of baptized Christians in educational ministry. The responses of the participants in the interviews suggest that the task of the church is to work toward providing the baptized with lifelong opportunities for Christian education. Furthermore, the interview responses highlight the important linkage between education and pastoral ministry in order to meet the needs of the baptized.

Although this book is concerned with confirmation ministry, this particular chapter considers educational ministry in the broader context of the human life cycle. The educational enterprise surrounds our lives from birth to death, from the limited experiences and exposures of childhood to the complex and differentiated experiences of young, middle, and older adulthood. More specifically, even though confirmation ministry is a part of the church's educational ministry, too often congregations, pastors, and catechists act as though it were "the educational ministry of the church" or "the crown" of educational ministry in the life of the baptized. In this chapter we look at confirmation ministry as a part of the broader framework of lifelong educational ministry in the biography of all persons. It is part of a lifelong process in which individuals interact and engage with family, pastors, associates in ministry, diaconal ministers, and lay leaders. Individuals are also connected to agencies and institutions within and outside of the congregation that assist them on their journeys of faith. Thus educational ministry is integral to pastoral ministry.

Setting the Boundaries of Lifelong Education and Pastoral Ministry

A popular notion assumes that education and learning take place solely within a classroom. This educational enterprise emphasizes an accumulated amount of knowledge, the development of skills, graduation, and employment. Although this description is essentially true, it is also limited. The educational experiences of all people go beyond the classroom and the teacher or lecturer. The various persons, agencies, and societies at work in an educational ecology meet the needs of students. These people, agencies, and societies intersect throughout the learners' lives. Although some educational practitioners equate lifelong learning with adult education, lifelong learning takes place from the beginning to the end of our lives—including adulthood. Dejnozka and Kapel suggest lifelong learning or education has the following characteristics:

- It is a lifelong (birth to death) activity.
- It involves all community agencies working as educational partners with the school.
- The educational program is sufficiently flexible to meet the needs of diverse, yet motivated, learners who possess a range of abilities and interests.
- Education is provided at the time it is needed.[1]

Michael Galbraith states that a discussion of lifelong learning and education involves the growth and development of the human being. In addition, the person is involved in "a process of transforming experience into knowledge, skills, and attitudes through a variety of processes." He sees this learning as experiential and distributed among a number of community-based providers including religious institutions, vocational institutions, and family.[2] Margaret Krych in reflecting on lifelong learning in the church states that we are equipping people throughout their lives in the faith community to be the baptized people of God in the world.[3]

The assisting, equipping, and helping of baptized children, youth, and adults into a way of lifelong learning occurs through the work of teachers, mentors, and facilitators in the educational process. Although we sometimes relegate Sunday school classes to lay volunteers and confirmation and adult classes to rostered persons, lifelong education in the parish demands a more inclusive perspective. Leadership includes people who are part of a pastoral team—people who nurture, care for, support, and instruct persons in the faith journey. The pastoral team in a broad sense includes parents and guardians, sponsors, pastors, associates in ministry, diaconal ministers, and laity. All these persons assist the baptized in their course of life. Each of these groups of people assists the baptized in service to the gospel of Jesus Christ.

In sum, lifelong educational ministry takes place along with pastoral ministry. It includes intentional care, concern, support, and challenges for the baptized though the various stages, styles, and passages of life. H. George Anderson, presiding bishop of the Evangelical Lutheran Church in America, states that as members of the church we might see our task as assisting the baptized to probe and examine the issues of life so that "the faith dimensions of those issues are revealed."[4]

A congregational ministry that incorporates educational ministry and pastoral ministry is not a twentieth-century phenomenon. It is a lifelong ministry woven into the very fabric of our lives as baptized people gathered in congregations through the ages. Lifelong learning and pastoral ministries are located in the gathered community of Christians. As baptized members of the body of Christ we celebrate a lifetime of learning and growth:

> By water and the Holy Sprit we are made members of the Church which is the body of Christ. As we live with him and with his people, we grow in faith, love, and obedience to the will of God.[5]

The promises of the sponsors and parents at the baptism of young children also reflect this lifelong ministry to the baptized. The sponsors and parents promise to

> . . . bring them to the services of God's house, and teach them the Lord's Prayer, the Creed, and the Ten Commandments. As they grow in years, you should place in their hands the Holy Scriptures and provide for their instruction in the Christian faith.[6]

These words indicate that baptism is not a once and for all event that rests in the past. The words indicate that all the questions and issues in the life of the Christian are not answered with the sacrament of baptism. Incorporation and initiation into the church provides the means for continued reflection and learning as one goes through the stages and cycles of life. Scripture is a helpful starting point for our investigation.

The encounter of Philip with the Ethiopian eunuch (Acts 8:26-40) is illustrative of the educational and pastoral dimensions that can guide our lives within the church. Philip is on the road between Jerusalem and Gaza where he meets the Ethiopian official who is reading from scripture as he returns to his home from Jerusalem. Philip is moved by the Spirit to greet him and upon approaching, hears the Ethiopian reading aloud from Isaiah. Philip asks, "Do you understand what you are reading?" The Ethiopian replies, "How can I, unless someone guides me?" The Ethiopian invites Philip to journey with him.

This first section of the encounter between these two men gives us an example of the educational or the catechetical life. This passage suggests that the life of the Christian is one of interpreting and proclaiming, of witnessing to the gospel. The church needs interpreters, teachers, mentors, and models—those who want to engage, to share, and to guide others in the word of God. Are Christians willing to walk beside, ride along with, share, and encounter others in their ongoing reflection and interpretation of the scripture? Of life in the church?

Paul reflects this lifelong process in 1 Corinthians 13:11-12:

> When I was a child, I spoke like a child, I thought like a child, I reasoned like a child; when I became an adult, I put an end to childish ways. For now we see in a mirror, dimly, but then we will see face to face. Now I know only in part; then I will know fully, even as I have been fully known.

Paul reminds us that in the human life span we cannot and will not have all the answers for living in relationship with God and our neighbor. All our endeavors are temporary, not permanent; partial, not complete. Years of study, reflection, and action remain for us. These activities are the core of lifelong education for the baptized Christian.

One of the legacies of the Reformation is the emphasis on the life of learning. We can see the connection between this educational interest and pastoral care among clergy and laity. Martin Luther understood the lifelong educational task. His words in the preface to the Large Catechism inform us about the ongoing task of reflection throughout the life of the baptized person:

> As for myself, let me say that I, too, am a doctor and a preacher—yes, and as learned and experienced as any of those who act so high and mighty. Yet I do as a child who is being taught the Catechism. Every morning, and whenever else I have time, I read and recite word for word the Lord's Prayer, the Ten Commandments, the Creed, the Psalms, etc. I must still read and study the Catechism daily, yet I cannot master it as I wish, but must remain a child and pupil of the Catechism, and I do it gladly.[7]

The emphasis in many congregations is to restrict catechetical instruction to the early adolescent and middle childhood years. Luther's comments indicate the continued value, relevance, and importance of ongoing reflection on the catechism. At the same time Luther calls on those in educational leadership to assist in this ongoing learning through preaching. Preaching takes place within worship with people who have come to hear God's word.[8] This union of catechetical study and preaching underscores the reciprocal relationship between lifelong education and pastoral care. Luther calls for a lifetime of catechesis and pastoral care.

Narrowly defined, catechesis is instruction.[9] In the early church catechesis was a period of Christian instruction for adults. The practice varied throughout the church. The duration of the instruction was from three months to three years. Adults learned the Ten Commandments, the Lord's Prayer, and the Apostles' Creed in preparation for baptism and participation in the eucharist.

John Westerhoff, however, defines catechesis more broadly. For him catechesis takes place in "a living, learning, worshiping, witnessing community of faith. To catechize is to participate with others in the lifelong pilgrimage of catechesis."[10] He goes on to connect catechesis with pastoral activity.

> Catechesis is pastoral ministry. It is a ministry of the Word, in which the faith is proclaimed and interpreted in verbal and nonverbal ways for the formation and transformation of the person and the community whose end is a lived love-relationship with God and neighbor.[11]

As a ministry of the word, catechesis is a dynamic relationship of the baptized with God and others. The formation and transformation of the person brings him or her into the marketplace of life. Lifelong learning has been a part of several ecclesiastical reports on confirmation. Lifelong learning or lifelong catechesis was examined in a 1970 study, in which Frank Klos wrote

> To help Christians grow in their capacity to love, the church has the obligation to serve them regardless of their ages through continual, intensive, pastoral and educational ministries. Change requires adjustments of all of us. Adjustments we often have a hard time making by ourselves. And only a sound educational program fired by a deep concern for the needs of people can guide individual Christians in interpreting and applying the gospel to contemporary situations. This is the underlying conviction supporting the church's idea of a lifelong catechumenate, of an unending catechetical process for everyone . . . Confirmation should mark a way station on the individual's educational journey through life. It should not be the end of the line.[12]

The theme of lifelong learning and pastoral ministry comes to the surface again in *The Confirmation Ministry Task Force Report* adopted by the 1993 Churchwide Assembly of the Evangelical Lutheran Church in America. It reaffirmed the 1970 understanding of confirmation by highlighting lifelong learning and underscored the fact that confirmation was not a onetime event but included all the baptized as co-learners.[13] Lifelong learning involves reflecting daily on dying and rising to new life, and equipping perceptive leaders who will take opportunities to engage individuals in instructional moments in parish life. Certainly, this ministry is part of the ongoing ministry of any congregation.[14] Educational ministry demands that congregational leadership take seriously the human being as a thinking creature.

The Lutheran World Federation also examined lifelong education and pastoral care in its study of confirmation ministry. LWF researchers identified the common worldwide themes such as the centrality of baptism, the partnership of confirmation ministry in the lifelong journey of faith, and the pastoral nature of the process in which the catechist provides a model of pastoral care.[15]

Furthermore, studies by several denominations on the adult catechumenate make references to lifelong learning and pastoral ministry. Paul Nelson of the ELCA says catechumenate "is a helpful term for a process of spiritual growth that extends from one's initial inquiry into the faith of the church to a committed life of Christian discipleship."[16] While a number of older adults might remember a time when a majority of people in neighborhoods or communities belonged to or identified with a faith community, many young and middle-aged adults have never been involved in any Christian community. Many adults have no connection with Christian congregational traditions, history, and education. This population of adults challenges congregations to develop a strong catechetical process that will address the issues and needs of these people. But issues, questions, and concerns arise throughout the life cycle. Such is also the case with catechetical instruction for early adolescent students who make up the bulk of catechetical programs in our congregations. Confirmation instruction comes at a time when these students are asking questions that involve their experiences as people of God in the congregation and general community. If we take Bishop Anderson's words about the questions of lifelong learning seriously, the result is an ongoing reflective activity on the part of the student. A. Roger Gobbel underscores this point in his analysis and critique of catechetical instruction:

> Catechetical instruction should have as its primary aim to initiate the young adolescent in learning a new thinking, in learning a new task of interpretation with the context of a faith community . . . Our failure to focus deliberately and directly on the learning of thinking and interpreting produces much of the frustration we encounter in our task and contributes greatly to an inane and insipid catechetical program.[17]

If the primary aim in catechetical instruction is to focus on the learning of thinking and interpreting, then we need to create an environment in which the important questions of all students are addressed in the learning environment created by the faith community. By extension, lifelong learning assists students to focus on a lifetime of questions. What are these questions? If our lives are rooted in baptism and we are constantly reflecting on that baptism, then the questions emerge from baptism. A. Roger Gobbel has stated that the two questions to which the baptized respond are "What is it for me this day to be a baptized person?" and "What is it for us together this day to be the people of God?"[18] In conjunction with the latter question, I offer a third, "What does it mean for us to be baptized Christians together in this world?" Let us look at the characteristics of the human life span and ponder these questions for each of the periods.

Early Childhood

This developmental period extends from the end of infancy to age five or six and is sometimes called the preschool years. It is during this period that "children learn to become more self-sufficient and to care for themselves, develop school readiness skills (following directions, identifying letters), and spend many hours in play with peers."[19] John Westerhoff describes this period of time as experienced faith. It is a time when children imitate, wonder, and experience the actions of the faith community. One can say that it is the beginning of Christian lifelong education. For denominations with infant baptism, children come to see the community in action. Westerhoff states:

> The child explores and tests, imagines and creates, observes and copies, experiences and reacts. Children's actions influence those with whom they interact, and the actions of others influence them. Their acts provide a mirror and a test for those with whom they interact.[20]

During this period the child experiences the community's worship, prayer life, singing, and story. It is during this period that the child does what she or he will do the rest of his or her life in the community. It is also during this period that the child begins his or her identity as a baptized Christian. She or he is claimed by God and marked for the rest of his or her life. The child learns to play with his or her classmates and begins simple prayers at Sunday school and, hopefully, in the home as well. The community and educational leaders within that community assist parents and guardians in their educational task. This assistance calls for sensitivity and intentional educational work in light of various configurations of households in the society. Educational leaders must deal realistically with single parent families, joint custody families, high numbers of teen parents, children living with grandparents, and children in foster care. In all these configurations, the children ask similar questions about identity with the community and their own life situations. At the same time that many church leaders are concerned and troubled by the difficulties faced in involving adults, they still must recognize the need to work with the variety of family patterns. What might be experienced or done educationally? Donald Ratcliff offers several suggestions for Christian education during the childhood years:

- Parent education classes in order to help prospective parents prepare for their responsibilities: These sessions would offer a time for the adults to reflect on the type of family heritage they want to pass on to their children.

- Providing media instruction for children from both secular and religious sources: It becomes important for the parent to discuss with the children the content of the program as well as probe the child for the meanings that emerged for him or her.

- The family huddle: This entails the meeting of the family on a regular basis to discover, study, and pray. The components include:

    Discovery. Members of the family share the events in their lives for that particular day.

    Values. The behaviors of the family are clarified as to their values.

    Teaching and affirmation of religious values. This might include eliciting material from scripture or using devotional books.

    Discussion of actual behavior as compared with the values of church, the Bible, the family, and the individual. The use of stories for illustrations can be helpful to the parent.

    Commitment to bring real living into greater congruence with the ideal.

- The checkup: This activity with children as early as four years of age provides the parent or guardian with private time with the child and asks the question, "How am I doing as a parent?" Here the opportunity is given for the child to share his or her feelings.

- Lifestyle: In this process, the parent or guardian uses the "teachable moment" to discuss religious topics. In this way, religion is seen as a part of the human enterprise. These moments can emerge through the observation of people, objects, and events. It is the integration of religion in life. It occurs through the ordinary actions within the home and neighborhood where Christian values can be highlighted.[21]

Lifelong education involves a number of people in the lives of the learner. In addition to educational leaders within the congregation, adults in the home are equally important for the nurture of the baptized. The emphasis is on conversation, dialogue, and reflection. These strategies can take place within the household. In examining a preliminary agenda for education in the parish the study "Effective Christian Education" states:

> Equip mothers and fathers to play a more active role in the religious education of their children, by means of conversation, family devotions, and family helping projects. This will probably require special efforts to strengthen the spiritual life of parents as well as efforts to devise practical strategies for promoting the faith development of children.[22]

Middle and Late Childhood

Middle and late childhood is the developmental period from age 6 to 11, the elementary school years. During this period children learn basic skills for lifelong learning including reading, writing, and arithmetic. The child's world is expanding beyond the family to the larger community, the world, and the culture. Santrock states that achievement is important during this period as well as the child's ability to be more self-controlled.[23] At the same time the child learns the basic skills for lifelong learning in school, he or she learns the basics of life in the faith community: the Bible, the tradition of the denomination, and behavior within the community. Children of this age respond positively to opportunities to participate in the worship life of the community and to explore the word of God in scripture. Here, we are talking about leadership development in the life of the child in the midst of the faith community. In the congregation where I worship, children participate in various ways in the worshiping community. Sometimes they read lessons at the gathering of the community. At other times they assist as ushers and worship greeters. In addition, the music and youth ministries programs integrate children and youth into the life of the community through vocal and instrumental music, drama, and service.

The baptized child receives his or her identity as a member of the body of Christ. In this period the child learns that she or he is loved by God. We as adult baptized people assist the child to know and love Christ Jesus. We assist the child in experiencing the actions and movement of the baptized in worship. We respond to questions that arise from the stories, hymns, and terms to which she or he is exposed.

As the child's world expands from family, to church, to neighborhood, the child knows that he or she has brothers and sisters in Christ around the world. These brothers and sisters live in different lands, speak a different language and dress differently. Yet we are all united in Christ. In middle or late childhood, children might share thoughts, questions, and insights with international friends. These worldwide connections are especially possible because many congregations and denominations are linked with other churches around the globe.

Transescence and Adolescence

Transescence and adolescence is the developmental period of transition from childhood to early adulthood, beginning at approximately 10 to 12 years of age and ending at 18 to 22 years of age. This period brings rapid physical changes, including gains in height and weight, changes in body contour, and the development of gender characteristics. At the same time, the pursuit of independence and an identity become important. In terms of cognitive development the person thinks more logically, abstractly, and idealistically. As his or her worldview expands, more and more time is spent outside the family.

In *The Quicksilver Years*, Benson, Williams, and Johnson report that religion is an important influence in the lives of young adolescents.[24] Yet, it is also a period when young adolescents question previous beliefs and actions within the faith community. Roehlkepartain and Scales point out they these young people have questions about themselves as well: Am I competent? Am I normal? Am I lovable and loving? These questions also parallel their religious journeys.[25]

Gobbel, Gobbel, and Ridenhour, in *Helping Youth Interpret the Bible*, examine the following questions that address the issues and tasks of the adolescent:

- Who am I? (attaining an identity)
- Who tells me who I am? (achieving an identity)
- Whose body is it, anyway? (accepting one's body)
- What is required of me? (achieving a value system)
- Am I my neighbor's keeper? (achieving social consciousness)[26]

These questions are important for living. It is my contention that these questions are not only the questions of youth but are also questions that span the human life cycle. Throughout the life span, students are addressing one or more of these questions. Perhaps certain questions will be considered more important at one particular stage of life, but the baptized person deals with these questions all the time. Many other questions can be added. These issues illustrate the ongoing questioning that lifelong learning assumes. How might lifelong education and pastoral ministry be described?

As they reflect on these questions, educational leaders need to provide a climate in which the adolescent feels free to inquire, question, and debate the critical issues in their lives. Seminarians preparing for various leadership roles in the church celebrate the openness of young people in youth groups and confirmation classes. On the other hand, those seminarians have also learned that the educational ministry within the congregation can only take place when they take time to acquaint themselves with the students and when they have taken time from a planned agenda to address adolescent issues from church, school, or extracurricular activities.

In a sense, that which takes place during the catechetical and post-catechetical instruction years can help to shape the young person's attitude toward lifelong learning. Hopefully, the educator or catechist engages the student in dialogue, offers possible responses, and allows for reflection on issues. The pastor or catechist can be seen as mentor, guide, confidant. Young persons deal with issues of sexuality, drugs, alcohol, and abuse (as victim or perpetrator). They have a need for safe places and trustworthy persons with whom they can converse. It should be noted that Lutheran youth reported that their congregations give a paucity of attention to issues surrounding drug use and adolescent sexuality. At the same time, these youth participate in at-risk behaviors.[27] Leaders in congregations must help young people confront a whole host of experiences. If religion is important to young people, the church and leaders in the church are a primary source for help in dealing with questions of life. We must take seriously the environment we provide for adolescents.

Gobbel, Gobbel, and Ridenhour speak of a safe environment that allows baptized youth to engage in conversation about the faith. In addition to their primary task of looking at biblical interpretation with youth, their suggestions are of importance to various encounters with young people. The description of the environment includes:

- Greeting and acknowledging adolescents as pilgrims with us—as we are all pilgrims in the faith.

- Abandoning all attempts to impose on adolescents fixed and static answers assumed to remain unchanged forever.

- Bringing appropriate biblical material to bear on the thoughts, feelings, and experiences of adolescents, which involves listening to the Bible as well as probing and asking questions from the text.

- Recognizing that biblical interpretation occurs in the context of the present. We all come with our own stories—past and present.

- Challenging adolescents to go beyond interpreting the information of the biblical text. The educator helps youth make sense out of the word.

- Giving space for new interpretations and understandings of self and the Bible in order to continue the conversation and go on to new conversations.[28]

Given the vicissitudes of life, the environment modeled during these critical years assists the young person in reaffirming his or her identity as a child of God and a person of worth. The young person can also know that she or he has a responsibility to care for the neighbor while recognizing that the values learned in the Christian community may clash with many of the popular values of the wider community.

To be together with the people of God, young persons need to experience a faith community that helps them think, reflect, and question previous assumptions about God, Jesus, and the Christian church. These young people should also experience life in a serving community, one that expects them to participate in making a difference in the lives of others. While a parish pastor at Advent Lutheran Church in Cleveland, I watched as youth group members eagerly joined a group to sing Christmas carols at the homes of members who were sick or shut-in. I have also observed young people learn to live together during confirmation retreats as they helped each other study, climb hills, and listen to each other as they learned to settle conflicts and ask for forgiveness.

It is hoped that during these years young people will gain a wider worldview and live as baptized people in that world. Anthony, the father of a teenage daughter, went on a work retreat to Mexico with members of his congregation. There the group built houses for persons who were living in substandard and inadequate housing. He returned very moved by the experience in which he worked, conversed with the indigenous people, and prayed and worshiped with the people in the village and the work team. He shared his experiences, pictures, and stories with his family. When the social ministry committee of his congregation announced another trip to Mexico, Anthony's daughter asked to be a part of the team. She wanted to share in the building of homes, the worship and living in the Mexican community. In her expanding worldview she is beginning to understand the role of the Christian church in service and in breaking down the barriers of language and culture.

Young Adulthood

The period of early or young adulthood begins in the late teens or early 20s and lasts through the 30s. It is a time of establishing personal and economic independence and a time of career development. For some, it is a time of selecting a mate, learning to live with someone in an intimate way, starting a family, and rearing children.[29] It may also be a time in Westerhoff's scheme when people are involved in a "searching" faith. The searching faith has three characteristics: doubt and critical judgment, experimentation, and commitment to persons and causes.[30] During this period of great change in status many young adults will question previous assumptions about their lives and their faith. They will search for other ways of fulfilling their lives and seek groups whose traditions are different from their own.

The challenge of ministering to this group has proven difficult for the church. Many young adults find it difficult to participate in religious education offerings. Their reasons for not participating vary, but research highlights busy schedules, family responsibilities, and conflicts with other organizations.[31] The challenge to educational leaders in the parish is to acknowledge these constraints and provide opportunities for the gathering of this population that accommodate their schedules. Spiritual nourishment is as important as social ministry. Topics for study groups must reflect interests and concerns of the group. Educational offerings that reflect the needs of the young adult, such as budgeting, money management, and sexuality, must be put in the context of theological and biblical insights.[32] These young people appreciate opportunities to delve into substantive faith and biblical issues.

As they adjust to adulthood, young adults can be assisted in the search for meaning in life. The young adult needs to know that she or he belongs to a community that will assist him or her during this search. Edith, a young adult, volunteered a number of hours with the Girls Scouts and a local children's home. When Easter neared and Edith learned that the children in the cottage had no place to eat Easter dinner, Edith announced to her mother that a group of children would be coming over for dinner. With the help of her mother and grandmother, Edith provided a day for the children with all the elements of a large family dinner.

While they are searching, young adults desire quality learning experiences. They seek a community of faithful people who listen to their questions and concerns as they seek to make sense of their new adult status. At the same time, they seek to experience full acceptance by the Christian community and to participate fully in a community that takes their opinions and issues seriously.

At the same time that the young adult is on a search for meaning in his or her life, he or she seeks to discover what it means to be a young adult Christian in relation to the world. The church can be a place for use of these new skills and abilities of this population for service in global ministry (such as international work camps and volunteer teachers).

Middle Adulthood

The period of middle adulthood, beginning at 35 to 40 and continuing into the 60s, is characterized by productive and expanding personal and social involvements. One task for those in middle adulthood is taking responsibility for assisting the next generation in becoming competent, mature individuals. In addition to personal growth, they are in the most fruitful years of their careers.[33] Self-inquiry also dominates this period: "What have I contributed to the next generation?" and "What am I going to do in the next years of my life before retirement?" are illustrative of the questions that are raised during this period of the life cycle. These years can be marked by crisis as well. In the scheme of lifelong learning, the church must provide opportunities for discussion and reflection on midlife crises that include marital stress and/or breakdown, death of close friends and family, aging, and alcoholism.[34]

Many of these adults are links between the younger and the older generations. While nurturing the growth and development of children who leave home for college, career, and marriage, the middle-aged adult may also have responsibility for the care of aging parents. Midlife adults also face the possibilities and limits of career and job mobility.

Lifelong learning and pastoral care are integral partners in the framework of a ministry that address midlife issues. Wickett asserts that the challenge in education ministry is to see the possible connections between the development tasks and spiritual or religious issues of midlife. In addition to the issues already mentioned, Wickett includes human relations with friends and colleagues, values clarification, financial planning, basic survival skills, creative problem solving, and stress management.[35] In response to the downsizing of corporate America, some congregations provide educational programs designed to help redirect persons who find themselves without employment for the first time in their adult lives. These courses can help people sharpen interview skills and assist with job placement. Along with the practical issues of finding new employment, questions of self-worth and identity emerge. Certainly a congregation's educational and pastoral ministries can address these issues through formal workshops and classes or individual discussions. These discussions are open-ended; the end point cannot be predetermined by either the teacher/facilitator or the participant.

Shirley was in her middle years. In the course of a six-month period she faced the death of two sons and her spouse. Although she worked at a hospital, her job could not fill the void or answer her questions about the losses. Her congregation offered a number of opportunities for Bible study. Although the Bible study included time for sharing, the important piece for Shirley was the studying and engaging the biblical texts.

For the middle-aged adult, reflection on his or her baptism offers a sense of identity at a time when so much around the person is changing. The promises of God become important to remember and reflect on as one watches the older generation (those of late adulthood) face the end of life. The middle adult is able to view the past and envision the future within the community. This special time can help one to know that the church is a reflecting community concerned about addressing the tensions involved in caring for two generations within a family.

As a Christian in the world, these adults are informed about the global work of the church. This time provides opportunity to establish contact with international neighbors who have similar interests. As the global village becomes more accessible through various forms of media and transportation, personal friendships and exchanges are possible. It is a time to visit the work of the churches away from one's native soil.

Late Adulthood

The late adulthood period begins in the sixties or seventies and lasts until death, and includes adjustment to decreasing strength and health, life review, retirement, and new social roles.[36] This population brings a host of resources and many years of experience that can be shared with the whole community. Linda Vogel asserts that too much has been said about the problems and needs of this group of adults and not enough about their unique resources.[37] Their lives and stories can be shared with other generations. The church can help as they make sense out of death and the meaning of life. Mrs. L., a retired public school teacher, was attending a series of adult forums I was presenting in a parish near the seminary. She told me that she had to miss the last session because she was asked by the high school youth to come to their class and discuss issues related to human sexuality. They wanted her input in a discussion of a topic that is sensitive in most congregations.

Although most people in this period of life are retired, they are still vital members of congregations and communities. Their career and life skills are valuable to congregations in a variety of ways. While I was a vicar (intern), Mrs. Benjamin, who had spent her adult life as a parish worker in the church, shared with me her experiences of pastoral care over her 78 years. She taught me how to listen, care for, and visit those who were sick, ailing, emotionally troubled, and dying. It was a special gift she shared with me as well as my supervising pastor.

We must learn to respect the older adult as an adult and not relegate to them meaningless tasks. They continue to be active members of the congregation. They continue to bring their unique gifts and abilities to the center of community life. Vogel reminds us that older adults do not want to be manipulated or talked down to, lose control of their lives, or be seen as having nothing to offer the community. The environment that we provide for education needs to include activities that build on the life experience of older adults. Teachers can use visual images and mental pictures from which the older adult can make associations from prior learning. Older adults appreciate being able to work at their own pace and having a clear focus that avoids distractions. Encourage older adults to use their verbal abilities and problem-solving skills. Use ongoing evaluation that allows the learners to shape the future of the class.[38]

As baptized Christians, older adults can continue to see themselves as children of God. As members of the body of Christ, older adults know they are in a community that still considers them valuable contributors to the life of the congregation. When they are nurtured by the community, they continue to nurture the community with wisdom and insight.

To be a Christian in the world and with easy access to global transportation, older retired adults can explore other regions of the world on behalf of the church. Those who are able can give a year or more of service to the work of the church. Mrs. B was a retired librarian who had always wanted to venture across the seas to observe the missionary work of the church. Through contact with her denomination's global mission office she spent two years in a West African country. There, sharing her skills as a librarian, she helped with educational programs.

Intentional Engagement

In each of these periods of life, educational issues must be addressed. The focus throughout must be on lifelong learning so that children, youth, and adults engage in a process of ongoing reflection. At the same time, congregational leaders who work with people in the various life stages must discern their roles in educational leadership. The whole community is involved in educational ministry by providing personal care and involvement in this ministry. Nathan Jones highlights this responsibility when he writes,

> Pastoral catechesis will be concerned with the totality of life and reflection on our experience in the light of Christian faith. Catechists help people bring into awareness and clarity aspects of life which might not otherwise be noticed. There is more available to be discovered.[39]

Indeed, pastoral ministry in lifelong education as ministry points to God's future, the coming of the kingdom of God. Such education equips and assists people for a life of service and discipleship. What becomes important throughout the lives of Christians is the hope and vision shared by the people of God. This vision is particularly important for adults because they have the ability to reflect, interpret, and respond to the issues of living within the community, society, and world. Therefore, the pastoral team must always engage the people with a vision. The late Grant Shockley wrote,

> Recognizing that persons learn throughout life, life-span education should be provided and encouraged to assist adaptation to changing conditions and a rapidly changing world. Proportionately, as much time will be spent on adults as on children and youth as they face increasingly complex and difficult decision-making situations.[40]

Shockley suggests an intentional engagement model for the Christian community. This model is helpful for all Christians throughout the life span as they reflect on their lives in the congregation and the world. This model has six characteristics:

1. *Self-awareness:* At this level, one comes to an authentic understanding of self in terms of identity, determination, and direction. This author sees this level as rooted in the sacrament of baptism and nurtured through study and reflection on the word of God and the eucharist.

2. *Social awareness:* At this level learners view the social, political, economic, and political conditions that might oppress them.

3. *Systematic engagement:* At this level the learner develops his or her ability to do constructive critique.

4. *Transformation:* At the transformation level churches exemplify the liberation of the gospel in the lives and ministries of the people.

5. *Praxis:* Praxis is action, reflection, and action strategy that center on accountability to the congregation, family, and denomination. It is education for mission and involves persons working in and through the faith community.

6. *Role of community:* At this level the community becomes the curriculum-planning guide for the church in all facets of ministry: preaching, worship, fellowship, teaching, outreach, and social action.[41]

The viability of this paradigm is a major consideration: Can an intentional engagement model work? I respond affirmatively but realize the large amount of time and work required of the leadership. The model involves the immersion of congregational members in continuous reflection as baptized people of God. At Epiphany Lutheran Church in Brooklyn, New York, Pastor Robert Gahagen and the congregation developed a program called Re. In a yearlong emphasis the congregation, through education in Sunday school, liturgy, Bible study, and summer programs, involved all baptized members in questioning, reflecting, and action. Concrete reminders of the theme were provided through buttons, bulletin inserts, and temple talks. The sermons reinforced what the people experienced (and would experience) by exploring subtopics such as rejoice, renew, renaissance, request, reply, and respond. The theme engaged the baptized in mission within the congregation and the community through committees on reflection (Bible study), responding (witness), refurbishing (building), retreats, review (evaluating the ministry), and revival. This type of program demands vision on the part of the pastoral and educational leadership team. The intentional engagement model communicates to the children, youth, and adults (young, middle, and older) that they, as baptized people of God, can make a difference in the world.

Pastoral leadership provides a vision when it is not afraid to

- serve as an agent of the promises of God's story;

- become an advocate of vision in the Christian story;

- encourage development of the congregation's involvement and interface with the religious dimension of life;

- be mediators for the judgments integral to the vision.[42]

Lifelong education and pastoral ministry are integral partners in this vision.

Conclusion

Lifelong education and pastoral ministry are two facets of a ministry for the baptized that continues from birth to death. As the baptized ask "What does it mean for me to be a baptized Christian?" they connect baptism with a life involved with the story of God's promises. Lifelong learning and pastoral care

- assist the people of God to respond to the issues of life that they face as baptized children, youth, and adults within their homes, communities, and world;

- assist baptized people to discern between the values espoused by the general community and those hoped for and embraced by the faith community;

- equip the baptized for service within the faith community, the greater community, and the world;

- prepare and engage the baptized in ongoing reflection and interpreting, thereby providing the roots for leadership within the faith community and in individual vocations;

- are engaged in witnessing to the future.

Notes

1. Edward L. Dejnozka and David E. Kapel, eds., *American Educators' Encyclopedia.* (Westport, Conn.: Greenwood Press, 1982), 302.

2. Michael W. Galbraith, "Community-Based Organizations and the Delivery of Lifelong Learning Opportunities," presented to the National Institute on Postsecondary Education, Libraries, and Lifelong Learning, Office of Educational Research and Improvement, U.S. Department of Education, Washington, D.C. (April 1995), 5; available on the Internet at: http//www.ed.gov/pubs/PLLIConf95/comm.html

3. Margaret A. Krych, "The Gospel Calls Us," *Lifelong Learning*, Rebecca Grothe, ed. (Minneapolis: Augsburg, 1997), 21.

4. H. George Anderson, "Foreword," *Lifelong Learning*, 10.

5. *Lutheran Book of Worship* (Minneapolis: Augsburg Publishing House; Philadelphia: Board of Publication of the Lutheran Church in America, 1978), 121.

6. Ibid.

7. *The Book of Concord*, Theodore G. Tappert, trans. and ed. (Philadelphia: Fortress Press, 1959), 359; see also Marilyn J. Harran, *Martin Luther: Learning for Life* (St. Louis: Concordia Publishing House, 1997).

8. *The Book of Concord*, 359.

9. Geoffrey W. Bromiley, ed., *Theological Dictionary of the New Testament* (Grand Rapids, Mich.: Eerdmans, 1984), 422.

10. John H. Westerhoff, "The Challenge: Understanding the Problem of Faithfulness," *A Faithful Church* (Wilton, Conn.: Morehouse-Barlow Co., 1981), 3.

11. Ibid., 5.

12. Frank W. Klos, *Confirmation and First Communion: A Study Book* (Minneapolis: Augsburg Publishing House; Philadelphia: Board of Publication of the Lutheran Church in America; St. Louis, Concordia Publishing House, 1968), 110.

13. Division for Congregational Ministries, *The Confirmation Ministry Task Force Report* (Chicago: Evangelical Lutheran Church in America, 1993), 9.

14. Ibid., 14.

15. *Confirmation Ministry Study: Global Report.* LWF Document No. 38 (Geneva: LWF, 1995), 49–50.

16. Paul Nelson, "Introduction," *Welcome to Christ: A Lutheran Introduction to the Catechumenate* (Minneapolis: Augsburg Fortress, 1997), 7.

17. A. Roger Gobbel, "Catechetical Instruction: An Invitation to Thinking," *Seminary Bulletin,* vol. 60 (Winter 1980): 32.

18. A. Roger Gobbel, "Christian Education: An Exercise in Interpreting," *Education for Christian Living,* Marvin L. Roloff, ed. (Minneapolis: Augsburg, 1987), 152.

19. John W. Santrock, *Life-Span Development* (Madison, Wis.: Brown and Benchmark, 1997), 20.

20. John H. Westerhoff, *Will Our Children Have Faith?* (New York: Seabury, 1976), 91.

21. Donald Ratcliff, "Social Contexts of Children's Ministry," *Handbook of Children's Religious Education,* Donald E. Ratcliff, ed. (Birmingham, Ala.: Religious Education Press, 1992), 25–28.

22. *Effective Christian Education* (Minneapolis: Search Institute, 1990), 66.

23. Santrock, 20.

24. Peter Benson, Dorothy Williams, and Arthur Johnson, *The Quicksilver Years* (Minneapolis: Search Institute, 1987), 111.

25. Eugene C. Roehlkepartain, *Youth Development in Congregations* (Minneapolis: Search Institute, 1995), 18.

26. A. Roger Gobbel, Gertrude Gobbel, and Thomas Ridenhour, Sr., *Helping Youth Interpret the Bible* (Atlanta: John Knox Press, 1984), 10.

27. *Effective Christian Education,* 23.

28. Gobbel, Gobbel, and Ridenhour, 60–61; see also Jerry Aldrige, "Preadolescence," *Handbook of Youth Ministry,* Donald Ratcliff and James A. Davies, eds. (Birmingham: Religious Education Press, 1991), 97–118.

29. Gobbel, Gobbel, and Ridenhour, 20.

30. Westerhoff, 96–97.

31. Harley Atkinson, "Participation of Young Adults in Religious Education Activities," *Handbook of Young Adult Religious Education,* (Birmingham, Ala.: Religious Education Press, 1995), 84.

32. Sharan B. Merriam and Trenton R. Ferro, "Working with Young Adults," *Handbook of Young Adult Religious Education,* Nancy Foltz, ed., (Birmingham, Ala.: Religious Education Press, 1986), 79.

33. Santrock, 20.

34. R. E. Y. Wickett, "Working with Middle-Aged Adults," *Handbook of Adult Religious Education* (Birmingham, Ala.: Religious Education Press, 1986), 90.

35. Ibid., 99.

36. Santrock, 20.

37. Linda Jane Vogel, "Working With Older Adults," *Handbook of Adult Religious Education* (Birmingham, Ala.: Religious Education Press, 1986), 108.

38. Ibid., 117–118.

39. Nathan W. Jones, "Pastoral and Catechetical Methodologies: An African American Perspective," *God Bless Them* (Washington, D.C.: U.S. Catholic Conference, 1995), 49.

40. Grant S. Shockley, "Black Pastoral Leadership in Religious Education" *The Pastor as Religious Educator*, Robert L. Browning, ed. (Birmingham, Ala.: Religious Education Press, 1989), 192–193.

41. Grant S. Shockley, "From Emancipation to Transformation to Consummation: A Black Perspective," in *Does the Church Really Want Religious Education?* (Birmingham, Ala.: Religious Education Press, 1988), 245–246.

42. Charles R. Foster, "The Pastor: Agent of Vision," *The Pastor as Religious Educator* (Birmingham, Ala.: Religious Education Press, 1989), 22–30.

CHAPTER 10

Educational Approaches and Teaching Methods

Donald R. Just

Earlier this year I participated in a memorial service for my closest boy-hood friend. We went to Sunday school, confirmation, and high school together. We were teammates on the high school baseball, track, and football teams. Although college took us in different directions, we kept in touch. He became a physical education teacher and coach and served in those capacities for more than 30 years. Eulogies by his children and friends portrayed him as a caring father, a faithful and loving husband. Many at the service applauded his work as a dedicated and caring teacher and coach. He was remembered for his lengthy service to the community as a volunteer athletic coach. In the homily, his pastor noted that my friend knew he was dying but was confident of salvation through his Lord and Savior, Jesus Christ.

Since the memorial service, I have recalled conversations he and I had as catechumens preparing for the rite of confirmation. I remembered that we were both a bit overwhelmed by the seriousness of the promise we would be making before the congregation during the rite of confirmation—the promise to be faithful. However, we found much comfort in the words "with the help of God." At the memorial service, I was able to say to those assembled that I had witnessed his confirmation promise some 40 years earlier and that it appeared to me that he had indeed kept it "with the help of God." More importantly, my friend knew that God keeps the promise of baptism.

I believe that my friend's life reflects the enduring effects of a meaningful parish education program in which catechetical instruction is a key piece. Over the years, we had regularly discussed ethical and moral issues that we faced in our lives. We were often the other's confidant and counselor on such matters. Confirmation instruction was the learning context that gave us a systematic framework for the language of faith—a context that fostered a life-long discussion about how best to live out our faith. Confirmation classes had taught us the language of faith and initiated us to a higher level of theological discourse.

In retrospect it is possible to see that much more was going on in our catechetical experience than a mere mastering of a prescribed set of answers. The pastor had a meaningful pastoral relationship with each catechumen's family. He was respected by the congregation and community. His teaching authority was grounded in his life as a pastor in the community. He addressed the catechetical task in a way that conveyed divine possibilities in the process. He willingly shared his faith journey and the struggles it embodied for him. Indeed, his vulnerability may have been best displayed during his attempts to play right field during our occasional youth softball games. He demonstrated Ken Smith's understanding of Christian authority as "grounded in the capacity of the teacher to authentically, genuinely, and really illustrate the mystery of death and resurrection in his/her own life."[1] His pastoral presence made the classroom an extension of the church and worship space. It was clear to us that the responsibility of study was deserving of the same respect as that given to worship—the shared center of each activity being the word of God. The purpose for our catechetical class was akin to at least one aspect of worship, exploring the meaning of divine proclamation for our lives. When seen as a whole it seems that this 1950s experience met a standard for confirmation later set by a 1993 ELCA Confirmation Ministry Task Force:

> Confirmation ministry is a pastoral and educational ministry of the church that helps the baptized through Word and Sacrament to identify more deeply with the Christian community and participate more fully in its mission.[2]

Confirmation ministry, rightly done and rightly understood, is a means by which God's work begun at baptism is awakened and strengthened so that the believer is equipped to give witness to that faith throughout his or her life. It seems that my friend's life of witness and service, rooted in the approach to confirmation ministry of the 1950s, met the standard set by the task force in 1993. Additionally it nicely met the first two of four recommendations of the 1993 report:

1. That congregational confirmation ministry be Gospel-centered, grace-centered both in content and in approach.

2. That such a confirmation ministry be tailor-made with an emphasis on community building and faith to convey the Gospel in the congregation's particular context.

3. That congregations create or designate a confirmation ministry team to give shape and direction to the planning and coordination of a pastoral and educational confirmation ministry.

4. That synods, the churchwide organizations, and seminaries be in partnership with congregations in developing a broad variety of support resources, such as materials, networks, and trained leaders for confirmation ministry.[3]

Continuity and Change

We bring to the task of catechetical instruction the enduring effects and memories of our own learning experiences. What can or should be retained of the methods used in our instruction deserves consideration based on its demonstrated effectiveness. Luther's Small and Large Catechisms together with the Bible must remain primary texts for Lutherans. If they do not use the catechisms themselves, then congregations need to use published materials that utilize Luther's catechisms as primary texts. Indeed, materials based on the catechisms can be written in language more appropriate for younger adolescents whose cognitive skills may not be sufficiently developed to grapple with the classical theological language contained in the catechisms. The catechisms serve to maintain a continuity with the past on such key theological formulations as law and gospel, the centrality of holy scripture, justification by faith, the priesthood of all believers, and the real presence in the eucharist.

As educators we must be conscious of the need to balance concerns for both continuity and change. Continuity is affirmed by remaining grounded in the essential biblical and catechetical truths that have guided the church and its educational ministries. Change is affirmed when we take seriously the application of biblical truths in relation to specific cultural, social, and personal realities. Perhaps the notion of continuity and change in the church is best seen in our most recent service books, *Lutheran Book of Worship* and *With One Voice*. Greater emphasis on baptismal theology and more involvement by the laity in the leadership of worship reflect changes in our contemporary understanding of worship. These service books reflect and implement these changes without violating or diminishing what has been constant in five centuries of Lutheran worship.

On the educational side of congregational life, significant changes in our understandings of how children and adolescents learn signal the need for changes in educational approaches. Additionally, the 1993 *Report* observed that contemporary society offers some unique challenges to the church's educational ministry:

- American youth engage in many at-risk behaviors;

- pluralism in society;

- the changing nature of households;

- the demands of an increasingly complex world.[4]

Considering the changes in understanding of how young people learn, the social challenges and modern developments in educational technology, we have a reasoned call for new approaches to our educational ministries. However, while the call for new approaches to teaching is a sound one, the changes must not abandon what is good and enduring in our biblical and confessional tradition.

Implementing an Effective Confirmation Ministry in the Congregation

The Confirmation Ministry Task Force Report adopted by the ELCA in 1993 called for the establishment of a confirmation ministry team in each congregation. The purpose of the congregational team is to tailor-make a confirmation ministry program that is gospel-centered, grace-centered, and that conveys the gospel in the congregation's particular context. The report notes that congregations continue to see the confirmation rite as important even though the meaning at times appears ambiguous. Therefore a primary responsibility of each confirmation ministry team will be to define what confirmation means to their community of faith. Congregational mission statements need to be examined and current practices reviewed with a eye toward congruence between mission and practice.[5]

Identifying a Congregation's Approach to Education

Some excellent work has been done by researchers of religious education regarding congregational approaches to education. A 1975 study by Harold Burgess identified four approaches to teaching: traditional, contemporary-theological, social-cultural, and social service.[6] A more recent analysis by Jack Seymour and others identified five approaches: religious education, faith community, spiritual development, liberation, and interpretation.[7] The five approaches described by Jack Seymour and his collaborators are not seen as exclusive of one another nor are they presented as exhaustive of all the ways by which Christian education can be defined. They are presented to "illustrate primary metaphors used to understand the task of Christian education."[8] Seymour cites Ian Barbour's notion "that human beings construct models, paradigms, and myths which serve as interpretive frameworks to help them limit, organize and act upon impressions."[9]

The approaches presented by Seymour and others serve as interpretive frameworks and metaphors by which we identify particular approaches to education and, in particular, catechetical education. First a brief look at the five approaches.

RELIGIOUS INSTRUCTION

Broadly understood, the users of this approach view the learning process as consisting of "the transmission of Christian religious beliefs, practices, feelings, knowledge, and effects on the learner, and the context is the church's educational programs."[10] Correct belief and proper understanding are the primary concerns of educators taking this approach. The key concepts in the process of religious education are understanding, deciding, and believing:

- understanding—"in order that people might understand the gospel and understand themselves and others in relation to the gospel, truth";[11]

- deciding—"moving thinking and understanding into decision";[12]

- believing—"the activity of helping persons come to believe, always relating that which is reasonable to believe to truth."[13]

With this approach, learning environments are structured in ways that best assist learners in acquiring the desired understanding of the gospel and its application to daily living. Learning materials and learning settings are chosen on the basis of their usefulness in conveying a particular belief system. Therefore the curriculum will most likely consist of traditional materials, and the classroom is most often the formal classroom setting.

FAITH COMMUNITY

This approach looks to the faith community for clues to the appropriate procedures for education. "The unique contours of the faith community itself become the contours of the education program."[14] The purpose of education is the building up of the community of faith. Learner edification takes place though his or her participation in the faith community's heritage, rituals, traditions, and lifestyles as well as its thinking and values. In order for learning to take place, the learner must be engaged in the life of the community. The goal of education in this approach is to facilitate a process that enables development of skill, and an acquiring of wisdom that leads to responsible participation in the community.[15]

Catechesis done using this approach is a pastoral activity rather than an educational one. The teacher functions as a kind of priest to the learning community. The learner is one who is seeking to identify with the community and needs to acquire an understanding of its rituals and lifestyles in order to participate fully in the community's life. The learning setting can be virtually any of the various contexts of the community.

SPIRITUAL DEVELOPMENT

As the title implies, the development of the learner's spiritual life is the primary purpose and context for education. The proper focus of education is on the religious experience and the religious quest of the individual. Development theorists such as Jean Piaget, Erik Erikson, Lawrence Kohlberg, and James Fowler inform much of the thought for this approach.

Contemporary understandings of the processes of cognitive, moral, emotional, and spiritual development are applied to religious education. The goal of the spiritual development approach is to provide an environment that stimulates individual spiritual growth. Metaphors such as spiritual director, coach, mentor, observer, and guide describe the role of the teacher. The learner is viewed as one in the process of moving through developmental stages. Learning settings can be any context that fosters spiritual growth and maturation. Materials are evaluated on the basis of their appropriateness for the learner's stage of development. The teacher as spiritual director has the task of nurturing learning at and through the various life crises in an individual's life journey.

LIBERATION

Liberation thought in education and theology grew out of a Latin American context where both oppression and poverty are realities. The educational methodologies of theorists such as Paulo Friere were developed in contexts where learners were often illiterate.

Even though an important goal of liberation education is to combat illiteracy, reform of political and social structures is also a priority. Some proponents of this educational approach believe that the education process "demands our active struggle for humanizing life."[16] Under this approach, lifestyle is an important matter to be addressed by religious education. Beliefs, values, and attitudes, demonstrated by the way one chooses to live, provide the focus of this approach.

Learners are expected to be involved in social action. The role of the teacher is understood as that of a colleague who challenges the learner to reflect critically on lifestyle in light of the Christian faith. Goals include helping the learner grow in awareness of social justice, structures of power, and actions that will lead to social transformation.

INTERPRETATION

The interpretation approach holds that religious education's primary task is to connect faith and life. It resolves "the Bible as the primary resource" versus "life experience as the primary resource" dispute with the contention that religious education must include both.

> The task of Christian education is to engage the faith-story and the experience of living into a dialogical relationship from which meaning for living emerges.[17]

The teacher is an interpreter or guide who is present to help the learner interpret and understand the meaning of human experience in the light of the Christian story. The learner is one seeking to find meaning in personal experience and religious truth. An appropriate setting is any context that fosters reflection about the meaning of faith and experience.

Five approaches to educational ministry, while not differing completely from each other, represent different frameworks for defining and organizing an educational program. Each approach is designed to teach, form, and initiate persons into Christian life and faith. Together, they provide a continuum of learning objectives ranging from assimilation of prescribed religious beliefs and practices to more individualistic and subjective interpretations of biblical and personal narrative. The breadth of thought and focus manifested by the five approaches explain, at least in part, the principle that no single way is the correct way to do educational ministry.

Goals Determine Methodology

Iris Cully writes that method includes "everything which a teacher does to teach and through which a pupil learns."[18] Nowhere is the goal of method more true than in confirmation ministry with its blending of the educational and pastoral elements of parish life. Cully further reminds educators that "the teacher has the option of deliberately planning methods or drifting into them."[19] She underscores what ought to be obvious to every catechist: effective methodology presupposes clearly articulated and established goals. Yet as important as they are, goals and objectives by themselves do not eliminate all the problems and challenges that accompany the teaching of confirmation. No one methodology will automatically take care of discipline problems in the classroom or ensure the regular attendance of catechumens.

Catechists and confirmation ministry teams must decide what they want to accomplish in the relatively short window of opportunity that confirmation education provides. Ideally, confirmation is one segment of a lifelong parish educational program. When lifelong education is the case, confirmation does not have the burden of addressing the whole spectrum of religious education. In the context of the total educational program, decisions are made regarding the particular focus of the confirmation experience. Gracia Grindal writing in defense of confirmation ministry comes to mind here:

Confirmation, at its best, is a time to stop, review and test to see whether or not our young people are rooted and grounded in the word. Family devotions and Sunday schools should aim toward it; Sunday morning and Monday morning should be built upon it. Train up your children in the way they should go, and when they are old, they will not depart from it.[20]

When we complete a program of confirmation instruction, what do we want catechumens to know and what do we want them to have experienced about the faith and their church?

In summary, the goals of confirmation ministry are shaped by:

- congregational self-understanding;
- the lives of the catechumens and their families;
- human and community resources;
- lifelong emphasis of education;
- baptismal theology.

Given the vision, resources, and theology of a particular congregation—what are the desired outcomes of confirmation ministry? Using the language of the five approaches, a congregation faces the following questions:

- Is religious instruction the primary goal? Does mastery of the text mean a particular understanding of the content of faith?
- Do the desired outcomes include meaningful involvement in the community of faith?
- How important is the individual spiritual development of the catechumens?
- Is an appreciation of liberation thought and the development of a congruent lifestyle high on the list of desired outcomes?
- Is meaning making and ability to interpret the meaning of life in light of sacred text a primary desired outcome?

Is it helpful to prioritize desired outcomes and then determine an educational methodology that will most effectively reach that goal? Perhaps the religious instruction approach offers a baseline by which we ensure that learners have a grasp of the language of faith as drawn from the key texts of faith. The language of faith then becomes the vehicle for participation in the faith community and for individual interpretation and meaning making. Faith development might best be understood as a lifelong journey.

Acquiring the language of faith then equips the learner for that process of faith development in which catechists serve as important mentors and guides. Which approach best characterizes the congregation's educational mission? Perhaps the most appropriate approach for a community of faith is one that best represents the unique vision of the people in that community of faith.

Characteristics of Gospel-Centered, Grace-Centered Confirmation Ministry

The 1993 ELCA task force identified common characteristics of effective programs:

- a focus on grace, affirmation of baptism, mission, discipleship, and vocation;
- a focus on the Bible and the Small Catechism;
- the use of resources and guidelines provided by the church;
- involvement of a committee or group composed of lay people, youth, pastor(s), parents, and council and educational committee members in the development of the program;
- an emphasis on human relationships within the congregation;
- an integration of the program into the worship life of the congregation;
- a continuation of the program after the rite of affirmation of baptism with an emphasis on maintaining key relationships with the newly confirmed;
- an understanding of affirmation of baptism as a lifelong process rather than a once-in-a-lifetime event.[21]

Models of Confirmation Ministry

Confirmation programs in the church range from traditional programs in congregations of all sizes to individualized self-paced designs directed by tutors in learning centers in large congregations to "campfirmation" programs conducted by clusters of small congregations. Chapter 2, "The Changing Face of Confirmation," reviews some of the models developed in recent years. The models chronicle the responses of congregations and denomination publishing houses to the changing needs of learners and the insights of cognitive theory and developmental research.

Most congregations still provide two years of dedicated study centered on weekly classes that are often augmented with service projects and other learning experiences. In most congregations, the rite of affirmation of baptism takes place on festival Sundays: Passion/Palm Sunday, Pentecost Sunday, or Reformation Sunday. At this time the young people affirm their baptism before the congregation. In other congregations, affirmation of baptism occurs when an individual confirmand is ready to give public witness to the faith before the congregation. Confirmation ministry is practiced in a variety of ways throughout the church. Tradition, needs, and beliefs about confirmation are determinants in each location.

My confirmation experience during the 1950s featured Saturday morning classes that met throughout the academic year. Course methodology consisted of presentations and lectures given by the pastor, class discussion, and the recitation of assigned memory work. Our study texts were the Bible and an edition of Luther's Small Catechism that contained short explanations.[22] We studied selected books of the Bible and the six parts of the catechism. Assignments each week included the memorization of key parts of the catechism with Luther's meanings and selected supporting biblical passages used as "proof texts" for the doctrines being taught. The pastor had high expectations regarding the seriousness with which we would approach our study as well as our ability to understand the material. These expectations were shared and reinforced by our parents. Mine were not the only parents who made completion of the assigned homework and memorization a prerequisite for participation in Friday evening school or community activities. A few days before the rite of confirmation, we faced a much dreaded "public examination" before the congregation. The dread we experienced proved to be unwarranted. The pastor, knowing each of us well, was selective in the questions each of us was asked, thereby ensuring that we could demonstrate to the congregation a sufficient understanding of the Christian faith. The examination event was a time of triumph for each of us as we were then considered prepared and enthusiastically invited to become "confirmed members" in the life of the congregation. By modern standards the educational process of 40 years ago seems archaic. The method of lecture, discussion, and recitation was modeled after Martin Luther's question-and-answer method. The process was almost totally content-centered. We were expected to memorize and recite verbatim the answers contained in the catechism. No published catechetical materials other than the Luther's Small Catechism and Bible were available.

The only audiovisuals were some black and white filmstrips on Bible stories.

In this chapter we will take a look at a number of congregational models:

- traditional/classroom;
- expanded/later and longer;
- individualized/self-paced model;
- home-based learning;
- retreat/campfirmation;
- presentation/discussion.[23]

TRADITIONAL/CLASSROOM

In this confirmation model students typically meet weekly in a classroom-style setting with a catechist, or instructor. It most closely approximates the religious instruction approach. Content generally includes a mastery of a particular body of knowledge based on the Bible, catechism, and books of worship. Study may also include heroes of the faith such as Augustine, Francis of Assisi, Martin Luther, and Martin Luther King Jr.

This model most often involves a two- or three-year program that meets for 30 weeks coinciding with regular school terms. The age level is typically seventh through eighth or ninth grades.

Instructional methods include formal presentations of key concepts drawn from the Bible, catechism, or books of worship. Reading and work assignments are made from the texts, which may include published student workbooks. Memory work is frequently a part of the learning experience. The traditional classroom model lends itself to audiovisual presentations, guest speakers, mentors, and computer-assisted instruction. Extracurricular activities might include field trips, retreats, service projects, and cluster learning with other congregations or ecumenical partners.

The traditional/classroom model, besides being the most popular model, is also the most "tried and true." It can be effective as I believe the experience of my boyhood friend demonstrates. However, as the discussion of my own experience indicates, it worked at least in part because catechetical expectations were strongly reinforced by parents and because the pastor enjoyed meaningful pastoral relationships with each learner. Additionally, much of the weight of success depends on the catechist's teaching ability. Not all catechists have such gifts and therefore may not be effective with a model so highly dependent on the ability of the catechist to make presentations and sustain the interest of the learners. This model certainly leaves room for varied methods of presentation that employ creative educational technology as well as creative discussion strategies.

The traditional/classroom model, while most comparable to the religious instruction approach, is not limited to it. Instruction and activities can lean toward integrating each learner into the faith community. Catechists can be vitally interested in the faith development of each learner. Depending on the congregational setting and theological bent of the catechist, issues raised by liberation thought can be addressed in a traditional setting. Finally, acquiring the language of faith and a working knowledge of the biblical witness makes possible interpretation of faith for daily living.

EXPANDED/LATER AND LONGER

Confirmation ministry with this approach may begin in early childhood and continue well into the high school years. By its very nature this model demonstrates that affirmation of baptism is a lifelong event rather than a once-in-a-lifetime event. It addresses the "confirmation as graduation" problem by "affirming" the catechumens at various points throughout the extended process. Occasions for affirmation of baptism include an initiation event at the beginning of an extended confirmation program, the presentation of a Bible sometime during the early grades, and first communion sometime in the middle grades. The rite of affirmation of baptism in this model is frequently delayed until the later high school years.

This model draws on a wide range of educational methods. It has the advantage of using age-appropriate packaged materials at the various stages of cognitive and spiritual development. The extended period of instruction offers many opportunities for a variety of learning activities such as learning in small group settings, retreats, service projects for older students, and intergenerational events involving both congregation and family members.

This model seems to take more seriously a lifelong view of educational ministry by incorporating the baptized into the worship, educational, communal, and service life of the congregation in particular ways. Catechetical study, beginning in the lower elementary school years, could well continue for a lifetime. This model gives opportunity for study during the earlier grade school years to focus on content such as the Lord's Prayer and the Commandments. Classes for adolescents may then feature a more concen-

trated study of the Bible and catechism and include an emphasis on participation in worship and the service activities of the congregation.

INDIVIDUALIZED/SELF-PACED MODEL

This model generally prescribes both a body of knowledge to be mastered and
a core of learning experiences to be completed. One feature is to give the
learner greater control over the pace of learning by inviting student participation in decisions over when and how learning takes place. The core learning experiences often include the somewhat traditional requirements such as
a basic understanding of the Bible, key parts of the Small Catechism, and
aspects of worship. Options may be offered as electives based on individual
interest, skill, and spiritual gifts.

Programmed learning focuses on instructional content packaged into sets
of materials that allow the learner to proceed at an individual pace. The self-
paced program may include learning centers staffed by learning facilitators.
Learners may work individually or in groups at these centers. Much of the
material can be packaged in audio- or videotape form. Such a format would
also invite the use of computer technology in the learning experience. While
this model makes it possible for learning to be highly individualistic, it need
not necessarily be solitary. Where learning centers are available and staffed,
learning can be collaborative. This model fosters close working and learning
relationships with tutors and mentors. Learning experiences can be designed
to facilitate active participation in the worship and service activities of the
congregation. Other learning experiences can be designed to foster learning
and devotional activities within the family setting.

HOME-BASED MODEL

This model takes seriously Martin Luther's intent in writing the Small
Catechism: that the "head of the family shall teach" the fundamentals of the
Christian faith to the household in "plain form."[24] This model is deliberate in
making the family the "first church" and therefore the single most important
conveyer of religious values. The possibilities for family involvement is limited only by the extent to which the family is willing to participate in the catechetical experience. One variation of this approach features in-home packets
for parents. The packets contain study materials, suggested learning formats,
and suggestions for family-based projects. Possibilities for using audiovisual

materials and computer-based materials are endless and only limited by family and parish budgets.

Another variation features a deliberate emphasis on involving parents and family members in the learner's congregation-based catechetical classes and activities. Family members are included in activities in retreat settings, worship contexts, and service projects.

CAMPFIRMATION

This model features a series of weeklong camping events over two or three years. These weeks at camp are designed for the purpose of catechetical instruction. The camp events include instruction segments by trained leaders or teams of leaders, a series of age-appropriate worship activities often designed around selected themes, group meal and recreation times, and the experience of living in "camping families" under the guidance of camp or cabin counselors.

This model is often utilized and organized by clusters of congregations in geographic regions of the church. Some clusters have merely added confirmation instruction to preexisting camping programs. In other areas, outdoor ministry agencies of the church have developed camp-based confirmation programs for congregations in their region. They are deliberate in engaging pastors in the development and implementation of these programs. These programs can be especially attractive to children and youth. The program offers a variety of learning possibilities that are unique to the outdoor setting of the camp.

PRESENTATION/DISCUSSION

This model utilizes both small and large group learning strategies. Sessions frequently begin with a gathering of the total group. This gathering time may feature worship and other large group activities that address the focus and theme for the session. Gathering activities may include a presentation of a particular theme through skits, readings, audiovisual presentations, and planning events. Small group activities follow the gathering time. These small group settings offer time for prayer, discussion, personal sharing, crafts, and other activities that apply the theme. Small groups may invest part of their time together in designing presentations to be made to the larger group.

A variation on this model has the small groups gathering frequently at regularly appointed times. Small group gatherings may take place in a variety of settings including homes. The large group, combining all the small groups, meets less frequently but also at regularly appointed times. Small groups are invited to be creative and engage in a variety of activities that include service projects and recreational activities in addition to formal learning settings for confirmation instruction.

Conclusion

Each congregation is a unique and particular collection of gifts and resources for educational ministry. Congregations acknowledge and celebrate those gifts and resources when they see them as the means by which God would have them do confirmation ministry in their particular context. The congregation's vision of educational ministry is informed by its resources, the needs within the community of faith, and its understanding of the faith as informed by scripture and the Confessions.

Effective educational programs are the result of a regular assessment of gifts and resources together with regular assessments of the educational needs of the membership. Out of those assessments emerge the important questions for confirmation ministry: What does the particular collection of gifts and resources in the community of faith tell us about God's intentions for education ministry? What do the particular needs of the people tell us about appropriate goals and objectives in this context? What educational approaches will best equip the baptized for lives of faithful service? It would seem that the resources address the "how" of educational ministry, and needs inform the "what" of educational ministry.

My experience of catechetical instruction in the 1950s served me and my fellow students well. My childhood friend's life was evidence of an effective program in a rural context utilizing the particular gifts of a 1950s congregation and its pastor. Learning the language of faith and acquiring the habits of faithful worship and service were the key objectives of that program. The religious instruction approach to catechetical ministry effectively utilized the resources at the congregation's disposal and met its concern for "correct belief and proper understanding," while equipping the catechumens for a life of faith in a changing, postwar America.

Fifty years later, the concerns remain essentially the same. How do we meet a congregation's concern for basic religious instruction while equipping

participants for life in the twenty-first century? Realities such as diverse mul-
ticultural communities, a global economy, two-income households, and
cyberspace suggest approaches that prepare catechumens for faithful worship
and lives of service in these new contexts. The new realities require that we
address matters of social justice, acculturation, and spiritual development in
ways appropriate to these contexts. The particular questions raised in each
context will determine the most appropriate approach. In whatever time or
whatever context we do catechetical ministry, we will still need to ask what
approach or method will most effectively ensure that those in the learning
experience are being addressed by the living word of God.

Notes

1. Ken Smith, *Tools for Teaching Confirmation* (Chicago: Evangelical Lutheran Church
in America, 1993), 7.

2. *The Confirmation Ministry Task Force Report* (Chicago: Evangelical Lutheran
Church in America, 1993), 1.

3. Ibid., 14.

4. Ibid., 3.

5. For a resource that guides the work of a congregational confirmation ministry
team, see Thomas K. Johnson, *Confirmation: A Congregational Planner* (Minneapolis:
Augsburg Fortress, 1999). See also Ted Schroeder, *Creating a Central Purpose for Your
Christian Education Ministry: A Workshop Design* (Chicago: Division for Congregational
Ministries, Evangelical Lutheran Church in America, 1995).

6. Harold Burgess, *An Invitation to Religious Education* (Birmingham, Ala.: Religious
Education Press, 1975).

7. Jack Seymour et al., *Contemporary Approaches to Christian Education* (Nashville:
Abingdon, 1982).

8. Ibid., 11.

9. Ibid., 13.

10. Ibid., 16.

11. Ibid, 43.

12. Ibid.

13. Ibid., 47.

14. Ibid., 19.

15. Ibid., 65.

16. Ibid., 110.

17. Ibid., 124.

18. Iris V. Cully, *Ways to Teach Children* (Philadelphia: Fortress Press, 1965), 8.

19. Ibid., 9.

20. Gracia Grindal, "Confirmation Embraced (. . . If Done Right)," *Word and World*, vol. 11, no. 4 (Fall 1991): 405.

21. *The Confirmation Ministry Task Force Report* (Chicago: Evangelical Lutheran Church in America, 1993), 1.

22. *A Short Explanation of Dr. Martin Luther's Small Catechism: A Handbook of Christian Doctrine* (St. Louis: Concordia Publishing House, 1943).

23. See also Kennith Smith, *Six Models of Confirmation Ministry* (Chicago: Evangelical Lutheran Church in America, 1993), and *Confirmation: More Than Just Business as Usual!* (Chicago: Evangelical Lutheran Church in America, 1998).

24. *The Book of Concord*, Theodore G. Tappert, trans. and ed. (Philadelphia: Fortress Press, 1959), 342.

APPENDIX A

The Confirmation Ministry Task Force Report

(Adopted by the Third Biennial Churchwide Assembly
of the Evangelical Lutheran Church in America, September 1, 1993)

PREFACE

In 1988 the Church Council of the Evangelical Lutheran Church in America and board of the Division for Congregational Life, responding to a recommendation of the former church bodies, approved a study of confirmation ministry. A pre-study committee drafted a preliminary process, then the board of the Division for Congregational Life named a Confirmation Ministry Task Force to lead the study. From the start, this task force concentrated on two major items. First, drawing on the 1970 report of the *Joint Commission on the Theology and Practice of Confirmation,* in which the Lutheran Church in America, the American Lutheran Church, and The Lutheran Church—Missouri Synod conducted an intense study of confirmation ministry, the task force worked with a definition of confirmation ministry, which reads:

> Confirmation ministry is a pastoral and educational ministry of the church that helps the baptized through Word and Sacrament to identify more deeply with the Christian community and participate more fully in its mission.

Secondly, this task force identified a focal question for its study process:

> What is the role of the congregation in affirming youth in Christian faithfulness with an emphasis on lifelong learning and discipleship?

What follows is informed and shaped by these two concerns and is addressed to both pastors and lay leaders in congregations to help them develop in their setting a grace-centered vision for confirmation ministry.

The report has three parts. Part One responds to the question "What is confirmation ministry?" and offers an understanding of what confirmation, at its most vital, truly is. It begins with a look at the background of recent studies of confirmation ministry, followed by what is seen as the challenge and opportunity of this ministry. Part One concludes with a discussion of confirmation's baptismal basis.

Part Two addresses the questions, *What does this mean for us?* and *How do we respond?* It offers practical, concrete suggestions for creating an effective confirmation program in the parish. It looks at the role of the congregation in confirmation ministry, confirmation's grace-centered nature, and the importance of lifelong learning within the community of faith. Part Two discusses rites of affirmation of Baptism and offers ways of implementing and assessing confirmation ministry in congregations.

Part Three summarizes the report and makes recommendations.

What Is Confirmation Ministry?

Part One

UNDERSTANDINGS FROM RECENT STUDIES

As we enter the twenty-first century, the Evangelical Lutheran Church in America can be thankful for a theology and a tradition rooted in an understanding and experience of the grace of God. Our grace-centered ways of thinking and talking about God and our traditional Lutheran ways of responding to God's Word are gifts to be shared with all Christians.

Much of this classic heritage has been emphasized anew since the 1970 *Report of the Joint Commission on the Theology and Practice of Confirmation.* This current study recognizes and applauds that work as a comprehensive examination of the history and theology of confirmation and the precedent for a number of major studies by other Christian denominations.

Several themes of the 1970 report are of particular importance:

- the centrality of Baptism to our faith,
- the separation of first Communion from the rite of confirmation,
- the need for a lifelong process of learning, greater emphasis on the entire congregation's pastoral care of young people,
- the challenge to provide genuine opportunities for more profound attachment of youth to the Christian community, and
- the provision for a variety of rites at significant times in life.

Additionally, since 1970 there have been a number of changes in congregational perception and practice regarding confirmation ministry, including:

- responsibility for confirmation ministry is more and more shared by both lay and clergy,
- catechetical instruction has broadened to include issues of the wider world,
- instruction in the Bible and the Small Catechism has recently returned to the fore,
- increased awareness of learning styles and contexts has generated a variety of approaches, strategies, and techniques,
- increased understanding regarding developmental stages in both faith and cognition affects both what is taught and how it is taught,
- though a large majority of congregations invite members to take part in Communion before they are confirmed, the age for first Communion varies,
- congregations continue to see the confirmation rite as important even though the meaning remains ambiguous,
- the confirmation rite is seen as an affirmation of Baptism, not a completion of it or its competitor, and
- catechetical instruction has been a valued opportunity for experimentation.

These themes and understandings have provided a good base from which to begin discussion of confirmation ministry.

THE CHALLENGE OF CONFIRMATION MINISTRY

What is the role of faith in the lives of today's young people? What is the role of confirmation ministry in the life of today's church? These two questions are intertwined and generate an agenda for the Evangelical Lutheran Church in America as we seek to be faithful in our ministry. In exploring them, we discover both challenge and opportunity for confirmation ministry.

While it is true that confirmation is a practice not mentioned in Scripture (although it is grounded in Baptism, as we shall see), it was created by the church as a valuable tool for growth in faith. Because of its work through the centuries in helping to shape a Christian's faith, confirmation ministry remains important to Lutheran congregations today. Its changing form and function over the years is an attempt to address better the needs of the young people of the day.

As we look at confirmation ministry today, there is much to celebrate. Today's young Christians bring to congregations exuberance, talents, diverse perspectives, and insight. They are not simply the church of the future, they play an important role today. They are ready and eager to probe their identity, to appraise the traditions of family, church, and wider community, and to put their experiences into the context of faith in Jesus Christ. Their invigorating commitment, in addition to the emergence of new models in educational ministry and the restoration of Baptism to the center of Christian experience, offer tremendous hope and opportunity for a vital confirmation ministry.

Moreover, our Lutheran heritage presents great reassurance and resources to use in ministry with young people, especially as we share an understanding of life that differs from that of society's. We live with the assurance that although we may at times feel our Lord's grace is too good to be true, even our weakness cannot diminish the actions God has taken to redeem us. Ours is a theology and a tradition rooted in the grace of God.

But society presents challenges. Its trends are disturbing. American youth, whether active in church or not, engage in many at-risk behaviors: thoughts of suicide, drug and alcohol abuse, aggression, and abuse of sexual expression, to name only a few. Furthermore, the pluralism in society, the changing nature of households, and the demands of an increasingly complex world require review of confirmation ministry so that it remains a vital ministry of the church.

The challenge confirmation ministry faces becomes even greater when one realizes that, as a recent study shows, many adult Lutherans have difficulty in accepting salvation as a gift. Confirmation ministry today must address this inconsistency between what our church teaches about salvation and what Lutherans young and old say they believe.

Yet, in all of this we have hope. God continues to send the Holy Spirit to bear the good news of God's gracious love to us through the Word and sacraments. Individual members of all ages, in actions toward one another, daily affirm God's grace. Baptized into Christ, young people feel themselves drawn into the Christian community, and, empowered by their active role in a worshiping community, are better equipped to venture into a fast-paced, pluralistic society, bringing a message of God's grace to share with others. The church is free and challenged to change and enhance confirmation ministry so that it best serves individuals of all ages in our congregations.

THE BAPTISMAL BASIS FOR CONFIRMATION MINISTRY

The practice of confirmation is not mentioned in Scripture. If flows out of Baptism. It is an implication of Baptism, a ministry to help Christians realize Baptism's gracious benefits: forgiveness of sins, deliverance from death and the devil, and the bestowal of everlasting salvation to all who believe what God has promised, as Luther said in the Small Catechism.

When the New Testament describes how the triune God saves people, it relates salvation to the death and resurrection of Jesus, who died for our sins and was raised for our justification, gave his life as a ransom for many, and offered for all time a single sacrifice for sin. Jesus' whole life culminates in his death on the cross and God's raising him on the third day (Mark 10:45, Rom. 3:25, 4:25, 1 Cor. 15:3-5, 1 Tim. 2:6, Heb.10:12).

Our relation to Jesus' death is all-important. In the Gospel of John, the cross is where Jesus draws all people to himself. In Matthew, Mark, and Luke, after predicting his own death, Jesus tells his followers they are to take up their own crosses. In his letters, the apostle Paul speaks of being joined to Christ's death, of dying with Christ, and of being crucified with Christ (John 12:32, Mark 8:34-35 and parallels, Rom. 6:4-8, Gal. 2:19).

The Gospel, which is the power of the triune God for salvation, is the proclamation that God was, in Christ, reconciling the world, a reconciliation freely given to us because God is gracious. God's Spirit leads us to trust this good news that God in Christ has established a right relationship with us. This is the heart of the New Testament's idea of salvation, and it gives form to believers' lives. We are to die to sin, to the old age, and to our old selves. As we are joined to Christ's death, so also will we be joined to his resurrection. A new creation will be raised as Christ lives in us and we abide in him. This is given already in faith and one day will be brought to completion in a new resurrection body (Rom. 1:16, 3:24,3-5, 6:1-11, 2 Cor. 5:19, Gal. 1:4, Eph. 4:22, John 15:4, 1 Cor. 15).

This biblical pattern of the new life in Christ stands in contrast to both ancient and modern schemes of self-fulfillment. It focuses on the death of our old sinful self, the forgiveness of sins, the presence of the Holy Spirit, and newness of life in Christ. We are saved or put right with God by God's graciousness, not by our own achievements, and are set free from a preoccupation with our own well-being. Now we are free to love our neighbors and the world that God creates.

God brings us into this new relationship by joining us to Christ in Baptism. Through water and the Word, "and our trust in this Word," as Luther wrote in the Small Catechism, God incorporates us into the crucified and risen Christ and his body, the Church. Baptism is one of the "means of grace" God's Spirit uses to create saving faith in people. Whether faith is generated in adults or older children who hear the Gospel and are then baptized, or infants are brought by believing parents to be baptized, faith in Christ follows Baptism. The Spirit uses the proclamation and teaching of the Word and the Sacrament of Holy Communion in the assembly of believers to create and sustain faith in those who are baptized.

Baptism is a lifelong reality, as well as a rite. When the early Christians heard the word baptize, they would think of an everyday action, not primarily a religious ritual. Literally, baptize means "wash," "immerse," and "cleanse." It also was used metaphorically in New Testament times to mean "drown," "sin," or "throw down one's opponent in wrestling." Therefore, it is not surprising that in the only two places in the New Testament where Jesus speaks of his own Baptism, he refers not to his being washed in the Jordan River by John, but his impending death. Baptism refers to what Jesus must undergo. It began when he was washed and received the Holy Spirit and his commission from God, but it did not end there. It culminated in his death on the cross (see Luke 12:50 and Mark 10:40-45).

As Christians we are baptized into his death. We too are given a divine commission. This reality continues in our lives until we die. We are no longer our own, but we belong to Christ, so that we now walk in faith and hope. As Luther reminds us in the Small Catechism, we are to remember our Baptism daily in the walk of life. In doing this, we gain courage and guidance for a life of mercy and justice. We are assured that God's love for us is concrete, real, and immediate.

These insights lead us to understand that Baptism is the basis for Christian education and nurture, including confirmation ministry. The Church is to help baptized Christians to live out their Baptism, to grow in knowledge, insight, and faithfulness as servants of Christ. Baptized Christians need to be nurtured in lives of faith, hope, and love, grounded in the pattern of death and resurrection.

Confirmation ministry does not *complete* Baptism, for Baptism is already complete through God's work of joining us to Christ and his body, the Church. In him is salvation. Moreover, confirmation ministry does not *compete* with Baptism, because confirmation ministry does not save anyone.

Identity, mission, discipleship, and vocation, important issues addressed in confirmation ministry, proceed from Baptism. Being baptized into the Church, we find our *identity* as God's children, forgiven sinners, members of Christ's body. Because it comes by God's action, this identity takes precedence over other aspects of who we are: ethnic background, gender nationality, class, or culture. Not that these aspects are denied; rather they are claimed for Christ and God's mission in the world. Confirmation ministry is an important time for young Christians to reflect on their identities as Christians in their particular time and place.

Being baptized involves us in Christ's *mission,* through the Church, to bring the Gospel to all people. Because salvation is a gracious gift of God, no human characteristics qualify or disqualify a person. This church's pastoral and educational ministry, including confirmation ministry, is to assist its members in this mission (Matt. 28:18-20 and Eph. 4:11-13).

Furthermore, this mission requires church members of all ages to be *disciples,* that is, followers of Jesus. Disciples are members of Christ's body with a mission. Like Jesus, we deny ourselves for the sake of others. Because such living will put us in conflict with many of society's norms and expectations, we need the fellowship of believers, involved in worship, study, prayer, and conversation, to sustain and direct us as disciples. We need the forgiveness of sins and regular participation in the means of grace to sustain us in faith, hope, and love. As baptized youth participate in the congregation, confirmation ministry gives shape to discipleship and opportunity to reflect on the mission of the Church.

As baptized people, we see our daily life as a place to carry out our *vocation,* our calling. All aspects of life, home and school, community and nation, daily work and leisure, citizenship and friendship, belong to God. All are places where God calls us to serve. God's Word and the Church help us to discover ways to carry out our calling. Youth, especially, face far-reaching decisions about education, marriage or singleness, citizenship and occupation. Confirmation ministry addresses this time of decision-making. It can empower young people to trust their own experiences of Christ's faithfulness as they identify those values and beliefs for which they are willing to suffer. Confirmation can help young people determine how they want to live now and in the future.

To summarize, confirmation ministry is an opportunity for congregations to renew the vision of living by grace, grounded in Baptism. This vision is especially important for ministry with young Christians, but it also has lifelong implications. Through identity with the baptized community, we grow in mission, discipleship, and our vocations in daily life. The congregation, of course, plays a vital role in this ministry.

What Does This Mean for Us? How Do We Respond?

Part Two

THE ROLE OF THE CONGREGATION IN CONFIRMATION MINISTRY

The Congregation's Ministry of Word and Sacrament

Living with Christ means living with other people of God and helping one another grow in faith, love, and obedience to God's will. Therefore, confirmation ministry must be understood to include not only formal classroom instruction, but the entire life of the whole Church and of the congregation.

The task of confirmation ministry is not only to reflect on the familiar questions and answers of the Christian faith, but to deepen our trust in God's promises, to strengthen our sense of Christian vocation, and to equip us better to live out that vocation in witness and service in the world.

Confirmation ministry will vary from place to place, but it will always be an educational and pastoral ministry of the entire community of faith. To describe confirmation ministry as the responsibility of the entire congregation suggests that faith matures by virtue of the Holy Spirit working through a rich fabric of caring relationships.

The focus of this life together is worship. In gathering to hear God's Word and to receive the Sacrament of Holy Communion, we are nurtured and encouraged in faith throughout life. In the pattern of weekly worship, we are called together to hear again and celebrate the good news of God's grace in Jesus Christ, and then are sent forth to respond to our identity as those who have been baptized into the death and resurrection of Jesus Christ.

Within communities of faith we learn from each other. Each person has something to offer and much to receive. While we have commonly thought of confirmation ministry as consisting of one or more adults giving instruction to youth, the nature of belonging to a community of faith suggests the process is multidirectional and involves people throughout their lives. The quickened faith of the young, their good questions, the witness of their experiences with God, and their expressions of service challenge the baptized of all ages.

Confirmation ministry must facilitate the lifelong learning of the baptized. The ability to express faith changes as we grow in years, and the understanding of our Christian identity and vocation is clarified and refined by new experiences. We never graduate from the need to be renewed in the promise of our Baptism, which, through our daily dying and rising with Christ, enables us to face new trials and temptations.

First Communion

Because Christian identity begins with God's action in Baptism and continues throughout life, the 1970 *Report of the Joint Commission on the Theology and Practice of Confirmation* was able to recommend that one's first Communion no longer be tied to status as a confirmed member of the Church. During the past two decades, congregations of the ELCA have chosen a variety of ages at which to prepare children for receiving this sacrament. The 1990 reports from ELCA congregations suggest that while grade five is now the usual time for admitting baptized children to the Lord's Table, there is a variety of practice throughout the country.

The 1970 report calls for flexibility in such practice. We agree. That study and the subsequent *A Statement on Communion Practices,* adopted by The American Lutheran Church and the Lutheran Church in America in 1978, both recommend age 10 or fifth grade as a time of readiness for first Communion; but the statement also notes that such readiness may occur earlier or later. The 1978 statement indicates that, within certain guidelines, "The responsibility for deciding when to admit a child is shared by the pastor, the child, the family or sponsoring persons, and the congregation." Our confessional writings also provide for a degree of freedom and flexibility concerning readiness for Communion, while mandating instruction so that the baptized may receive the sacrament with a living and discerning faith.

Commitment to a process of instruction before receiving the sacrament does not imply that one becomes worthy by understanding or merit. Holy Communion is as much the free gift of God as the Word and Baptism. Honoring the gracious nature of the sacraments is what stands at the heart of our evangelical perspective.

Attention to Youth

The baptismal pattern of death and resurrection shapes the life of each Christian and gives meaning to life's experiences, particularly at times of personal transition, such as adolescence. The years from ages 12 through 22, or even later, are a time of complex life changes for youth, requiring heightened care and attention from this church. Therefore, congregations are called to provide age-appropriate educational and pastoral ministry to youth throughout their adolescent years, regardless of the particular shape of confirmation ministry, or the age at which young people are confirmed. Furthermore, a continued emphasis upon learning from the Small Catechism and the Scriptures is an expectation of confirmation ministry, for it enables Christian young people to meet life's turbulent transitions with an informed faith. Opportunities for spiritual growth and prayer are also a significant element in confirmation ministry.

Confirmation Teachers

Who is to teach our young people? The centrality of the pastor's role has long been recognized in the Lutheran tradition. In bearing a public responsibility for Word and sacraments in the faith community, the pastoral role has been largely defined by a concern for teaching the Scriptures, church doctrine, and theology. Equally important is the unique role the pastor plays as an adult model of faith and ministry.

Adult lay persons play an increasingly important role. They are chosen by virtue of the maturity of their own faith, their skills for relating to young people, and their commitment to the community of faith. Especially where there are opportunities for training and regular support, lay catechists have much to offer. Some have great experience and expertise as educators, others have special gifts in community building and unique abilities to enhance the relational aspects of confirmation ministry.

Lay catechists should model what it means to be faithful to Jesus Christ. It is important that young people see such catechists playing a role not only in special confirmation ministry settings but also in the ongoing life of the congregation. Lay catechists are able to give credibility to the way in which a lively understanding of vocation can shape the life of an adult Christian.

In addition to pastors and lay catechists, parents and guardians have a large share of the responsibility for the nurture of their children in the Christian faith. Congregations should encourage and equip parents and guardians, starting from the birth and the baptism of their children, to be models of faithfulness and guides in Christian life and understanding. Especially if a young person does not have a parent or guardian who can serve as a model of Christian faithfulness, congregations should consider supplying a surrogate mentor. An increasing number of congregations have found mentors useful for all confirmands. Not only are such adults able to personalize confirmation through a one-to-one relationship with the student, but, like lay catechists, mentors also witness to the importance of vocation.

Finally, we must not neglect the fact that young Christians themselves have significant gifts to share with each other. Intentional development of peer relationships, whether structured between confirmands or involving older youth, can provide students an enriching and supporting environment in which to face life's transitions.

GOSPEL-CENTERED, GRACE-CENTERED CONFIRMATION MINISTRY

The strength of our Lutheran heritage is rooted in our insistence that God be understood as the good and gracious one who brings us to faith through the Gospel, and who, in Baptism, unites us with the death and resurrection of Jesus Christ. The role of the congregation is formed by an understanding that the Word and sacraments are gifts freely given.

Each congregation shapes confirmation ministry to address the needs and resources of a particular setting. In doing this, the primary question to be asked is: How can this congregation best bring the Gospel to its young people and nurture them in lives of faith? When a congregation plans a program centered on Scripture, doctrine, and the Small Catechism, and intentionally involves youth in worship, service, and witness for the sake of the Gospel, the congregation is responding to God's gracious gift. Synods and the churchwide expression of this church, and seminaries, play an important role in assisting congregations in this task. Materials, networks, and trained leaders are resources that they are able to provide the local congregation.

Congregations tailor their programs by using available resources: their Christian community, individual members, their time, and the gifts they bring. A confirmation ministry team, discussed in detail below, is a helpful means of organizing and utilizing these resources.

Three Basic Needs

As congregations strive to bring the Gospel to young people and nurture them in lives of faith, they should consider the following three basic needs often expressed by young people:

The Need for Self-Worth and Personal Identity. A variety of experiences shape self-worth and personal identity, two issues that need careful attention in work with youth, who often see themselves as unworthy and incapable of measuring up. Our society's emphasis on competition and achievement, the dilemma between having and not having, the media images of perfection, and adult expectations contribute to young people's negative feelings about themselves.

The Need for Relationships. Personal identity is linked to a sense of belonging to a group. Young people need relationships with each other, with adults, and with God. Friendship-making and group decision-making skills are important. Exposure to various styles of family life, persons of different ages, and adult mentors can help young Christians feel important and needed. Youth especially need to be needed. They need to be valued as contributing members of the church, capable of being partners in the Gospel.

The Need for Time. Sometimes adults appear to have too little time for young people. Unfortunately, many young people also have too little time for themselves. Yet, growing up takes time, pressure-free time, to observe, participate, reflect, and question repeatedly amid dramatic physical, emotional, and spiritual changes. Having time for personal growth in the context of patient love is essential to emotional well-being.

Grace-centered confirmation ministry addresses these basic needs of young people in light of the resources available to the congregation. It can respond to those youth who may have been closed out of the life of the congregation. An experientially based, cooperative learning program can integrate all young people.

Characteristics of Gospel-Centered, Grace-Centered Confirmation Ministry

Over the past two years, this task force has gathered information, ideas, and perspectives from a variety of sources. Included was a study of 30 exemplary confirmation ministry programs throughout this church. They reveal exciting possibilities for integrating grace-centered confirmation ministry into the daily life of ELCA congregations.

Deciding how the Gospel can be brought to a particular congregation involves important congregation-based choices. In shaping its own approach to confirmation ministry, the congregation is assisted by published resources as well as synodical and churchwide suggestions and programs.

In the programs studied, several elements were identified as common characteristics of a strong program:

- a focus on grace, affirmation of Baptism, mission, discipleship, and vocation,
- a focus on the Bible and the Small Catechism,
- the use of resources and guidelines provided by the church,
- involvement of a committee or group composed of lay people, youth, pastor(s), parents, and council and education committee members in the development of the program,
- an emphasis on human relationships within the congregation,
- an integration of the program into the worship life of the congregation,
- a continuation of the program after the rite of confirmation with an emphasis on maintaining key relationships with the newly confirmed, and
- an understanding of affirmation of Baptism as a lifelong process rather than a once-in-a-lifetime event.

AN INVITATION TO LIFELONG LEARNING

Given the lifelong nature of God's act in Baptism and the continuous need for God's Word of grace offered in the shared life and conversations of believers, confirmation ministry is more than education for youth. Issues relating to God's will, faith, and discipleship are important whatever one's age.

An invitation to lifelong learning emphasizes the needs and contributions of young people on the one hand while insisting that, in community, people of all ages can benefit from being co-learners. In every congregation, mature members bring the stability of lifelong experiences of living by God's grace. Youth bring exuberance and fresh questions of the faith. Relationships, when nurtured across generations and among peers, can allow for significant learning and growing in faith together.

While our Baptism into Christ occurs only once, complete and unalterable, the baptismal experience of dying and rising to new life in Christ is experienced daily. It calls forth a need to reflect on our faith commitments, to grow in trust, and to hear God's assurance in the midst of insecurity. Thus, transitions in life, and the times between, can become "learning moments": moments in which the Church has the opportunity to direct us again to the baptismal ground of our faith in Jesus Christ. Ministry should be intentionally focused on these learning opportunities.

Leaders of already established programs (circles, Bible studies, issues forums, support groups, visitation groups) engage in confirmation ministry to all ages by calling attention to these learning moments. This helps members return to their Baptism and see these experiences in light of God's grace. These moments are also prime occasions to ask again the familiar catechetical question: "What does this mean?"' Such ministry, whether in the context of informal exchanges between Christian sisters and brothers or in more formal or public contexts, could turn these times of loss or newness into *baptismal moments.*

RITES OF AFFIRMATION OF BAPTISM

A rite that is truly an affirmation of Baptism can be of great benefit to the congregation, as the community of faith seeks to minister to members experiencing life's transition. The Church discerns and proclaims God's movement in people's lives as they experience endings and beginnings, connecting these significant transitions with the baptismal understanding of our dying and rising with Christ. These rites mark moments when the faith given in Baptism finds new expression, and the spiritual gifts given in Baptism are stirred up to meet new challenges.

In all its forms, including the adolescent confirmation rite, the rite of affirmation of Baptism is a creation of the Church, not a sacrament instituted by Christ. We have much freedom in designing and celebrating such rites. The practice of affirmation of Baptism should recall and honor Baptism itself. Elements of a baptismal event may be used in affirmation without overshadowing Baptism. For instance, those making affirmation may enter the nave holding their already lit baptismal candles, or may wear albs to recall the white garment worn or put on at Baptism. Water may be lifted from the font so it can be seen and heard during the vows.

While Baptism happens only once, affirmation of Baptism and prayer for the baptized can happen many times. One way to encourage the lifelong return to Baptism is to hold regular rites of baptismal affirmation for the whole congregation on baptismal festivals such as the Easter Vigil or the Baptism of Our Lord, or on other appropriate days, such as rally day or congregational anniversaries.

When there are changes in a Christian's life, rites of affirmation of Baptism and intercessory prayer could mark the passage. Depending upon the situation and pastoral sensitivity, these rites could be held in small group settings, such as a support group or a circle of friends. Moving into a nursing home, beginning parenthood or grandparenthood, choosing or changing an occupation, moving out of the parental home, the diagnosis of a chronic illness, the end of one's first year of mourning, the ending of a relationship, and retirement are all examples of life's transitions that could be acknowledged by these rites.

The confirmation rite is preceded by years of instruction, relationship, and growth. Other rites of affirmation at other stages in people's lives also would involve preparation, perhaps in the form of pastoral conversation, in order to connect their faith with their transitions. Like the adolescent confirmation rite, these rites would not be graduation but rather commencement ceremonies, marking the beginning of a new stage of life. The congregation should make every effort to continue support following the rite. A continuing relationship with a mentor, continued involvement in fellowship and leadership in this church, and ongoing opportunities for study and reflection are important, especially during the teenage years.

Several elements might be included in rites of baptismal affirmation at times of transitions: presentation by names of those affirming their faith; recognition of those participants in the process leading to the rite; a reminder of God's baptismal promises; public profession of the creeds; affirmation of Baptism responses appropriate to the stage in life; prayer, including a prayer for the stirring up of the Spirit's gifts; and laying on of hands for those affirming faith.

Like all rites of the Church, rites of affirmation of Baptism should have certain characteristics. They should be: evangelical (displaying and proclaiming the grace, love, justice, and beauty of God), baptismal (linked with Baptism in word, symbol, action, and timing), honest (reflecting the experience, beliefs, and context of those making affirmation, and placed within the faith of the whole Church), communal (involving as much of the community as feasible, in both planning and celebration), voluntary (assuring willing, not coerced, participants), and contextual (reflecting a sensitivity to the cultural context, history, and piety of the congregation).

IMPLEMENTING AN EFFECTIVE CONFIRMATION MINISTRY IN CONGREGATIONS

Models of Gospel-Centered, Grace-Centered Confirmation Ministry

In listening to ELCA congregations and Lutheran churches in other parts of the world, a number of confirmation program models that deserve consideration were discovered. Each approach could be adapted by several congregations working together in a coordinated program.

Longer and Later. An extension of confirmation ministry to include early childhood through high school years. Activities, spread out over many years, usually include in-home visitations, cooperative-learning groups, short courses, retreats, and parental covenanting.

Meeting of Young People. An emphasis on personal conversation and learning to use the faith to think and act. Sessions are described as meetings rather than classes. The pastor or catechist prepares an agenda and guides young people in weekly meetings about how the Bible and the catechism relate to their lives. This model uses experiential learning and usually includes one to two years of intensive work.

The Confirming Community. A system of relationships between confirmands and older youth who serve as peer helpers, tutors, and mentors. For example, eighth graders who are studying the sacraments help prepare fifth graders for first Communion; tenth graders counsel ninth graders, and both grades work as "counselors" in the church's VBS program. Adult mentoring and conversations with the pastor throughout the program provide time for reflection.

The Catechumenal Parish. Built on the historic catechumenal process, it moves the catechumen through a journey that involves the following stages: considering affirmation of the baptismal faith, enrolling as a confirmand or catechumen, studying and reflecting as part of a group and with a sponsor, receiving the Sacrament of Baptism or the reaffirmation of Baptism, and embracing congregational support after Baptism or confirmation. Movement through the process is ritually marked by the whole congregation.

The Renewed School. A structured catechetical program that revolves around regular classroom activities, with emphasis on learning the Small Catechism and Scripture. A strong relationship is fostered as teachers become mentors for young people, with special attention paid to helping students grow in self-esteem.

Vow-Driven Catechesis. Built on the vow made at the rite of confirmation, it develops five projects for each young person who is taking the vow. The development and completion of the five projects becomes the confirmation program for the young person.

(More complete information regarding these and other approaches is available by contacting the Division for Congregational Ministries, Evangelical Lutheran Church in America, 8765 West Higgins Road, Chicago, IL 60631.)

A Confirmation Ministry Team

Establishing and implementing an effective confirmation ministry program in a congregation takes time and effort. Selecting a confirmation ministry team is one of the best ways for a congregation to achieve success. But how should this team be structured? What are its purposes and responsibilities?

First, concerning structure, an effective team will reflect the congregation's size, makeup, and administrative structure. Team membership, determined by the size of the congregation or congregations, also should reflect the ministries of the parish. It might include the pastor, other congregational leaders (such as a council member, a stewardship or finance leader, a worship committee representative), educational leaders, youth, and parents. In larger congregations, a workable team size might be five or six members. In smaller congregations, the team might be as few as two or three people. Small congregations may want to work together in forming a joint team.

Second, concerning purpose, the team should: define what confirmation ministry means in the congregation, expand ownership of the ministry, guide planning and implementation to reflect a rich diversity of numbers, relate confirmation ministry to the congregation's total ministry, keep the program strong in periods of staff change, relate the church's tradition to the current program needs, and regularly review and evaluate the confirmation ministry program with regard to the overriding themes of faith, community, identity, and vocation.

Third, concerning responsibilities, the team will meet regularly to assess or monitor: the meaning and purpose of confirmation ministry in regard to the congregation's mission; the relationship between confirmation ministry and the church; the development of objectives and programs appropriate to the congregation, young people (including special learners), and leaders of the program (including pastoral and lay catechists' roles); and the resources required to carry out an effective ministry.

As the confirmation ministry team begins its work, here are some recommended tasks and guidelines:

- Study the congregation's mission statement and examine how confirmation ministry fits in terms of the total mission and ministry. Affirm the essential role of confirmation ministry, and assist in developing a long-range plan for moving into a grace-centered confirmation program.

- Identify tasks for lay persons and consider including these tasks on stewardship time-and-talent cards.
- Examine existing church programs for possible integration with confirmation ministry, especially Sunday school, youth programs, worship, camping, family events, social ministry, first Communion, pre- and post-Baptism sessions, new member classes, and evangelism programs.
- Identify members who are committed to teaching, administration, or curriculum development, and recruit them to assist in implementing the program.
- Examine the current financial support available to confirmation ministry, and wherever possible, place it in the congregational budget. Consider funding lay training and support.

Some special strategies the team might consider to help in transition to greater lay responsibility for the program include: invite a person to serve as confirmation ministry coordinator, with such responsibilities as teacher recruitment, budgeting, and scheduling and coordinating the program's service projects; advocate that confirmands be included as part of the congregation council and committees; increase publicity for confirmation; and link confirmation ministry with youth programs.

Involving Congregation Members in the Confirmation Ministry Program

The following are several ways to involve the congregation more fully in confirmation ministry:

- an adult mentoring program,
- leader training in experiential learning and techniques of cooperative learning (this also benefits other congregational programs),
- establishing a *community of learning* environment by incorporating fellowship and community building in catechetical content sessions. (Some suggestions: organize activity around a meal or snack that involves other youth and adults; hold youth group meetings in conjunction with confirmation ministry sessions to provide for interaction, tutoring, or mentoring across grade levels; provide time for one-to-one sessions with pastors to discuss personal concerns and theological or spiritual questions, thus establishing a trusting bond.),
- establishing caring relationships with families in the congregation through in-home visits in the elementary years, following the model of Longer and Later programs,
- connecting confirmation ministry with other dimensions of congregational life. (Some suggestions: Use the catechism in Sunday school units; offer courses with sufficient flexibility to include adults, parents, and youth; have pastors work to develop strong relationships with post-catechetical youth; encourage the youth to help teach younger congregational members.),
- initiate a program of contracts for learning, service, and covenant relationships, which would develop clear expectations of roles and responsibilities of parents and youth in agreements or covenants, and
- promote biblical literacy across all age levels.

Assessing Confirmation Programs

As existing congregational confirmation ministry programs were considered in this study, several elements in effective programs emerged. To each of these elements, which are listed below, we offer one possible guideline and reflective question(s) to assist congregations in assessing their confirmation programs.

- The program attempted to focus on grace, affirmation of Baptism, mission, discipleship, and vocation. *Guideline:* Affirm the centrality of Baptism. *Question:* How are we reminding our young people of their Baptism and helping them use the tools of faith to make decisions about their lives as baptized people?

- The program focused on the Bible and the Small Catechism. *Guideline:* Recognize Scripture as the basis of all Christian teaching, emphasizing that the source of authority is the Word. *Questions:* How are we making use of the classic "question and answer" format of catechesis? How are we helping our youth to formulate contemporary life questions and answers modeled after Luther's Small Catechism? How are we using catechetics as a process of moral formation?

- The program was developed by the congregation using resources and guidelines provided by the church. *Guideline:* Examine confirmation ministry through the lens of congregational life and the congregation's mission statement. *Question:* Are expectations for students and families clearly formulated and known to all involved?

- A committee or group within the congregation was involved in the development of the program. *Guideline:* Provide stability by building a program that will last many years. *Question:* What happens to our program if our pastor leaves?

- The group included lay people, youth, pastor(s), parents, and representatives of the council and education committee. *Guideline:* Integrate confirmation ministry with the congregation's total ministry. *Questions:* How do we value ministry as the responsibility of the priesthood of believers? Is our laity actively involved in our ministry?

- The program emphasized human relationships within the congregation. *Guideline:* Provide opportunities for relationships with other "forgiven sinners" who facilitate learning: adult sponsors, hosts, or guides who invite others to a new level of vocation, who serve as examples, and who empower others to achieve their visions. *Question:* How is each confirmand linked to an adult significant in his or her life?

- The program was integrated into the worship life of the congregation. *Guideline:* Link the congregation's education and worship ministries so they support each other. *Question:* What opportunities do we provide confirmands to be actively involved in worship, so they may experience reverence and thanksgiving and the stability of tradition?

- The program continued after the rite of confirmation with an emphasis on maintaining a key relationship. *Guideline:* Provide a safe place for young people to examine and explore their faith journeys as Christians. *Question:* How do our members, both youth and adults, see confirmation ministry as a part of the lifelong process of being (not becoming) faithful church members?

- The program began to think of affirmation of Baptism as a lifelong process rather than a once-in-a-lifetime event. *Guideline:* Draw on life's baptismal rhythms of dying and rising in organizing ministry in the congregation. *Question:* How are we encouraging our youth to see confirmation ministry as a lifelong process?

To summarize, a confirmation ministry team will assist the congregation in developing a Gospel-centered, grace-centered confirmation ministry.

Summary and Recommendations

Part Three

This report's definition of confirmation ministry emphasizes the pastoral and educational ministries of this church that help the baptized through Word and Sacrament, to identify with the Christian community and to participate in its mission. A key question has been: What is the role of the congregation in affirming youth in Christian faithfulness with an emphasis on lifelong learning and discipleship? This definition and question have led to several understandings.

First, everything involved in confirmation ministry flows from Baptism. The faith that follows Baptism is the focus for congregational life. In this life together, the Bible, the Small Catechism, and worship for all members, including young persons, are vital. A Gospel-centered, grace-centered approach to confirmation ministry conveys a community grounded in Christ.

Second, confirmation ministry happens in a living community of faith and is the responsibility of the whole congregation, not only the pastor. Confirmation ministry is better able to respond to the concrete needs of youth when it is tailored to fit particular contexts.

Third, effective confirmation ministry involves use of a variety of persons and approaches. Youth are helped to mature in faithfulness through learning with peers and persons of all ages and cultures, including catechists, mentors, pastors, and parents or guardians. For such learning to take place, congregations must be hospitable places for youth.

Fourth, young people benefit from confirmation ministry programs that include diverse models of learning. Young Christians should not be isolated from the ministry of the rest of the congregation, for confirmands are called to lifelong learning in worship, identity, mission, discipleship, and vocation. Confirmation ministry thrives where adult involvement in education and service is a high priority. In other words, it is as important for adults to participate in education as it is for children and youth to be involved in congregational worship.

RECOMMENDATIONS

1) *That congregational confirmation ministry be Gospel-centered, grace-centered both in content and in approach.* Recognizing the many dimensions of the lives of young people, we call upon congregations to intentionally address the need to hear the Gospel as refreshing, life-giving good news. Furthermore, because of the highly competitive and depersonalized environment of much formal schooling, congregations should make their *approach* to confirmation ministry grace-centered as well.

2) *That such a confirmation ministry be tailor-made with an emphasis on community building and faith to convey the Gospel in the congregation's particular context.* Recognizing the diverse settings in which members live, we affirm the congregation's freedom to work singly, or with neighboring congregations, to develop a confirmation ministry which addresses the needs of their specific young people. Such an approach provides the flexibility to address the varied ages, maturity, and skills of young people.

3) *That congregations create, or designate, a confirmation ministry team to give shape and direc-tion to the planning and coordination of a pastoral and educational confirmation ministry.* Recognizing that reforming confirmation ministry is an on-going task, we urge that specific members of the congregation be designated to provide oversight and continuity.

4) *That synods, the churchwide organization, and seminaries be in partnership with congregations in developing a broad variety of support resources, such as materials, networks, and trained lead-ers for confirmation ministry.* Recognizing that our approach to confirmation ministry places greater responsibility at the congregational level, we call upon others in this church to work together to provide support and resources.

MEMBERS OF THE STUDY TASK FORCE
Patricia Lull, Chair, Athens, Ohio
Marc Kolden, Vice-Chair, St. Paul, Minnesota
Dennis Bonikowske, Stevens Point, Wisconsin
Claudia Brookover, Humble, Texas
Robert Conrad, Chicago, Illinois
Beverly Conway, Chicago, Illinois
C. Richard Evenson, Northfield, Minnesota
Mary Hughes, Columbus, Ohio
Dorothy Jeffcoat, Columbia, South Carolina
Brian King, Dubuque, Iowa
Margaret Krych, Philadelphia, Pennsylvania
Donald Main, Lewisburg, Pennsylvania
Tito Moreno, Las Vegas, Nevada
Mark Oldenburg, Gettysburg, Pennsylvania
Rhoda Posey, Irvine, California
Elaine Ramshaw, Columbus, Ohio
Ruth Randall, Lincoln, Nebraska
John Seraphine, Oak Park, Illinois
Charles Sigel, Columbia, South Carolina
Kristin von Fischer, Chicago, Illinois

THE STAFF TEAM THAT WORKED WITH THIS TASK FORCE
Daniel Bollman, Wyvetta Bullock, Eldon DeWeerth, Rebecca Grothe, Mary Ann Moller-Gunderson, Kenneth Inskeep, Mark Knutson, Constance Leean, Susan Niemi, Marvin Roloff, and Ken Smith

Luther Lindberg, Columbia, South Carolina, was coordinator of seminary relations.

A P P E N D I X B

Bibliography

Browning, Robert L. and Reed, Roy A. *Models of Confirmation and Baptismal Affirmation*. Birmingham: Religious Education Press, 1995.

Coles, Robert. *The Spiritual Life of Children*. Boston: Houghton Mifflin, 1990.

Erikson, Erik H. *Identity: Youth and Crisis*. New York: W. W. Norton & Company, 1968.

Evangelical Lutheran Church in America, Division for Congregational Ministries. *The Confirmation Ministry Task Force Report*. Chicago: Evangelical Lutheran Church in America, Division for Congregational Ministries, 1993.

Gilbert, W. Kent, ed. *Confirmation and Education*. Philadelphia: Fortress Press, 1969.

Kavanagh, Aidan. *Confirmation: Origins and Reform*. New York: Pueblo Publishing Company, 1988.

Klos, Frank W. *Confirmation and First Communion: A Study Book*. Minneapolis: Augsburg Publishing House; Philadelphia: Board of Publication of the Lutheran Church in America; St. Louis: Concordia Publishing House, 1968.

Lutheran World Federation. *Confirmation: A Study Document*. Geneva: Lutheran World Federation, 1963.

_____. *Confirmation in the Lutheran Churches Today*. Geneva: Lutheran World Federation, 1986.

_____. *Confirmation Ministry Study*. No. 38. Geneva: Lutheran World Federation, 1995.

Osmer, Robert O. *Confirmation: Presbyterian Practices in Ecumenical Perspective*. Louisville: Geneva Press, 1996.

Piper, Mary. *Reviving Ophelia: Saving the Selves of Adolescent Girls*. New York: Grosset-Putnam, 1994.

Pollack, William. *Real Boys: Rescuing Our Sons from the Myths of Boyhood*. New York: Random House, 1998.

Repp, Arthur C. *Confirmation in the Lutheran Church*. St. Louis: Concordia Publishing House, 1964.

Seymour, Jack et al. *Contemporary Approaches to Christian Education*. Nashville: Abingdon, 1982.

Smith, Kennith. *Handbook for Confirmation Ministry*. Geneva: Lutheran World Federation, 1998.

Tatum, Beverly Daniel. *"Why Are All the Black Kids Sitting Together in the Cafeteria?" and Other Conversations about Race*. New York: Basic Books, 1997.

INDEX